OPERATIONAL PROFITABILITY

OPERATIONAL PROFITABILITY

CONDUCTING MANAGEMENT AUDITS

ROBERT M. TOROK

PATRICK J. CORDON

JOHN WILEY & SONS, INC.

New York • Chichester • Weinheim • Toronto • Singapore • Brisbane

This text is printed on acid-free paper.

Copyright © 1997 by John Wiley & Sons, Inc.

All rights reserved. Published simultaneously in Canada.

This publication is designed to provide accurate and authoritative
information in regard to the subject matter covered. It is sold
with the understanding that the publisher is not engaged in
rendering legal, accounting, or other professional services. If
legal advice or other expert assistance is required, the services
of a competent professional person should be sought.

Library of Congress Cataloging-in-Publication Data:

Torok, Robert M.
    Operational profitability : conducting management audits / Robert
M. Torok, Patrick J. Cordon.
        p.   cm.
    ISBN 0-471-17225-1 (cloth : alk. paper)
    1. Management audit.   I. Cordon, Patrick J.   II. Title.
HD58.95.T67   1997
658.4—dc20   96-34964

Printed in the United States of America

10 9 8 7 6 5 4 3 2 1

PREFACE

THE MANAGEMENT OPERATIONS ANALYSIS

A Management Operations Analysis is an in-depth review of a business. It looks at the whole and how its individual parts and functions are interrelated to produce the overall results. A properly prepared outline for an analysis will bring together data in such a way that the business is seen as a single entity.

A management audit is not an organizational study. It goes far beyond questions of how the business should be divided into departments and how responsibilities should be assigned. It is not a departmental study. Although it does concern itself with issues important to individual functional departments in the company, the audit also focuses on how all these functions interrelate and how they are managed so the enterprise can effectively perform its economic function.

A financial audit is a snapshot in time, showing the results of prior operations of the firm and current financial health. These results are expressed in dollars, the language common to all businesses. A management analysis, being broader, looks at issues and conditions affecting the company's ability to operate well today, and also to meet its future goals. Because each firm is different, the standards of measurement must be different. They must reflect the unique character of the business and the environment in which it operates.

A company's management—the chief financial officers, chief executive officers, and other managers—have an obligation to understand and regulate the health of their business. The business's independent auditors—and other external consultants—play a critical role in this process. Because this information is extremely valuable to the client, it is important that they understand all the aspects of the client's business, in order to assist in identifying those areas that affect profitability.

The purpose of this book is:

1. To assist external auditors and business consultants in understanding what their clients need to know, and to give company management a step-by-step guide on what a properly conducted management audit entails, and how to plan for one.

v

2. To provide analytical tools to evaluate the companies' operations—for external advisors, these services represent additional revenue from existing clients, as well as an excellent opportunity for practice development and new business.

3. To serve as a basis for developing action plans and suggestions for improvements.

UNDERSTANDING THE ELEMENTS

It is important to realize that the management analysis is a tool for upper management. It is upper management that initiates and directs the scope and overall direction of the project. It is imperative that management is sure that the data gathered is factual and objective. The complete independence of the party conducting the management analysis, therefore, is a critical element of the management analysis process.

WHY CONDUCT A MANAGEMENT AUDIT?

In some organizations, upper management may decide that a management analysis should be conducted throughout the company every two or three years, even though no major problems may be evident. The philosophy of this approach is to reconfirm to upper management that the organization is working effectively. The "periodic" management analysis approach will often uncover potential problems, which, under normal circumstances, would be discovered only when the situation got out of control.

Other organizations (both small and large) initiate the management analysis approach to determine how the overall company and its individual units would grade out when compared against a set of objective standards for efficiency and effectiveness. The majority of companies that utilize this manual will fall into this category.

The management analysis may be used to evaluate a specific function within the organization to determine if the company is obtaining maximum cost efficiency from the way the function is currently performing. For example, a management analysis of an organization's purchasing department might uncover the fact that, because it did not obtain competitive bids when awarding major contracts, the firm lost significant sums of money.

Or, a management analysis of a firm's informational flow of key data might uncover the fact that, because of repeated delays in receiving important material on the company's clients and products, the organization is losing market share when it should actually be gaining.

In addition, the management audit may be initiated as the result of specific problems that develop in the firm. Management philosophies differ from company to company, as well as from industry to industry. But the following problem scenarios would be the type that would send danger signals to upper management, and indicate the need for an immediate management audit.

DANGER SIGNALS

Reduction of company profits may be an indication of operational inefficiencies that are increasing the cost of doing business and decreasing the quality of work, as well as the company's product. The management analysis process would define the specific causes of the problem, and evaluate potential solutions for each individual problem situation.

High turnover of personnel is another example of a negative symptom in the organization, which the management analysis process would help alleviate. High turnover may be caused by poor employee benefits, below-market salaries, or poor and inefficient working conditions. The management analysis process would define the source of the problem in such circumstances and, depending on the facts of the situation, recommend to upper management the action it must take to alleviate the problem.

Management analysis may be initiated as a direct result of a *specific operational problem,* which was uncovered by management. For example, you may discover that annual sales have been reduced because of the ability of the competition to sell an identical product to yours at a lower price. This finding dictates the immediate need to reevaluate your pricing strategy, including the direct and indirect costs associated with the product.

In another instance, company management may find that the *costs of suppliers, parts, materials, and service are extremely high.* The management analysis would review purchasing policies to determine if they are providing the best possible investment for the company. Such an audit may disclose that the company urgently requires a centralized purchasing system to monitor and control all major expenditures made by the company.

ROBERT M. TOROK
PATRICK J. CORDON

Cleveland, Ohio
December 1996

CONTENTS

1

THE BASIC APPROACH

It is important to note that, unlike the financial and operational analysis, which are limited in both scope and objectives, the management analysis is broader in its approach and objectives. The purpose of the broad approach in this manual is to allow flexibility throughout the course of the management analysis, since the specific problems have usually not been defined beforehand.

The professional management analysis will require various types of skills on the part of the individual or individuals involved. They should possess the ability to communicate effectively with all levels of the organization and to maintain a thought process that can critically evaluate each aspect of the organization. The management analysis approach will cross over various functions and management levels, and will require a basic knowledge of different disciplines.

The management analysis audit approach should follow certain basic steps for each engagement, even though the objectives of the various analysis will vary. The findings must be supported by facts and documented evidence. Each analysis should include the following features:

- *Definition of project scope.* Both upper management and the staff conducting the analysis must be in total agreement on the overall scope of the project. In some instances, the management analysis may be general in scope and the audit will include a detailed appraisal of each operational aspect of the organization. In other instances, a specific problem area may be defined (for example, the quality of the company's main product may be found lacking), and the management analysis will be initiated to document the causes and recommend corrective actions.

- *Planning, preparation, and organization.* When the project scope has been defined, the management analysis team will develop an action plan for conducting the assignment. The action plan documents the steps to be followed and estimates the time required to accomplish each step. This stage of the management analysis requires that each source of documentation relating to the area under review is thoroughly analyzed and updated.

- *Fact gathering and documentation update.* The next general phase of the management analysis includes the accumulation of all informational data relating to the areas defined in the scope of the project. This data is obtained from correspondence, policies and procedures, and all other informal information which can be obtained directly from employees through interviews.

- *Research and analysis.* The research and analysis stage is the most critical in the management analysis process. This phase of the audit accumulates the evidence and the facts which are necessary to support a final report to upper management.
- *Reporting.* The reporting phase of the management analysis includes a summarization of the work that was conducted, a description of the scope of the project, a detailed account of the major findings and a discussion of the alternatives which are available to upper management for eliminating the problem conditions which exist.

When the company is entering a period of new growth or major change, a management analysis can be useful to help set priorities for management attention.

CHECKLIST FOR A MANAGEMENT ANALYSIS

A full management analysis is a detailed survey of the entire business. For ease in assigning data collection and analysis, the checklist has been organized into 14 topics:

1. Background of the business, current problems, and outlook;
2. Ownership, capital structure, and investment policy;
3. Strategic concepts and competitive positioning;
4. Financial condition performance, and accounting;
5. Products (services), markets, and distribution;
6. Sales and marketing;
7. Operating policies, methods, and controls;
8. Manufacturing, inventory controls, and engineering;
9. Technical capabilities and development;
10. Organization, personnel, management development, and legal;
11. Purchasing;
12. Management systems, controls, and effectiveness;
13. Data processing; and
14. Special audits.

This checklist covers an in-depth analysis. A complete, but less detailed audit can be completed by using the same checklist only as a general guide.

HOW MUCH WORK IS INVOLVED?

Every company is different. Every management analysis is different. It is not possible to say exactly how much work is involved in a typical analysis. However, as a general estimate, an outside consultant might spend several person-months auditing a

$10–$20-million company. The same consulting firm might commit several person-years to an audit of a billion-dollar corporation.

Following are some important factors that influence how much effort is required for analyzing a particular firm:

- Company size and structure;
- Complexity of market and product lines;
- Customer geography and distribution channels;
- Diversity of facilities;
- Material control requirements;
- Technical base of operations; and
- Information needs for control.

SETTING UP THE MANAGEMENT ANALYSIS

In preparing to carry out a self-conducted management analysis, a company should first determine whether it needs a full analysis or wants to focus only on one or more of the major topics. This will help determine who in the organization is most appropriate to be assigned to this project and how much effort will be required.

Management should then establish specific timetables for collecting basic data as well as a schedule for obtaining answers to those questions that will involve discussion with managers and others in the organization. These timetables will help control the total effort and will, of course, influence the depth of the audit. As the audit proceeds, these schedules should be reviewed to find out if they are too tight to obtain all the information required, or if they are so loose as to allow the audit to consume too much time.

After the schedules are established and personnel identified, there should be a discussion of the analysis, its purposes, its schedules, and participants, with all members of the management staff. It is important that everyone understand what the project means, and the value of the project in improving their effectiveness and in enhancing the performance of the company. Their participation and their honest input will be critical. As the project proceeds, frequent input from the participants is essential, as is that of management staff and others in the organization regarding how well participants are performing in gathering information.

Trends in the data and weaknesses in the answers will reveal issues for further study. The answers not obtained are often more important than the answers that are. Lack of response will often point to the priority of the information collected and those items requiring action should be addressed.

It is important that all information collected is well documented, as even apparently unimportant papers and notes may be valuable in the analysis. They certainly will be necessary if there is a need to go back and check the information. They will also be helpful in the next audit to show what changes have occurred. Some historical data will not have to be collected next time.

The checklist is not perfect. It is oriented toward manufacturing firms, but is still useful for many other types of businesses. It can never be complete in its application to any one particular business.

GOALS AND EXPECTATIONS

Following is a synopsis of how to determine goals and expectations.

Goal   A means of establishing: what you want; when you want it; and how you want it.

Expectation   A means of communicating to others those goals you expect to be accomplished. It is a means of diminishing assumptions as to what one perceives things to be versus what others perceive things to be.

There are seven parts to consider when preparing Goals/Expectations:

1. Increase output, yield, equipment utilization, or other quantity of work;
2. Reduce costs such as for scrap, rework, personnel turnover, absenteeism, learning time, overtime, down time, maintenance, and supplies;
3. Obtain more suggestions for improving methods and procedures;
4. Reduce the number of rejects and complaints from inspection;
5. Complete a specific project by a certain deadline;
6. Develop trained replacements for specific jobs; and
7. Reduce medical aid, lost time, accidents, or employee grievances.

Exhibit 1.1 displays the roles of general management, middle management, and the role of supervisory management in planning goals and expectations.

SYSTEM COMPONENTS OVERVIEW

There are various components that must be reviewed—and defined in advance. Exhibit 1.2 graphically outlines those components.

EXHIBIT 1.1   Goals and Expectations—Management Plan

General Management	Middle Management	Supervision
Goal: What I want done		
Strategy: How and when I will get what I want ⟶	Goal	
Means: What I will do to achieve my goal	Strategy ⟶	Goal
Method: Implementation/Evaluation	Means	Strategy
	Method	Means
		Method

EXHIBIT 1.2   Basic System Components

Forecasting

Evaluation   Planning

Reporting   Execution

Follow-Up

Forecasting

Forecasting provides management with the ability to establish realistic goals based on plant capabilities and current requirements. Crew levels can be determined by the volume that is planned to be produced. This determination is used to create a more uniform production schedule, thus eliminating large production imbalances.

Planning

The purpose of the planning phase is to put manpower, materials, and machinery together in a coordinated effort to produce the required amount of production for each production period.

Execution

Execution provides management with ability to assign work schedules on a daily basis, as well as provide a means to monitor throughout each shift to ensure that the plan is being attained and to react immediately to off-schedule conditions and variances in order to minimize lost time and reduce production costs. The means for this activity is provided by the daily/weekly schedule, activity sheets, and daily schedule review meetings.

Follow-Up

Follow-up is the inspection phase of the system. Follow-up is the method that management uses to assure compliance to the plan, to identify problems, and initiate corrective action. It is a tool that will enable subordinates to feel secure that, if a problem develops, their management cares enough to be there to do something about it. It is a deterrent to creating perception problems between management and management; and management and labor. Follow-up is the assurance that the Execution phase is going as planned. Effective follow-up makes reporting a postmortem activity.

Reporting

Reporting will provide all levels of management with the current results of the day's accomplishments against the plan, so that effective steps can be taken to correct off-schedule conditions and to realistically plan the next production period. Reporting provides an avenue of communication between all levels of management, to discuss the results of the day's progress and the goals to be established for the next production period. Reporting assures that problem areas are highlighted and necessary decisions are made to resolve the problem.

Evaluation

Evaluation is a method of determining why something happened. It is an analysis conducted after results are reported, so that future activities can better be forecasted and planned. Evaluation occurs by thoroughly analyzing reporting documents. Overall performance is compared against plan. Specifically, we evaluate to determine:

- How costs were distributed (i.e., set-up, down time, changeovers, etc.);
- Where costs are higher than at other times;
- Why costs were higher one day than another;
- What can be done to achieve the same performance level as achieved on good days;
- Who is performing well and who isn't;
- What corrective action has occurred to solve negative variances;
- What corrective action is still required; and
- Where, when, and why lost time occurred.

In summary, evaluation is the important process dissecting past activities and performance, so that processes, procedures, and behaviors can be modified for future requirements.

EFFECTIVE MANAGER CHARACTERISTICS

The following system concepts have different manager characteristic efficiency requirements.

Forecasting

- Evaluates work openly and honestly;
- Accepts criticism as a basis for improvement;

- Sees the future as something one makes happen, not something that just happens;
- Judges ideas on the basis of merit, not on the basis of origin;
- Does not deny or excuse waste, inefficiency, or lost time;
- Sees the work of the department in relation to the larger organization.

Planning

- Sees the future as something one makes happen, not something that just happens;
- Judges ideas on the basis of merit, not on the basis of origin;
- Assigns work with due regard to production need and worker capabilities, rather than on personal biases, seniority, or custom;
- Delegates jobs and responsibilities to those who are subordinate;
- Defines goals, standards, and expectations for workers. Holds oneself and others to high, though realistic, goals;
- Is productivity-oriented and cooperates with new procedures to increase productivity.

Execution

- Assigns work with due regard to production need and worker capabilities, rather than on personal biases, seniority, or custom;
- Delegates jobs and responsibilities to those who are subordinate;
- Defines goals, standards, and expectations for workers. Holds oneself and others to high, though realistic, goals;
- Rejects unthinking obedience as an appropriate work orientation;
- Avoids judgmental thinking; does not judge co-workers on the basis of sex, race, or appearance;
- Relates to workers with consideration and understanding.

Reporting

- Sees worker alienation and its manifestations (absenteeism and turnover) as something that can be influenced through more effective supervision;
- Follows-up on work assignments to assure adequate performance;
- Communicates positive and negative feedback as appropriate;
- Confronts and counsels with employees when their work does not meet standards;
- Encourages workers to see themselves as members of a team, with each worker contributing to the achievement of team goals;
- Takes responsibility for developing stronger worker morale and motivation;
- Recognizes that people do their best work when they feel a sense of involvement.

LOST-TIME CAUSES

Lost time is nonproductive time. Lost time occurs whenever time that was designated to be used in the active production of a product or the delivery of a service is used for something else. Simply stated, lost time is any time that is used for some other activity other than accomplishing a production goal.

Lost time occurs for many different reasons but can generally be traced back to one of three points of origin:

- People problems;
- Machine problems; or
- Material problems.

These problems result from poor planning, ineffective communication, or lack of follow-up and confrontation.

Lost time prevents managers from meeting their goals. Lost time increases the cost of the product and, consequently, has a negative effect on the profit that the manager is expected to "earn" for the company.

Managers have the responsibility to:

- Recognize lost time;
- Identify its causes;
- Take corrective action to eliminate or minimize lost time; and
- Monitor actions to assure the steps taken have eliminated lost time.

Recognizing Lost Time and Identifying Causes

Some lost time is easy to recognize (i.e., material shortages, mechanical breakdowns, people loafing, or extending break periods). This is known as *obvious* lost time. Other lost time is more subtle, or *hidden*. Examples of this are "pacing" on the part of the workers, duplication of effort, undertrained employees, or lack of discipline. In order to help you become more effective in recognizing and identifying lost time and its causes, this book contains a list of things to look for in the work area.

Controlling Lost Time

Once a manager has recognized that lost time has occurred in a work area and has identified those factors that have caused it to occur, he or she must take corrective action to eliminate the cause. The manager becomes a problem solver and a decision maker. As will be seen in the next section, it is the manager who is sometimes the cause. This means that in some situations, in order to eliminate lost time, the manager must consider one's own behaviors and performance as a manager and set upon a course that will ultimately result in changing those behaviors. The passive manager, the manager who fails to set and communicate goals, the manager who fails to use or comply to systems, the manager who resists change, and the manager who does not use internal motivational techniques with people tends to have more lost time than managers who are more active and have a more positive outlook on their role and function.

Controlling lost time is not always easy, because hidden lost time occurs right in front of us. We must change our perceptions if we are to be able to recognize the symptoms and the cause of lost time. Lost time is the single greatest obstacle the manager faces to increasing productivity. Nonetheless, the effective manager must take the responsibility for eliminating lost time so that the goals of the company are met.

A List of Lost-Time Causes

Following are twenty-nine causes of lost time in the workplace.

1. *Layout of work area.* Poor layout requires more walking or other physical work than necessary to get work done.

2. *Layout of work facilities.* Poor layout causes too many people needing to use the same area at the same time.

3. *Not enough equipment.* High-use equipment needs to be used by too many people at the same time.

4. *Equipment use not scheduled.* Time for use of regular equipment is not planned.

5. *Improper equipment or tools.* This involves using the wrong tools for the job, either because the right ones are not available, or because they have not been taken to the job site.

6. *Poor work atmosphere.* Lighting, temperature, unnecessary clutter, or lack of cleanliness contribute to a poor working atmosphere.

7. *Mismatched capacities.* One operation, person, or group of people feeds work to another operation, person, or group of people at a lesser or greater rate than the rate at which the work can be performed.

8. *Pacing.* People or groups pace their work to exact amounts assigned to them, resulting in less than desirable work output, but an appearance of constant activity. This kind of lost time sometimes takes experience and observation of manload techniques to detect. In many operations, the last hour or two of work is paced to "fill out" the day.

9. *Lack of specific assignment.* The wrong work is done at the wrong time. This often results in lost time, because the work sequence is not as productive as is desirable.

10. *Assignment of work not equitable or demanding enough.* The supervisor allows each person to set his own pace. Often, in these situations, the worker has no understanding of what a reasonable work pace is, because it has not been defined to him by his supervisor. This results in inequities in the work pace among various people in the same group, and dissatisfaction on the part of the more energetic and ambitious people, causing them to slow down. The cost in payroll dollars can be very high.

11. *Lack of a "backup" assignment.* This occurs in situations where the input of higher-priority work fluctuates and the worker paces to do only the high-priority work. Here a supervisor can "even out" the work flow and eliminate productivity variances by making "backup" assignments to be accomplished during the slack period. The backup assignments are normally made in order of priority from the backlog of work in the section or department. This often results in a steady reduction or a constant control of the backlog.

12. *Lack of discipline.* This refers to a constant breach of company policy with regard to the time an employee should start work, break times, lunch periods, and quitting times. This can be very costly where discipline is relatively loose. Sloppy work habits causing faulty work which must be corrected and redone by others is also a major cause of lost time in an undisciplined operation. Also included are excessive time in personal conversations, or on personal phone calls, which are not of a legitimate emergency nature.

13. *Assumption that specialization is desirable.* The supervisor fails to train people to the point where maximum flexibility is gained. The result is small groups of specialists who cannot be used for other jobs when their own workload is lower than desirable.

14. *Failure to make use of inter-section or inter-departmental flexibility.* This is generally caused by failure to set up the communication channels and mechanics for shifting people from one major area to another, when this is desirable. Often a supervisor will "make work" in his or her own department, rather than temporarily shift a person to another area where needed. This is a natural tendency, often based on the feeling that the actual workload *could* increase at any time, and the transferred person or group *may* not be available to return. Lack of good mechanics to effect transfers is often quite costly.

15. *Uncontrollable use of overtime.* This occurs when a supervisor does not plan overtime based on accomplishing overtime work with a minimum of people at a desirable work pace. Sometimes the need for overtime is assumed rather than real. This occurs, for instance, when someone eligible for overtime pay works "just a few minutes more" (or hours) to finish a job, simply to finish it, not because it *had* to be finished. Another typical problem here is that the work pace is less than desirable, because the supervisor has gone home and is not available to assign work or solve problems.

16. *Failure of the supervisor to get into the detail of his operation.* In this situation, the employees begin to make their own rules and develop techniques and work habits that waste time. Often, if a supervisor fails to be accessible (this requires quite a bit of humility on the part of most supervisors to admit), employees do not ask questions that *could* result in time savings, and will often make assumptions that are not in the best interest of company management. A good supervisor *wants* to be "bothered" by employee's questions.

17. *Inadequate communications.* When requirements are not clearly communicated from one department to the next or within a department, lost time occurs when

the right work is not done at the right time. Lost time also occurs when too many or too few people to perform work are made available by a manager or supervisor, based on poor communications or failure to communicate changes in requirements from one area to another far enough in advance.

18. *Failure to recognize lost time.* Recognition of lost time requires training, thought and, most important of all, honesty and humility on the part of the manager or supervisor. This is especially true of technically, scientifically, or mechanically oriented supervisors who were made managers because their job knowledge was considered of equal or more importance than management skills. The manager feels that, because he or she has supervised an area for some time (often many years), he or she must justify its mode of operation, because to admit to any failings would be self-incriminating. Of course, nothing could be farther from the truth, because any company management always welcomes improvement, regardless of its relationship to the supervisor's time in service. In this case, the ego of the supervisor is a major deterrent to the detection and recovery of lost time.

19. *Poor definition of the supervisory role.* Most companies are guilty, to a certain extent, of failing to place the proper emphasis on the role of the supervisor as a time-conscious business man. In addition, many companies do not provide supervisors with the systems, mechanics, or training to minimize lost time in their areas of responsibility.

20. *Poor follow-up by higher management.* This occurs in cases where a supervisor or manager is motivated or even quite determined, to remove overtime from an area by taking a specific course of action that requires the approval or participation of higher management, but where higher management either does not approve or does not participate, due to simple procrastination or unwillingness to make a decision. In cases such as this, the reasons for avoiding decisions or "passing the buck" can be made to sound quite plausible, while costing the company significant payroll dollars.

21. *Breakdown in the execution of existing systems or procedures.* This is where existing systems and procedures are designed to highlight lost-time problems, but are not followed in spirit, or to the letter. Lost time goes undetected. In this case, additional lost time is created in the preparation of incomplete, ineffective, or useless reports and controls.

22. *Wrong emphasis in existing systems.* This is where existing systems do not keep pace with the changing character of a business operation. Time and dollars are lost, due both to lack of effective control and executing a system which has, in part or in total, no particular value.

23. *Duplication of effort.* These cases are not always obvious. Duplicate functions are often simultaneously performed in widely separated areas. An understanding of the concept and purpose of each function of each section or department is sometimes required before a manager can effectively erase all duplication of effort. Included in this type of lost time is needless cross-checks of predominantly accurate information. Sometimes work is generated within a department for the

use of that department, while another department is doing substantially the same work for its own use. Neither department managers nor higher management have any knowledge of the duplication.

24. *The supervisor does not identify with the goals of company management.* This problem can be a serious time and money waster in many ways, simply because the supervisor or manager is not motivated to control operations as if it were his or her own store and he or she were writing the payroll checks each week from their *own* personal bank account. In the day-to-day tangles with operating problems, boredom, laziness, and ego, somehow the reason for the existence of the company (to make money) becomes obscured.

25. *Inflexibility or lack of original and creative thought on the part of the manager.* This type of thinking can preserve lost time as if it were sealed in granite. If the manager does not understand that the most important function is continuous correction and improvement of the operation, the manager cannot operate effectively in a profit-oriented organization. At the point which a supervisor or manager believes the operation is near perfect or beyond improvement for all practical purposes, managerial effectiveness becomes seriously impaired.

26. *Fear.* When a supervisor is afraid to take charge as a leader of the operation, lack of discipline and lost time is the natural human result. Fear is usually based on the totally unnecessary conflict in the mind of the supervisor between the need to be "boss" of the operation and the desire to be "liked." The realization that a weak supervisor may be "liked" but is generally not respected by either the people or the company management can help correct this problem. It is human nature to respect and admire a demanding but fair and openly communicative manager. Fear of taking charge is often perpetuated, because the supervisor who has the problem characteristically will not admit fear, because the admission is such an ego-crushing experience. One will often go to great lengths to justify to oneself and to others motives for making less desirable demands on the people. Thus is perpetuated lost time in the operation.

27. *Training.* Lost time occurs when a worker is not fully trained to perform a job. It may result in machines and equipment being underutilized and work not being done as quickly as it should be.

28. *Scrap.* Any time an employee creates scrap, for whatever reason, lost time occurs because the time spent making scrap was not spent making a sellable product.

29. *Rework.* Rework situations result in doubling the effect of lost time. The time spent making a product that does not conform to quality standards is lost for the same reason as in scrap. In order to make the product "acceptable," time must be spent in a nonproductive activity. Often it takes more time to correct the quality of a product than it did to make it in the first place.

2

BUILDING THE ORGANIZATION
FROM THE BOTTOM UP

OBJECTIVES

Among the first questions to ask are, "What needs to be accomplished with organizational structure?" and "How to know when there is a good structure for the plant?" It is crucial to start with the objectives, and the broad answer is clear: the organizational structure must make its full contribution to the plant goals of quantity, quality, and cost. The specific answer is contained in this list of objectives for the plant organization. It must:

- *Accomplish the work.* Not only must it provide sufficient numbers of people with the ability to carry out the production tasks, but it must also furnish support personnel to move materials, judge quality, repair equipment, and supervise the operation.

- *Minimize cost.* Good organization structure can contribute mightily to reducing costs. It avoids wasting labor, just as a good production process avoids wasting material. Every task performed should be assigned to the lowest wage or salary level at which it can be performed competently. And, while the organization is providing sufficient numbers of people to do the work, it must not provide excessive numbers.

- *Maintain flexibility.* Every industrial plant experiences peaks and valleys of production output. Changes will occur in equipment, processes, and kinds of products manufactured. Key people may be absent for periods of time, ranging from a few days to months, or may suddenly leave the organization altogether. The organizational structure must provide maximum ability to meet these changing situations, without losing the ability to continue production, and without incurring excessive cost.

- *Provide clear-cut lines for authority and responsibility.* Unless each individual and group within the organization understands what his or her job is, and where his or her authority begins and ends, group performance will be damaged by confusion and internal friction.

- *Offer maximum opportunity for advancement.* People will leave when they see no chance to achieve higher positions and earnings. The organizational structure

13

can be built to encourage employees to broaden their skills, and to reward those who do; in return, it fosters employee loyalty and greater flexibility.

- *Harmonize with the physical layout of the plant.* An existing arrangement of buildings and heavy machinery dictates, to a large extent, the shape of the organization that will run it; to ignore the boundaries of departments and sections so determined is to create administrative problems for the foremen and supervisors who must later lead them. When a new plant is to be built, the physical layout should be adjusted to meet the requirements of good organizational structure; at this stage changes can be made at little or no cost, which will save many thousands of dollars in operating costs over the life of the plant.

SIX STEPS TO A MORE STRUCTURED ORGANIZATION

To build the organization from the ground up, follow the six steps listed below *in sequence.* Don't make the mistake of starting with a list of jobs to be filled; instead, go back into the most basic tasks that must be accomplished and work upward for them:

- List the tasks that must be performed by the organization.
- Combine the tasks into jobs which will be filled by workers.
- Group the workers into sections and departments.
- Develop the supervisory and managerial structure.
- Assign responsibilities to the sections and departments.
- Coordinate the activities of the sections and departments.

KEEPING SCHEDULE CHANGES DOWN

Once the schedule has been established, materials ordered, or work begun, sudden changes can have the following negative effects on plant operation:

- *Crowding* of operating floor with materials assembled for prior orders, which must now wait while the rush order is processed;
- *Overtime* costs, tend to increase production and quality errors;
- *Reduced plant efficiency* in output per person-hour;
- *Wasted time* of schedulers, foremen, and managers; and
- *Worker resentment* of sudden changes in assignments, especially when they result in waste of previous work.

The manager bears a double responsibility when schedule changes are demanded of the plant. It is the duty of the manager, as well as everyone else in the company, to serve legitimate customer needs. On the other hand, it is also the manager's duty to point out the additional costs of the negative effects listed above, and to probe the reasons for schedule changes. Often the reasons are poor—someone "forgot" an order, "lost a paper," or a clerk was absent and no one did his work. When such cases occur frequently, one can rightfully demand that these deficiencies should not be redeemed by increased plant costs.

MANAGING OTHER OPERATING FUNCTIONS

Guidelines on When to Use Overtime

Premium rates charged for overtime range from one-and-one-half to three times the base hourly rate, making a prima facie case for very close control and even elimination of overtime. Nevertheless, you know that you cannot simply do away with overtime by issuing an edict, and the cost decisions are not as simple as they first appear. Below are four guiding points to use in making overtime decisions:

1. Use overtime to keep the organization lean. When your person-hour calculations call for 9.5 people to staff a section, hire nine and make up the difference with overtime. Assuming that you pay for the 0.5 person at time-and-a-half, your cost liability is 0.75 at straight-time rates, rather than the 1.0 you would have paid had you hired the tenth person. Equally important, you will avoid hiring more people than you need, a practice which inevitably leads to loose work habits and hidden costs much higher than the overtime incurred.

2. Base overtime decisions on hard economic facts whenever possible. If holding a freight car another day will cost $75.00, but four person-hours of overtime at $10.50 times 1.5 can get it unloaded, then the decision is in favor of the overtime. If it will require a thousand dollars worth of overtime to meet a deadline on a job that will only return seven-hundred dollars in profit, the economic decision is against the use of overtime.

3. The cost of fringe benefits affects the economics of overtime decisions. Often the cost of these benefits, such as vacations, holidays, work clothing, and insurance, will total 30 percent of the base hourly rate, but does not increase because of overtime. Thus, when a choice must be made between having the existing force work overtime or hiring new workers at straight time, it is really between spending 1.5 times the base rate for the overtime work, and 1.3 times the base rate for the new workers.

4. Include unavoidable overtime in the budget. Sometimes you are required by forces beyond your control—sales policy, clerical mistakes in order handling, bad weather, the need to clean up for important visitors—to use overtime work. Although the individual occurrences cannot be foreseen with much accuracy, over a year their total costs tend toward a repetitive annual figure that can be predicted. The manager should insist that these costs be included in the budget.

MANAGING SHUT-DOWNS AND START-UPS

Throughout the year you are faced with a number of occasions requiring the planning of a shut-down or a start-up; holidays, slow production periods, vacations, maintenance turnarounds, and bringing new facilities on stream. It is imperative that these operations be carried out from written procedures, not only to prevent the omission of an important step, but also because the mere act of planning will uncover problems of coordination that must be answered ahead of time.

Shut-Downs

Use the following checklist of special preparations for a plant closing:

- *Building security:* Windows and doors locked, heating and ventilating systems adjusted properly;
- *Electrical systems:* Switches off, fuses pulled, breakers locked out;
- *Fluid systems:* Valves closed, vessels and pipes drained, depressured, or vented;
- *Sprinklers and other fire protection systems:* In working order, provisions for last-minute checks;
- *Freeze-ups:* Special protection, not only for outdoor equipment, but also for pipes that pass through or run close to cold walls;
- *Preparation for maintenance work:* If equipment repairs and overhauls are planned for the shutdown, be sure that the work area is cleaned up, process materials removed, and potentially dangerous conditions offset by safety precautions.

Start-Ups

The object is to get the plant running again quickly and smoothly. Consider the following points in planning the start-up:

- Bring maintenance and utility crews in early to have buildings, machines, and services ready when the production personnel start work.
- Coordinate material flow plan operations, especially in continuous and series-type production, so that production crews are neither idle, nor swamped by excessive work coming from previous steps in the process.
- Beware of pressure systems—steam, gas, and water lines may be carrying unusually high pressures because of zero demand during the shutdown period; valves must be opened more slowly and carefully than usual.
- Expect equipment problems. Lubricants will have drained from metal surfaces, pumps lost suction, fluid systems become airbound, and instruments that are off calibration or stuck in one position.

EMERGENCY PROCEDURES

As in the case of start-ups and shut-downs, emergency procedures must be thought out ahead of time, reduced to printed form, and widely disseminated to those who will actually put them into practice. It is an excellent idea to conduct drills and problem exercises in the use of power failure, flood, and fire emergency procedures, to be sure that plant personnel will react promptly and effectively should actual emergencies occur.

Power Failure

Prior to any actual emergency, examine all instruments and control devices to be sure that they are set for *fail-safe,* that is, when they are deprived of power they will cause cooling rather than heating, low rather than high pressure, to occur.

Shut off electrical, start–stop switches. Some types of electrical equipment can be damaged by a partial return of electric power and, in any event, the main breakers may cause a second power failure if they are overloaded with all equipment on when the power returns.

If the failure is in the steam system, take steps to protect the building against freezing. Close windows and doors, turn on emergency electric heaters if electricity is available. Decide at what building temperature workers will be sent home. Close steam valves at points in the system where process materials can be drawn into the pipes by vacuum, and where air can be drawn in.

Provide for emergency cooling. If your plant has a cooling tower for heat removal from process equipment, its fans and pumps will be shut down in an electrical failure. Arrange for emergency tie-ins to city water mains to accomplish enough cooling for safety purposes.

Fire

The first step in preparing an emergency procedure for fire is to decide what you want your employees to do first. Sound the alarm? Evacuate the building? Fight the fire with hand equipment until it is out or too big to handle? The answers to this question will vary with the type of plant you operate and the prevailing safety philosophy in your company. The important point is that the decisions be made ahead of time and incorporated into well-rehearsed procedures.

Shut-down decisions can be more complicated than they first appear. If there is a fire in one section of the plant, it would seem sensible to shut down operations in all other sections until the situation is under control. But, if a part of the plant is handling flammable liquids or gases, a sudden shut-down can cause venting of these materials, or perhaps spills, increasing the danger of fire. It may be safer to keep a department of this type running, unless the fire is very close to it.

The fire procedure will contain a description of the plant alarm system, its signals, and what to do if it fails. It should also spell out who is authorized to deal with the press and public in an emergency situation.

Flood

Flooding usually gives more warning of its arrival than do other types of emergencies, and the decision process can be spread out over a long period of time. If the plant is in the flood plain of a river, your state flood control agency or the U.S. Army Corps of Engineers can probably give you detailed data on the depth of water to expect and the frequency of flooding in the area.

Develop the procedure for evacuation. The primary questions are: Who makes the shut-down decisions? On what criteria? Which sections shut down first? and What are the composition and duties of emergency crews, if any?

Provide for protection of property. See that doors and windows are closed, and, if there is time, sealed. Electrical equipment should be de-energized, and delicate apparatus moved out of danger. Materials that can catch fire when exposed to water should be relocated.

Snow Emergency

The decision-making process is the key to a successful procedure, and should be detailed carefully in advance. Who makes the final decision on running or shutting down? Who must be consulted? Who sees the first information and warnings? How will the information be disseminated to employees?

Beware of hourly pay squabbles. Some union contracts (and even non-union plant rules) require that prior notice be given of a cancelled shift, or the workers are paid for the day anyway. Situations can arise in which one worker stays home and gets paid, while another reports, does a day's work, and gets the same pay; obviously the second worker will feel he is owed some kind of premium. To avoid such situations, one plant stays open if at least one supervisor can make it to the plant to assign workers; those who do report get paid for the work they do, while the absentees are not paid.

Communications. If the plant is to be shut down, employees must be notified in advance. Make arrangements with one or more local radio stations to broadcast your emergency announcements. Each fall post a notice telling employees which stations to listen to for emergency instructions.

HOLIDAY OPERATIONS

Some operations must run on holidays, either because their outputs cannot be stored or because they are too costly or complicated to shut down. Others that have the option of shutting down will usually do so, unless urgent customer needs or exceptional economic conditions dictate keeping the plant open. In either case, give special attention to these four points when considering holiday operations:

1. "Double-time-and-a-half" is not what it seems. You pay an employee eight hours straight-time pay whether he works the holiday or not; therefore, when he works the holiday your incremental cost is at time-and-a-half.

2. In prosperous times employees will generally resist holiday work, unless the nature of the operation obviously requires it. If the entire plant does not have to operate, it may be wiser to recruit a skeleton crew from among those who wish to volunteer for holiday work.

3. Holidays may bring increased incidence of drinking, sleeping on the job, and absenteeism; at these times the rules need to be firmly announced and impartially administered. Plant rules or the union contract should provide that an employee must work the day before and the day after the holiday in order to receive holiday pay.

4. Prepare for a lack of supporting operations both inside and outside the plant. The office is closed, clerks are gone, truck terminal dispatchers and railroad agents not available, fuel and food deliveries may not take place.

PUTTING THE PLANT ON SHIFT

Because of the many problems that face employees and management alike, the decision to schedule shift work for the plant is not made lightly but, for many operations, the need is compelling. This section examines such needs, the problems encountered, and what is involved in setting up shift operations.

Establishing Shift Operations

Following are four good reasons for setting up shift operations.

1. *Utilization of capital equipment.* When the cost of a machine is very high, compared with profit realized on each unit of production, the machine may have to be operated for more than eight hours a day, in order to justify its cost.

2. *High sales and production levels.* When they exceed one-shift capacity the workday must be extended to second and third shifts. Because it is time consuming to recruit and train supervision and operating personnel for additional shifts, this decision is usually made to run on more than a short-term basis, for at least a matter of months.

3. *Processes that cannot be shut down easily or economically.* High-heat furnaces, which take several days to reach operating temperatures, and complicated chemical processes, in which a raw material does not emerge as the finished product until a week after it has entered the process, are examples of operations that require shift work. Plant personnel will be more receptive to the idea of working shifts when the process itself makes the need obvious.

4. *Products that cannot be stored.* Transportation terminals and electric power plants are examples of plants whose "products" must be used at the instant they are created, and their need for shift work is obvious. Plants that make products for a daytime market, such as bakeries and dairies, are similarly affected.

Management Problems with Shift Operations

There are some problems, inherent to shift operations, that management will encounter.

Communications.   Direct contact between the upper levels of plant management and personnel of second and third shifts is limited to brief periods in the early morning and late afternoon; with some shift schedules direct contact can be almost nonexistent. To overcome the problem, written communications are used to a greater extent; the daytime superintendent or general foreman may leave a handwritten "night sheet," in which he gives detailed instructions for the work to be performed that night, any safety hazards he foresees, and minor notices of interest to the shift personnel. The shift foremen, in turn, keep a written log of their activities for the use of daytime supervision.

Management Control.   It is much more difficult for daytime plant management to be sure its procedures and plant rules are being observed when its members are not physically present to see what is going on. The use of rotating, rather than fixed, shift schedules can help management to overcome this problem.

Labor Shortages.   When employment rates are high in the surrounding area, it becomes difficult or impossible to staff night shifts. It may be necessary to offer very high wages and shift differentials to attract workers, and even these are not guaranteed solutions.

Cost of Shift Premiums.   When shifts are instituted, the cost of labor rises through the payment of a shift differential. Five percent of base wage is a typical level, but premiums in excess of 10 percent are not unheard of.

Reduced Worker Efficiency.   Many third-shift workers do not get full, satisfying rest; there are too many daytime household noises and distractions to permit uninterrupted sleep. The second-shift worker fares better, but is tempted to take a second job, or become absorbed in home projects during the day, showing up late and is disciplined by the production manager in the morning.

MAKING EFFECTIVE USE OF PERSONNEL

Chronic shortages of labor, and the high cost of available people, make compelling reasons for any manager to avoid wasting manpower in operations. Follow these seven lines of action:

1. Keep the work force flexible. The more kinds of work each employee can perform, the better the manpower utilization.

2. Have plans ready for slow periods. Cleanup, painting, repairs, and scrap rework all can be used to utilize manpower effectively when production operations are at an ebb.

3. Develop and maintain the attitude that all employees are expected to be engaged in useful activity during working hours.

4. If flexibility is not a prime consideration, then be sure that all plant work is performed at the lowest possible skill level.

5. Consider the use of manpower pools for the entire plant, rather than duplicate reserves of workers within each department.

6. Provide sufficient supervision. When the ratio of supervisors to workers drops too low, even the best motivated workers waste time trying to find someone to give them new assignments, or to whom they can report a production holdup.

7. Provide effective support services. Materials should be on time, machines in good repair, and tools and supplies readily available.

HOW TO CONTROL OUTSIDE WORKERS VISITING THE PLANT

It is inevitable that there will be people working in the plant who are not company employees—organization truck drivers, utility company workers, sales and delivery people, and cleaning service personnel. While deliberately hostile acts—theft, industrial spying, and disturbing regular employees—are rare, there is a significant danger from outside personnel not knowing the safety hazards and precautions required on the premises. Use the following three methods to keep control of the situation:

1. Designate one of your supervisors to be responsible for each kind of outside employee—maintenance foreman for utility workers, project engineer for contractors' personnel, personnel supervisor for vending machine servicemen. Your employees should know when outside personnel enter the plant, when they leave, and what they do while in it.

2. Identify visitors clearly. Use special visitor's badges; if safety hard hats are required in the plant, use a special color for visitors.

3. Issue written instructions to outside personnel. One company has a printed card, about 8 by 10 inches, which the gate guard hands to truck drivers and picks up from them as they leave. It tells the drivers where they can and cannot go in the plant, what facilities (lunchroom, rest room, smoking area) they may use, whether they can leave their engines running, and any safety precautions they must take.

When outside contractors' personnel first enter the plant to begin work, the project engineer should give them a one-page set of safety instructions and review them with each outside worker. All too often newspaper accounts of a serious plant fire end with ". . . authorities believe the blaze was ignited by an outside welder's torch."

ELEMENTS OF PLANT COSTS

Below are listed the major categories of plant costs, with the specific functions of those costs sublisted. Exhibit 2.1 outlines cost cutters in detail.

Labor
  Production
  Shipping
  Maintenance
  Materials movement
  Quality control
  Fringe Benefits
  Training
  Supervisor and
    administrative
Utilities
  Water
  Fuel
  Electricity
  Telephone
Depreciation
  Buildings
  Equipment
  Vehicles
Customer Returns of
  Defective Goods

Raw Materials
  Purchase price
  Freight in
  Handling and yield losses
Containers for Finished
Goods Supplies
  Production
  Shipping
  Maintenance
  Janitorial
  Office
Taxes and Licenses
Insurance
Support Services
  Fire protection
  Guard service
  Waste disposal
  Lunch/cafeteria
  Cleaning

EXHIBIT 2.1   Cost Cutters: Some Things to Think About

Planning
- Review operating statements and identify areas that offer best cost reduction potential.
- Flow-chart all major functions.
- Group-related functions should be under the same supervision.
- Shorten the chain of command; it improves communications and eliminate excess levels of supervision.
- Define responsibilities and authority; eliminate overlaps.
- Consider decentralizing and/or centralizing operations.
- Consider a profit-planning program.
- Try to measure benefits before spending.
- Make employees plan major jobs in advance.
- Defer all new actions until true needs are determined.
- Reduce the number of committees and length of meetings.
- Have an annual cost-reduction suggestion program.

Analyses of Departments and Activities
- Are all departments necessary? Should any be added?
- Are all officers and jobs necessary?
- Is the company magazine necessary?
- Are company-sponsored organizations necessary?
- Establish a word processing center.
- Reduce central filing.
- Centralize office services.
- Evaluate all major cost programs.
- Review the need for institutional type advertising.
- Eliminate duplicate records. Put a price tag on each report issued. The information will be surprising.
- Review all scrap, and see if any salvage value can be realized.

Personnel
- Set a good example for your staff.
- Promote from within to improve morale.
- Institute a hiring freeze for short periods.
- Review manpower requirements periodically.
- Review all educational and training programs.
- Have periodic performance reviews.
- Request periodic time-distribution reports from employees.

Efficiency
- Start and leave work on time.
- Utilize people to full capacity and qualifications.
- Permit carry-over of workload and level out peaks.
- Review all form designs for efficiency.
- Review quality of office equipment.
- Standardize equipment.
- Use more estimates in accounting.
- Have cycle billings.
- Close books quarterly; use estimated P/L statement monthly.
- Reduce quantity of reports.
- Use handwritten instead of typewritten memos.

(continued)

EXHIBIT 2.1 *(Continued)*

- Eliminate federal and trade reports where not required.
- Make a periodic review of files for retention necessity.
- Establish convenient "libraries" for manuals.
- Use combination requisition, purchase order, receiving report.
- Route reports rather than prepare multiple report copies.
- Use microfilm files to save space.
- Use computer to assist auditors.
- Use cheaper paper in duplicating machines.
- Use better machines for duplicating to cut down on waste.
- Reduce necessity for duplicating by use of common files.
- Do more internal printing of forms.
- Utilize copiers at strategic locations.
- Establish a form control manual; control quantities of forms.
- Review all forms for necessity and simplicity.
- Review all stationary costs.
- Reduce the size of annual reports, and number of colors.
- Purchase and issue office supplies in economical quantities.
- Reduce kinds of accounting paper carried in inventory.
- Control supplies and sundries.

Office Facilities
- Have forward planning of office layout.
- Have more modest offices.
- Eliminate offices for lower supervisory personnel.
- Use proper wattage and voltage.
- Use Fluorescent lighting.
- Turn out lights when not in use.
- Establish janitorial procedures that cycle the workload.
- Remove materials from desk nightly, to reduce janitorial work.
- Set standards for floor space allowances by classification of office employees.

Outside Services
- Hire temporaries for emergencies; no overtime.
- Utilize a supplier's free technical services.
- Cut out professional services where possible.
- Do your own building or garden maintenance.
- Use bank facilities to accumulate and pay freight bills, and to mechanically reconcile bank accounts.
- Self-produce costly supplies or material needed.
- Send paid freight and utility bills to outside audit agencies.

Communications
- Review all communication facilities.
- Start a telephone expense-reduction campaign.
- Reduce switchboard hours; close board earlier.
- Use one central mail room only.
- Install intraoffice mail and messenger service.
- Mechanize mail processing.
- Use lowest-class mail rate where feasible.
- Use lighter paper and envelopes.

EXHIBIT 2.1   *(Continued)*

- Don't use separate envelopes on interoffice mail.
- Mail dividend check with annual report.
- Eliminate the second proxy mailing.
- Don't mail statements to all customers.
- Reduce size of mailing lists.
- Don't use express mail unless necessary.

Meetings and Travel
- Strictly regulate all travel.
- Cut out executive cars.
- Cut out company airplanes.
- Use coach instead of first-class airfare.
- Use the airport bus instead of cabs.
- Stagger company hours to relieve congestion problems.
- Lease company cars instead of purchasing, and use compacts.
- Set up your own transport fleet.
- Reduce meeting and travel expense by a set percentage.
- Eliminate or reduce convention attendance.
- Use lower-priced hotels.
- Make contract travel arrangements with hotels in cities that are frequently visited by employees.
- Control moving expenses of people transferred.
- Eliminate expensive stockholders' meetings.
- Eliminate special stockholders' meetings by better planning.
- Cut down on lunchtime meetings.
- Have management meetings in corporate offices.

Payroll and Fringe Benefits
- Schedule overtime by priority.
- Dock employees for being late.
- Have shorter lunch hours.
- Eliminate oddball deductions for employees.
- Eliminate paychecks; have pay deposited in employees' bank accounts.
- Schedule varying pay dates to level load in payroll department and reduce payroll expenses.
- Review employee stock option plans.
- Eliminate Christmas gifts to employees.
- Eliminate or reduce coffee breaks.
- Have suggestion award system.

Funds
- Raise capitalization limits.
- Use lockbox banking.
- Keep petty cash funds to a minimum.
- Minimize number of bank accounts.
- Have bills paid by sight draft.
- Use idle funds.

(continued)

EXHIBIT 2.1   *(Continued)*

- Speed up billings.
- Review discount procedures.
- Hold payables for maximum time but pay for discount.
- Have salesmen and drivers deposit collections directly into banks.

Taxes and Insurance
- Move to lower tax areas.
- Renegotiate real estate taxes on idle facilities.
- Control inventories to reduce property taxes.
- Don't pay tax installments until due.
- Establish subsidiary corporations for branches in areas that tax on total company business.
- Review all insurance costs.
- Extend the use of "self-insurance."
- Negotiate insurance rates on a "package" basis.

Subscriptions and Dues
- Reduce memberships in outside societies, clubs, and associations.
- Eliminate duplicate memberships in organizations.
- Buy industrial and trade magazines at wholesale rates.
- Centralize magazine services.
- Reduce number of magazine and newspaper subscriptions.
- Develop bibliography of current periodicals to ensure review of latest ideas.

Miscellaneous
- Assemble all reports (internal) into a single book.
- Establish greater security to avoid inventory thefts.
- Obtain competitive bids for purchases of materials and supplies.
- Review purchase frequency for supplies and materials.
- Review technical magazines systematically for cost-saving ideas.
- Distribute useful "cost-cutters" to all personnel who might use them.

3

FINANCIAL RATIO ANALYSIS

Management is responsible for understanding the financial condition and performance of the organization. Such an understanding can be enhanced by interpreting a set of ratios from the existing financial statements. The evaluation of ratios should minimize the amount of time spent on interpreting the financial statements. This evaluation can provide answers to a broad range of questions, such as:

- How many times may the company's current liabilities be paid with its current assets?
- What is the average number of days for collecting accounts receivable?
- What is the average number of days for paying accounts payable?
- What portion of the company's assets is financed by its shareholders?
- What is the return on assets enjoyed by the company?
- What is the return on shareholders' equity?

Financial ratio analysis is a process of identifying, measuring, and evaluating financial relationships, or ratios, in the financial position and performance of the company. The advantage of the financial ratio is twofold. First, each ratio shows the relative size of two items, such as the amount of assets available to pay debts. Second, each ratio minimizes the effect of inflation when comparing results from one year with the next. For example, operating expenses may remain a constant percentage of sales, even as total expenses increase during inflation. Throughout the financial ratio analysis, a number of significant ratios will be presented. Some financial ratios will be individually evaluated as acceptable and others as poor, but each will provide essential information about the company's condition and performance.

Financial ratio analysis enables management to evaluate some attributes of the company, such as:

- Liquidity;
- Solvency;
- Profitability; and
- Ability to manage assets.

In the following pages, each of the sixteen key financial ratios is considered. The nine secondary ratios yield important information about the company's fundamental financial condition and its competitive position, but do not indicate causes of comparative strength or weakness.

Let's examine the seven primary, or causal, ratios:

1. Net Profit to Net Sales;
2. Net Sales to Total Assets;
3. Collection Period of Accounts Receivable;
4. Cost of Sales to Inventory;
5. Net Sales to Fixed Assets;
6. Net Sales to Net Worth; and
7. Long-Term Liabilities to Total Noncurrent Assets.

RATIO SUMMARIES

For the ratio summaries that appear at the ends of the following sections, we use the terms *favorable* and *unfavorable* in a conservative context. Of the two extremes, the favorable side is characterized by high profit, low debt, and high liquidity. Actually, for relatively small companies, the most favorable financial structure may be near the middle of the competitive pack. The underlying assumption is that most firms gain their greatest advantage from concentrating on their special talents—tool making, designing and manufacturing furniture, distributing electrical equipment, wholesaling produce, selling men's clothing, exterminating pests, marketing and installing cable television—or whatever their business purpose may be. From this perspective, financial management, clearly a critical element in business success, is seen as a means of keeping a company out of trouble and enabling management to sleep better at night. For credit grantors, financial analysis is viewed as the most effective means of avoiding problems—and, of course, sleeping better, too.

Unless a company's decision makers are familiar (and comfortable) with techniques of financial management and specific means of achieving a comparative advantage, maintaining the business's financial structure in line with that of typical competitors is generally a good idea. Particularly with respect to working capital sufficiency and financial leverage, experimentation with a novel financial approach can be dangerous. By following common industry practice in most financial matters, management can concentrate on achieving excellence in the business's basic operations—attaining a high level of profit and outstanding officers'/owners' compensation through superior performance in the company's specific areas of expertise. Only one ratio, *Net Profit to Net Sales,* is regarded as having a consistently favorable direction: The higher the better. But even this ratio must be viewed with some caution. High *Net Profit to Net Sales* may be the result of a disinvestment strategy that cannot be sustained—a strategy of short-term cost minimization that will jeopardize the company's competitive position in the future.

As a practical matter, financial management involves balancing risk and reward. If management has reason to consider a comparatively high-debt, low-liquidity, or low-profit strategy for well-defined operational or strategic purposes, ratio analysis will be helpful in evaluating both the potential risks and the likely rewards.

Some ratios, such as *Long-Term Liabilities to Total Noncurrent Assets,* have a narrow range of common experience, because of the nature of the relationship they represent. Borrowing only a small proportion of the purchase price of fixed assets and other noncurrent assets is not ordinarily a wise practice; on the other hand, few lenders are willing to advance funds in excess of 80 percent or 90 percent of book value. Consequently, this ratio is generally found in the 0.5 to 0.7 range. The values for *Net Sales to Fixed Assets,* on the other hand, vary widely from industry to industry.

THE SEVEN CAUSAL RATIOS

Below is a summary of basic financial principles.

1. *Maintain an adequate profit percentage on sales volume.* High *Net Profit to Net Sales* affords a protection against losses in the event of increased price competition or a general decline in demand. As a causal ratio, it also increases return on equity and tends to reduce financial leverage (depending on management policy with respect to retention of earnings).

2. *Manage total assets carefully in relation to sales volume.* High *Net Sales to Total Assets* tends to reduce costs associated with asset management (bad debts, inventory handling costs, inventory write-downs, depreciation, insurance, property taxes, and interest expense). As a causal ratio, it also reduces financial leverage and/or increases return on equity.

3. *Collect accounts receivable at least as rapidly as competitors—unless there is profitable advantage in extending special terms.* Low (short) *Collection Period of Accounts Receivable* tends to reduce bad debts, collection costs, and interest expense. As a causal ratio, it also strengthens working capital balance, reduces financial leverage, and/or increases return on equity.

4. *Hold inventory to the same or lower level (in relation to cost of sales) as competitors—unless there is a profitable advantage in maintaining a greater variety of stock on hand, carrying more raw material, or accepting orders that involve slower throughput (higher work-in-process).* High *Cost of Sales to Inventory* tends to reduce occupancy costs, handling costs, inventory write-downs, insurance, local and state taxes (in some jurisdictions), and interest expense. As a causal ratio, it also strengthens working capital balance, reduces financial leverage, and/or increases return on equity.

5. *Achieve a comparatively high level of net sales in relation to fixed assets—unless there is a profitable advantage in greater modernization, automation, a prestige location, or an unusual array of mechanical capabilities.* High *Net Sales to Fixed Assets* tends to reduce depreciation, occupancy costs, insurance, property taxes, and interest expense. As a causal ratio, it also strengthens working capital sufficiency and balance, reduces financial leverage, and/or increases return on equity.

6. *Maintain an adequate level of net worth (owners' equity) to support sales volume.* Low *Net Sales to Net Worth* tends to reduce interest expense. As a causal ratio, it also reduces financial leverage and tends to strengthen working capital sufficiency and working capital balance (depending on management policy with respect to accounts receivable and inventory versus fixed assets). On the other hand, low *Net Sales to Net Worth* tends to reduce return on equity.

7. *Finance fixed assets and other noncurrent assets with long-term liabilities.* High *Long-Term Liabilities to Total Noncurrent Assets* may increase interest expense (depending on the availability of "free" money such as accounts payable, and on long-term versus short-term interest rates). A high ratio, however, exerts a favorable influence on the secondary ratios by improving working capital sufficiency and strengthening working capital balance.

If all seven causal ratios are equal to their respective industry medians, the nine secondary ratios listed later in this chapter will also be in line with the industry norms.

Causal Ratio 1: Net Profit to Net Sales

Popular Names	*Return on Sales Ratio; Net Profit Margin; Profit Percentage; The Bottom Line*
Purpose	Measures a company's ability to generate profit on its average sales dollar.
Calculation	Divide net profit by net sales, then multiply result by 100, converting ratio to a percentage.
Example	Your company's net profit was $35,000 and your net sales were $1 million during your last fiscal year. What was your *Net Profit to Net Sales?*
	Solution: 35,000 divided by 1,000,000 = 0.35; then 0.35 $\times$ 100 = 3.5%.
Financial Impact	A *high* percentage exerts a *favorable* influence: It increases return on equity and tends to decrease financial leverage.
Operational Impact	A *high* ratio tends to reduce interest cost (provided that earnings are retained to reduce debt) and promote greater operating freedom; however, a high ratio may indicate a disinvestment or "harvesting" strategy that cannot be sustained.
Definition	Net profit *before taxes* is ordinarily used by bankers and other credit grantors as the basis for measuring comparative profitability (versus previous performance or external standards). Net profit *after taxes* is the true "bottom line," but the effect of state and local income taxes, as well as federal income tax credits and carrybacks, can distort

comparative performance. Net profit *from operations* (before non-operating income, non-operating expense, and extraordinary items) and net profit *before officers'/owners' compensation* are also useful measures.

Special Reminder
: *Net Profit to Net Sales* is expressed as a percentage, not as a simple ratio.

Critical Value
: A *negative* percentage, which shows a net loss for the period, causes a negative return on equity and tends to increase interest cost and financial leverage.

Range of Common Experience
: 2.3% to 4.4% (before income taxes).

Causal Ratio 2: Net Sales to Total Assets

Popular Names
: *Asset Utilization Ratio; Asset Management Ratio*

Purpose
: Measures a company's ability to generate sales volume on the assets it employs, or from another perspective, its ability to control assets in relation to sales. Summarizes the combined influence of the individual asset utilization ratio—particularly *Collection Period of Accounts Receivable, Cost of Sales to Inventory,* and *Net Sales to Fixed Assets.*

Calculation
: Divide net sales by total assets.

Example
: Your company's net sales during your last fiscal year were $1 million, and your total assets at year-end were $410,000. What was your *Net Sales to Total Assets?*

: *Solution:* 1,000,000 divided by 410,000 = 2.4.

Financial Impact
: A *high* ratio exerts a *favorable* influence: It reduces financial leverage and/or increases return on equity.

Operational Impact
: A *high* ratio tends to reduce interest cost.

Range of Common Experience
: 1.9 times to 2.8 times.

Causal Ratio 3: Collection Period of Accounts Receivable

Popular Names
: *Collection Period; Days' Sales in Receivables*

Purpose
: Measures a company's control of accounts receivable in relation to net sales volume; indicates the average number of days required to convert accounts receivable to cash.

Calculation
: Multiply accounts receivable by 365, then divide result by net sales; express ratio as whole number.

Example

Your company's accounts receivable were $130,000 at year-end, and net sales for your last fiscal year were $1 million. What was your *Collection Period of Accounts Receivable?*

Solution 1 (for the calculator): $130,000 \times 365 = 47,450,000$; then 47,450,000 divided by 1,000,000 = 47.45 days.

Solution 2 (for greater understanding): Average daily net sales = 1,000,000 divided by 365 = 2,740; then 130,000 divided by 2,740 = 47.45 days of net sales outstanding as accounts receivable.

Financial Impact

A *low* ratio exerts a *favorable* influence: It increases asset utilization, reduces financial leverage, and/or increases return on equity.

Operational Impact

A *low* ratio tends to reduce record keeping and verification costs and also lowers the probability of loss due to bad debts (customer insolvency or unwillingness to pay); on the other hand, a *low* ratio may also indicate an unduly restrictive credit-and-collection policy that is reducing potentially profitable sales to otherwise creditworthy customers.

Range of Common Experience   24 to 48 days.

Causal Ratio 4: Cost of Sales to Inventory

Popular Name

Inventory Turnover Ratio

Purpose

Measures a company's control of inventory in relation to cost of sales; indicates how many times inventory "turns" in a year.

Calculation

Divide cost of sales by inventory.

Example

Your company's cost of sales during your last fiscal year was $750,000, and your inventory at year-end was $155,000. What was your *Cost of Sales to Inventory?*

Solution: 750,000 divided by 155,000 = 4.8.

Financial Impact

A *high* ratio exerts a *favorable* influence: It increases asset utilization, reduces financial leverage, and/or increases return on equity.

Operational Impact

A *high* ratio tends to reduce storage, record keeping, verification, and interest costs and lowers the probability of loss due to physical deterioration or obsolescence; however, in wholesaling, retailing, and make-to-stock manufacturing, a *high* ratio also tends to increase ordering costs and raises the probability of stock-outs and customer dissatisfaction because of limited product selection. This ratio is not applicable to distributors and service industries that do not maintain inventory.

Range of Common Experience   4.1 times to 8.2 times.

Causal Ratio 5: Net Sales to Fixed Assets

Popular Name

Fixed Assets Activity Ratio

Purpose

Measures a company's control of fixed assets in relation to net sales volume or, from another perspective, indicates a company's ability to produce net sales from use of its fixed assets (land, buildings, leasehold improvements, machinery, equipment, furniture, fixtures, and vehicles).

Calculation

Divide net sales by fixed assets.

Example

Your company's net sales during your last fiscal year were $1 million, and your fixed assets at year-end were $210,000. What was your *Net Sales to Fixed Assets?*

Solution: 1,000,000 divided by 210,000 = 4.7.

Financial Impact

A *high* ratio exerts a *favorable* influence: It increases asset utilization, also reduces financial leverage, and/or increases return on equity.

Operational Impact

A *high* ratio tends to reduce depreciation and interest costs; however, it also tends to increase costs related to operating leases (by substituting leased facilities and equipment for acquired assets), personnel (due to lack of automation, crowded sales space, etc.), and travel or delivery expenses (when less costly facilities are acquired in outlying areas).

Range of Common Experience: 6.8 times to 22.4 times.

Causal Ratio 6: Net Sales to Net Worth

Popular Names

Investment Adequacy Ratio; Trading Ratio

Purpose

Measures the adequacy of a company's net worth in support of its net sales volume or, from another perspective, the multiplier effect of "trading on equity" to achieve a higher percentage return on shareholders' investment.

Calculation

Divide net sales by net worth.

Example

Your company's net sales during your last fiscal year were $1 million, and your net worth at year-end was $160,000. What was your *Net Sales to Net Worth?*

Solution: 1,000,000 divided by 160,000 = 6.25.

Financial Impact

A *low* ratio exerts a *favorable* influence in one respect: It reduces financial leverage. However, a *low* ratio is *unfavorable* in another respect: It reduces return on equity.

Operational Impact

A *low* ratio tends to reduce interest cost.

Definition

Net worth, called "owner's equity" in a sole proprietorship (IRS Schedule C), "partners' capital" in a partnership (IRS Form 1065), and "stockholders' equity" or "shareholders' equity" in a corporation (IRS Form 1120, 1120-A, or 1120S), equals total assets minus total liabilities.

Special Reminder

A *low* ratio shows a *high* level of net worth to support net sales.

Critical Value

When total liabilities are greater than total assets, net worth will be in a deficit position and a meaningful ratio cannot be calculated. In such a case, treat *Net Sales to Net Worth* as a very large number for comparative purposes. Deficit net worth is a serious condition that warrants close management attention.

Range of Common Experience

4.8 times to 8.4 times.

Causal Ratio 7: Long-Term Liabilities to Total Noncurrent Assets

Popular Name

Long-Term Financing Ratio

Purpose

Measures a company's use of long-term borrowing to finance acquisition of fixed assets and other noncurrent (miscellaneous) assets.

Calculation

Divide long-term liabilities by total noncurrent assets.

Example

Your company's long-term liabilities were $55,000, your fixed assets were $100,000, and your other noncurrent assets were zero at year-end. What was your *Long-Term Liabilities to Total Noncurrent Assets?*

Solution: Total noncurrent assets = 100,000 + 0 = 100,000; then 55,000 divided by 100,000 = .55.

Financial Impact	A *high* ratio increases working capital sufficiency and tends to increase working capital balance. From a conservative viewpoint, high debt is ordinarily an unfavorable condition; but for this ratio, the benefit of strengthening working capital must be considered.
Operational Impact	A *high* ratio may increase or decrease interest cost, depending on two factors: (1) the company's need for short-term bank borrowing, and (2) short-term versus long-term interest rates.
Critical Value	A ratio *greater* than 1.0 shows long-term borrowing in excess of the book value of fixed assets and other noncurrent assets.
Range of Common Experience	0.5 times to 0.7 times.

THE NINE SECONDARY RATIOS THAT MEASURE EFFECT

By studying the nine secondary ratios, you will gain a clear comprehension of *cause and effect,* the most important concept in the effective use of ratio analysis. An understanding of the cause-and-effect element allows you to examine any financial statement and, within minutes, pinpoint the precise nature of any lack of balance reflected in that statement. Ignorance of cause and effect will leave you jousting with windmills, concentrating on entirely incidental factors.

One important aspect of financial management is represented by each of the nine secondary ratios. By definition, these measures are not as influential as the seven causal ratios, but they are entirely necessary for gaining a sound understanding of a company's basic financial structure. Improvement in operating performance and financial structure can only be achieved through changes in the seven causal ratios, but the extent of that improvement is measured by the nine secondary ratios. In fact, certain of the secondary measures—particularly *Current Assets to Current Liabilities, Total Liabilities to Net Worth,* and *Net Profit to Net Worth*—are among the first ratios examined by credit grantors and investors because they serve as highly convenient summaries of a company's competitive strengths and weaknesses. The interest of outside analysts in the secondary ratios is, in itself, good reason for management to become familiar with these key financial measures.

Examine the nine ratios that measure effect:

1. Net Profit to Net Worth;
2. Total Liabilities to Net Worth;
3. Current Liabilities to Net Worth;
4. Net Sales to Working Capital;
5. Current Assets to Current Liabilities;
6. Cash and Short-Term Investments plus Accounts Receivable to Current Liabilities (the Quick Ratio);

7. Total Noncurrent Assets to Net Worth;

8. Long-Term Liabilities to Working Capital; and

9. Net Profit to Total Assets.

The Secondary Ratios

Following is a summary of basic financial principles.

1. Reinvest sufficient *profit* in relation to *net worth* (in order to support future *sales* volume).

   - High *Net Profit to Net Worth* enables a company to increase owners' equity at a comparatively rapid pace for the purpose of supporting sales growth. The actual percentage increase in net worth depends on the effective tax rate, as well as management policy with respect to retaining net profit. If owners' equity is expanded at a more rapid rate than sales volume, *Total Liabilities to Net Worth* will decline at an even faster rate than *Net Sales to Net Worth*.

   - *Net Profit to Net Worth* can be increased through changes in two causal ratios: Boosting *Net Profit to Net Sales* and/or raising *Net Sales to Net Worth*.

2. Manage *financial leverage* in relation to *return on equity*.

   - Although high *Total Liabilities to Net Worth* reflects relatively great pressure from creditors, it also tends to increase *Net Profit to Net Worth* (depending on the availability of "free" money, such as accounts payable, as well as the rate of interest on any funds borrowed from commercial lenders). Management must determine the extent to which the advantage of a higher percentage of profit on owners' equity is offset by actual or implied restrictions on management's operating freedom.

   - *Total Liabilities to Net Worth* can be reduced through changes in two causal ratios: Lowering *Net Sales to Net Worth* and/or increasing *Net Sales to Total Assets*. If high *Net Sales to Total Assets* is coupled with high *Net Profit to Net Sales,* a company may enjoy low financial leverage as well as high return on equity.

3. Maintain sufficient *working capital* to support *sales* volume.

   - Low *Net Sales to Working Capital* indicates that cash flow problems are relatively unlikely. On the other hand, achieving a high degree of operating freedom by maintaining a high level of working capital in relation to sales volume tends to reduce *Net Profit to Net Worth*.

   - *Net Sales to Working Capital* can be reduced (showing stronger working capital in relation to net sales) by changes in three causal ratios: Lowering *Net Sales to Net Worth* (which lowers return on equity), increasing *Long-Term Liabilities to Total Noncurrent Assets* (which may reduce return on equity, depending on interest rates on short-term debt versus long-term debt and the availability of non-interest-bearing trade credit), and increasing *Net Sales to Fixed Assets* (which will have a positive effect on return on equity if such higher fixed asset activity reflects improved asset management, but may have a negative effect on return on equity if the increase results from failure to modernize and a willingness to operate with obsolete, nearly fully depreciated facilities).

4. Maintain an adequate balance between *current assets* and *current liabilities.*

   • High *Current Assets to Current Liabilities* shows a comparatively great ability to absorb possible bad-debt losses or write-downs of inventory without failing to meet current obligations. Nevertheless, achieving such a favorable balance from a conservative perspective may result in a reduction of return on equity.

   • A company with low *Net Sales to Working Capital* will automatically enjoy high *Current Assets to Current Liabilities* if other key financial factors are equal. With no change in *Net Sales to Working Capital, Current Assets to Current Liabilities* may be increased through changes in two causal ratios: Reducing the *Collection Period of Accounts Receivable* (which will have a positive effect on return on equity from the decrease in accounts receivable) may reflect improved credit policies and collection procedures, but may have a negative effect if the reduction results from restricting sales to fast-paying accounts. Furthermore increasing *Cost of Sales to Inventory* may have a positive or negative impact on return on equity, depending on improvements in inventory management versus reductions of stock on hand or restrictions on production. In fact, a company with low working capital sufficiency—high *Net Sales to Working Capital*—can achieve high *Current Assets to Current Liabilities* by means of a very low *Collection Period of Accounts Receivable* and/or very high *Cost of Sales to Inventory.*

Secondary Ratio 1: Net Profit to Net Worth

Popular Name	*Return on Equity*
Purpose	Measures a company's ability to produce profit on owners' investment (original investment plus retained earnings) and to increase net worth for future sales growth.
Calculation	Divide net profit by net worth, then multiply result by 100, converting ratio to a percentage.
Example	Your company's net profit was $35,000 for the year, and your net worth was $150,000 at year-end. What was your *Net Profit to Net Worth?*
	Solution: 35,000 divided by 150,000 = .230; then .230 × 100 = 23.007.
Financial Impact	A *high* ratio is a *favorable* result: It shows a comparatively high rate of return on owners' equity, which, in turn, tends to decrease financial leverage. However, a high ratio may be a symptom of low investment adequacy.
Operational Impact	A *high* ratio tends to reduce interest cost over time; however, a high ratio may occur when both total debt and interest cost are on the high side.

Definitions	Net profit *before taxes* is ordinarily used by bankers and other credit grantors as the basis for measuring comparative profitability (versus previous performance or external standards). Net profit *after taxes* is the true "bottom line," but the effect of state and local income taxes, as well as federal income tax credits and carrybacks, can distort comparative performance. Net profit *from operations* (before non-operating income, non-operating expense, and extraordinary items) and net profit *before officers'/owners' compensation* are also useful measures.
	Net worth—called "owner's equity" in a sole proprietorship (IRS Schedule C), "partners' capital" in a partnership (IRS Form 1065), "stockholders' equity" or "shareholders' equity" in a corporation (IRS Form 1120, 1120-A, or 1120S)—equals total assets minus total liabilities.
Special Reminders	Net profit is expressed as a percentage, not as a simple ratio relative to net worth.
	Net worth is stated at book value, not market value, which is often significantly higher. Consequently, *Net Profit to Net Worth* at actual market value may be substantially lower than *Net Profit to Net Worth* at book value.
Critical Values	A *negative* percentage, which shows a net loss for the period, tends to increase *financial leverage*. When total liabilities are greater than total assets, net worth will be in a deficit position and a meaningful ratio cannot be calculated. In such a case, treat *Net Profit to Net Worth* as a very large number for comparative purposes. Deficit net worth is a serious condition that warrants close management attention.
Range of Common Experience	15.2% to 21.3% (before income taxes).

Secondary Ratio 2: Total Liabilities to Net Worth

Popular Names	*Financial Leverage Ratio; Debt-to-Equity Ratio; Debt-to-Worth Ratio*
Purpose	Measures a company's funds from creditors (suppliers, banks, and other lenders) against the investment of owners (original investment plus retained earnings); indicates the pressure of total debt (current and long-term) relative to equity.
Calculation	Divide total liabilities by net worth.

Example	Your company's total liabilities were $250,000, and your net worth was $160,000 at year-end. What was your *Total Liabilities to Net Worth?*
	Solution: 250,000 divided by 160,000 = 1.6.
Financial Impact	A *low* ratio is a *favorable* condition from a conservative perspective: It shows comparatively little dependence on outside sources in relation to owners' equity. However, a low ratio may be unfavorable in another respect: It may be related to a low return on equity.
Operational Impact	A *low* ratio tends to reduce interest cost and lower the probability of disadvantageous changes in credit terms or interference in management prerogatives by creditors.
Definition	Net worth—called "owner's equity" in a sole proprietorship (IRS Schedule C), "partners' capital" in a partnership (IRS Form 1065), "stockholders' equity" or "shareholders' equity" in a corporation (IRS Form 1120, 1120-A, or 1120S)—equals total assets minus total liabilities.
Critical Value	When total liabilities are greater than total assets, net worth will be in a deficit position and a meaningful ratio cannot be calculated. In such a case, treat *Total Liabilities to Net Worth* as a very large number for comparative purposes. Deficit net worth is a serious condition that warrants close management attention.
Range of Common Experience	1.4 times to 2.1 times.

Secondary Ratio 3: Current Liabilities to Net Worth

Popular Names	*Current-Debt-to-Equity Ratio; Current-Debt-to-Worth Ratio*
Purpose	Measures a company's funds from short-term creditors (ordinarily trade suppliers and banks) plus the current portion of long-term debt in relation to the investment of owners (original investment plus retained earnings); indicates the pressure of current debt relative to equity.
Calculation	Divide current liabilities by net worth.
Example	Your company's current liabilities were $200,000, and your net worth was $160,000 at year-end. What was your *Current Liabilities to Net Worth?*
	Solution: 200,000 divided by 160,000 = 1.25.

Financial Impact	A *low* ratio is a *favorable* condition from a conservative perspective: It shows comparatively little dependence on short-term obligations in relation to owners' equity. However, a low ratio may be unfavorable in another respect: It may be related to a low return on equity.
Operational Impact	A *low* ratio tends to reduce interest cost and lower the probability of disadvantageous changes in credit terms or interference in management prerogatives by creditors.
Definition	Net worth—called "owner's equity" in a sole proprietorship (IRS Schedule C), "partners' capital" in a partnership (IRS Form 1065), "stockholders' equity" or "shareholders' equity" in a corporation (IRS Form 1120, 1120-A, or 1120S)—equals total assets minus total liabilities.
Critical Value	When total liabilities are *greater* than total assets, net worth will be in a deficit position and a meaningful ratio cannot be calculated. In such a case, treat *Current Liabilities to Net Worth* as a very large number for comparative purposes. Deficit net worth is a serious condition that warrants close management attention.
Range of Common Experience	Insufficient industry data.

Secondary Ratio 4: Net Sales to Working Capital

Popular Name	*Working Capital Sufficiency Ratio*
Purpose	Measures the sufficiency of a company's working capital—the excess of current assets over current liabilities—in support of its net sales volume.
Calculation	Subtract current liabilities from current assets to obtain working capital, then divide net sales by working capital.
Example	Your company's net sales were $1 million during your last fiscal year, your current assets were $300,000, and your current liabilities were $210,000 at year-end. What was your *Net Sales to Working Capital?*
	Solution: Working capital = 300,000 − 210,000 = 90,000; then 1,000,000 divided by 90,000 = 11.11.
Financial Impact	A *low* ratio is a favorable condition from a conservative perspective: It shows a comparatively large

	spread between current assets and current liabilities in relation to net sales.
Operational Impact	A *low* ratio tends to reduce the probability of bill-paying difficulty from irregularities in cash flow; however, a low ratio may increase interest costs if comparatively high long-term liabilities are used to increase working capital.
Definition	Working capital equals current assets minus current liabilities.
Special Reminder	A *low* ratio shows a *high* level of working capital to support net sales.
Critical Value	When current liabilities are greater than current assets, working capital will be in a deficit position and a meaningful ratio cannot be calculated. In such a case, treat *Net Sales to Working Capital* as a very large number for comparative purposes. Deficit working capital is a serious condition that warrants close management attention.
Range of Common Experience	8.6 times to 25.3 times.

Secondary Ratio 5: Current Assets to Current Liabilities

Popular Name	*Current Ratio*
Purpose	Measures a company's ability to cover its current liabilities (obligations due within one year) from its current assets (cash and short-term investments plus the other assets, accounts receivable and inventory, expected to turn into cash within one year); indicates a company's ability to meet day-to-day obligations within terms and to withstand operating difficulties or possible write-downs of inventory or accounts receivable.
Calculation	Divide current assets by current liabilities.
Example	Your company's current assets were $300,000, and your current liabilities were $210,000 at year-end. What was your *Current Assets to Current Liabilities?* *Solution:* 300,000 divided by 210,000 = 1.43.
Financial Impact	A *high* ratio is a *favorable* condition from a conservative perspective: It indicates a comparatively great margin of safety for payment of current liabilities from the conversion of current assets into cash (in the course of normal operations or in the event of liquidation of assets).

Operational Impact	A *high* ratio tends to increase operating freedom and reduce the probability of bill-paying difficulty from write-downs of accounts receivable or inventory.
Range of Common Experience	1.3 times to 1.7 times.

Secondary Ratio 6: Cash and Short-Term Investments Plus Accounts Receivable to Current Liabilities (Quick Ratio)

Popular Names	*Quick Ratio; Acid Test Ratio*
Purpose	Measures a company's ability to cover its current liabilities (obligations due within one year) from its liquid assets (cash and short-term investments plus accounts receivable); indicates a company's ability to meet day-to-day obligations within terms without the need to convert inventory to cash and to withstand operating difficulties or possible write-downs of accounts receivable.
Calculation	Add cash and short-term investments to accounts receivable, then divide the sum by current liabilities.
Example	Your company's cash and short-term investments were $20,000, your accounts receivable were $130,000, and your current liabilities were $200,000 at year-end. What was your *Quick Ratio?*
	Solution: Liquid assets = 20,000 + 130,000 = 150,000; then 150,000 divided by 200,000 = 7.5.
Financial Impact	A *high* ratio is a *favorable* condition from a conservative perspective: It indicates comparatively little dependence on the salability of inventory to meet current obligations.
Operational Impact	A *high* ratio tends to increase operating freedom and lower the probability of bill-paying difficulty from write-downs of accounts receivable.
Range of Common Experience	0.6 times to 1.0 times.

Secondary Ratio 7: Total Noncurrent Assets to Net Worth

Popular Name	*Noncurrent Assets Equity Ratio*
Purpose	Measures a company's ability to support its acquisition of fixed assets and miscellaneous (other noncurrent) assets by means of owners' investment (original investment plus retained earnings).
Calculation	Divide total noncurrent assets by net worth.

Example

Your company's fixed assets were 100,000, your miscellaneous assets were zero, and your net worth was $160,000 at year-end. What was your *Total Noncurrent Assets to Net Worth?*

Solution: Total noncurrent assets = 100,000 + 0 = 100,000; then 100,000 divided by 160,000 = .625.

Financial Impact

A *low* ratio exerts a *favorable* influence from a conservative perspective: It increases working capital sufficiency and tends to increase working capital balance. However, a *low* ratio may be *unfavorable* in another respect: It may be related to a low return on equity.

Operational Impact

A *low* ratio tends to reduce interest costs.

Definition

Net worth—called "owner's equity" in a sole proprietorship (IRS Schedule C), "partners' capital" in a partnership (IRS Form 1065), "stockholders' equity" or "shareholders' equity" in a corporation (IRS Form 1120, 1120-A, or 1120S)—equals total assets minus total liabilities.

Critical Values

When total liabilities are *greater* than total assets, net worth will be in a deficit position and a meaningful ratio cannot be calculated. In such a case, treat *Total Noncurrent Assets to Net Worth* as a very large number for comparative purposes. Deficit net worth is a serious condition that warrants close management attention.

A ratio *greater* than 1.0 shows that net worth is not sufficient to fund fixed assets and miscellaneous (other noncurrent) assets. Consequently, long-term liabilities are required to achieve a positive working capital position.

Range of Common Experience

0.5 times to 1.3 times.

Secondary Ratio 8: Long-Term Liabilities to Working Capital

Popular Name

Working Capital Dependency Ratio

Purpose

Measures the extent to which a company's working capital is dependent on long-term liabilities; from another perspective, measures a company's ability to repay long-term liabilities by reducing working capital.

Calculation

Subtract current liabilities from current assets to obtain working capital, then divide long-term liabilities by working capital.

Example	Your company's current assets were $325,000, your current liabilities were $200,000, and your long-term liabilities were $50,000 at year-end. What was your *Long-Term Liabilities to Working Capital?*
	Solution: Working capital = 325,000 − 200,000 = 125,000; then 50,000 divided by 125,000 = .40.
Financial Impact	A *low* ratio is a *favorable* condition from a conservative perspective: It indicates comparatively low dependence on long-term debt to hold current liabilities below current assets.
Operational Impact	A *low* ratio tends to decrease interest cost.
Critical Values	When current liabilities are greater than current assets, working capital will be in a deficit position, and a meaningful ratio cannot be calculated. In such a case, treat *Long-Term Liabilities to Working Capital* as a very large number for comparative purposes. Deficit working capital is a serious condition that warrants close management attention.
	A ratio greater than 1.0 shows that long-term borrowing was required to achieve a positive working capital position (due to total noncurrent assets greater than net worth).
Range of Common Experience	Insufficient industry data.

Secondary Ratio 9: Net Profit to Total Assets

Popular Name	*Return on Assets*
Purpose	Measures a company's ability to produce profit on assets employed.
Calculation	Divide net profit by total assets, then multiply result by 100, converting ratio to a percentage.
Example	Your company's net profit was $35,000 for the year, and your total assets were $400,000 at year-end. What was your *Net Profit to Total Assets?*
	Solution: 35,000 divided by 400,000 = .0875; then .0875 × 100 = 8.75%.
Financial Impact	A *high* ratio is a favorable result: It indicates a comparatively high rate of return on assets employed.
Operational Impact	A *high* ratio tends to reduce interest cost over time.
Definition	Net profit *before taxes* is ordinarily used by bankers and other credit grantors as the basis for measuring comparative profitability (versus

previous performance or external standards). Net profit *after taxes* is the true "bottom line," but the effect of state and local income taxes, as well as federal income tax credits and carrybacks, can distort comparative performance. Net profit *from operations* (before non-operating income, non-operating expense, and extraordinary items) and net profit *before officers'/owners' compensation* are also useful measures.

Special Reminder

Net profit is expressed as a percentage, not as a simple ratio.

Critical Value

A *negative* percentage shows that operating policy and asset management resulted in a net loss for the period.

Range of Common Experience

5.3% to 9.0% (before income taxes).

4

IMPACT OF THE SEVEN CAUSAL RATIOS ON THE NINE SECONDARY RATIOS THAT MEASURE EFFECT

The seven causal ratios discussed in Chapter 3 exert a predictable influence on the nine secondary ratios that measure effect. A comparatively low *Collection Period of Accounts Receivable* will, for example, reduce *Total Liabilities to Net Worth* and increase *Current Assets to Current Liabilities*. In many companies, however, the impact of one causal ratio will be favorable, while a second causal ratio will push the business in an unfavorable direction. The net result, which is always reflected in the nine secondary ratios, will depend on the relative importance of each of the causal ratios within the company's financial structure. The concern's comparative standing will also be affected by the importance of the components of each ratio in relation to the other financial statement items for the typical company in its line of business activity. A wide numerical variation from the industry norm with respect to *Cost of Sales to Inventory* may, for example, have only a minimal impact on the secondary ratios of a company when it operates within an industry that is generally characterized by a very small inventory level in relation to net sales. On the other hand, a seemingly minor difference in *Net Sales to Fixed Assets* may have a noticeable influence on several of the nine ratios that measure effect whenever the company's line of business activity involves major investment in physical facilities and equipment. The following outline is provided for your consideration.

CAUSAL RATIO 1: NET PROFIT TO NET SALES

If the other causal ratios remain unchanged at the same sales volume, an *increase* in *Net Profit to Net Sales* will have the following impact on the secondary ratios:

Net Profit to Net Worth	*Increase:* Greater return on equity because of rise in net profit.
Total Liabilities to Net Worth	*Decrease:* Lower financial leverage because of expansion of net worth.*

Current Liabilities to Net Worth	*Decrease:* Lower current liabilities in relation to net worth because of expansion of net worth.*
Current Assets to Current Liabilities	*Increase:* Greater cushion between current assets and current liabilities because of the rise in current assets and/or reduction of current liabilities.[†]
Cash and Short-Term Investments Plus Accounts Receivable to Current Liabilities (Quick Ratio)	*Increase:* Greater coverage of current liabilities from liquid assets because of rise in cash and accounts receivable and/or reduction of current liabilities.[†]
Net Sales to Working Capital	*Decrease:* Greater working capital sufficiency in relation to net sales because of rise in current assets and/or reduction of current liabilities.[†]
Total Noncurrent Assets to Net Worth	*Decrease:* Lower proportion of net worth used to support fixed assets because of expansion of net worth.*
Long-Term Liabilities to Working Capital	*Decrease:* Lower dependence of working capital on long-term liabilities because of rise in working capital.[†]
Net Profit to Total Assets	*Increase:* Greater return on assets because of rise in net profit.

* Assuming retention of at least some portion of the additional profit.
[†] Assuming that a portion of retained earnings will be used to increase cash and short-term investments or other current assets—or to reduce current liabilities.

CAUSAL RATIO 2: NET SALES TO TOTAL ASSETS

If the other causal ratios remain unchanged at the same sales volume, an *increase* in *Net Sales to Total Assets* will have the following impact on the secondary ratios:

Net Profit to Net Worth	*Increase:* Greater return on equity (assuming a net profit) because less owners' equity is required to support a lower level of assets; interest-bearing debt may be reduced, increasing net profit.
Total Liabilities to Net Worth	*Decrease:* Lower financial leverage because reduced assets require less borrowing; decrease based on assumption that total liabilities would be paid down at a faster rate than net worth would be reduced through dividends or other distribution of equity.
Current Liabilities to Net Worth	*Decrease:* Lower current liabilities in relation to net worth due to (1) reduced current assets (assuming

that current liabilities would be paid from at least a portion of funds released) and/or (2) smaller current maturities of long-term debt used to finance fixed assets.*

Current Assets to Current Liabilities

Increase: (1) Greater coverage of current liabilities and current assets because current liabilities would be reduced at a faster rate than current assets and/or (2) greater cushion between current assets and current liabilities by virtue of lower current maturities of long-term debt.*

Cash and Short-Term Investments Plus Accounts Receivable to Current Liabilities (Quick Ratio)

Increase likely, but depends on asset items responsible for increase in *Net Sales to Total Assets,* as well as whether *Quick Ratio* is greater or less than 1.0.*

Net Sales to Working Capital

Decrease likely, but depends on asset items responsible for increase in *Net Sales to Total Assets.**

Total Noncurrent Assets to Net Worth

Decrease likely, but depends on asset items responsible for increase in *Net Sales to Total Assets.**

Long-Term Liabilities to Working Capital

Decrease likely, but depends on asset items responsible for increase in *Net Sales to Total Assets.**

Net Profit to Total Assets

Increase: Greater return on assets (assuming net profit) because of lower asset base.

---

* A review of the next three causal ratios—the *Collection Period of Accounts Receivable, Cost of Sales to Inventory,* and *Net Sales to Fixed Assets*—will provide more specific guidance with respect to influences on these secondary measures.

CAUSAL RATIO 3: COLLECTION PERIOD OF ACCOUNTS RECEIVABLE

If the other causal ratios remain unchanged at the same sales volume, a *decrease* in the *Collection Period of Accounts Receivable* will have the following impact on the secondary ratios:

Net Profit to Net Worth

Increase: Greater return on equity (assuming a net profit) because less owners' equity is required to support a lower level of assets; interest-bearing debt may be reduced, increasing net profit.

Total Liabilities to Net Worth

Decrease: Lower financial leverage because reduced assets require less borrowing; decrease based on assumption that total liabilities would be paid down at a faster rate than net worth would be reduced through dividends or other distribution of equity.

Current Liabilities to Net Worth	*Decrease:* Lower current liabilities in relation to net worth because reduced assets require less borrowing; decrease based on assumption that current liabilities would be paid down at a faster rate than net worth would be reduced through dividends or other distribution of equity.
Current Assets to Current Liabilities	*Increase:* Greater coverage of current liabilities and current assets because current liabilities would be reduced at a faster rate than current assets (assuming that this ratio is greater than 1.0 and that a portion of the cash generated by the reduction in accounts receivable would be applied to lowering current liabilities).
Cash and Short-Term Investments plus Accounts Receivable to Current Liabilities (Quick Ratio)	*Depends* whether the ratio is greater or less than 1.0: Increase (greater coverage of current liabilities from liquid assets) will result if the ratio is greater than 1.0 because current liabilities would be reduced at a faster rate than liquid assets; decrease (reduced coverage of current liabilities from liquid assets on a proportionate basis) will result if the ratio is less than 1.0 because current liabilities would be reduced at a slower rate than liquid assets.
Net Sales to Working Capital	*No change* (assuming that a portion of the reduction in accounts receivable would be applied to lowering current liabilities).
Total Noncurrent Assets to Net Worth	*No change.*
Long-Term Liabilities to Working Capital	*No change.*
Net Profit to Total Assets	*Increase:* Greater return on assets (assuming a net profit) because of lower asset base.

CAUSAL RATIO 4: COST OF SALES TO INVENTORY

If the other causal ratios remain unchanged at the same sales volume, an *increase* in *Cost of Sales to Inventory* will have the following impact on the secondary ratios:

Net Profit to Net Worth	*Increase:* Greater return on equity (assuming a net profit) because less owners' equity is required to support a lower level of assets; interest-bearing debt may be reduced, increasing net profit.

Total Liabilities to Net Worth	*Decrease:* Lower financial leverage because reduced assets require less borrowing; decrease based on assumption that total liabilities would be paid down at a faster rate than net worth would be reduced through dividends or other distribution of equity.
Current Liabilities to Net Worth	*Decrease:* Lower current liabilities in relation to net worth because reduced assets require less borrowing (and also assuming that current liabilities would be paid down faster than net worth would be decreased through dividends or other distribution of equity).
Current Assets to Current Liabilities	*Increase:* Greater coverage of current liabilities by current assets because current liabilities would be reduced at a faster rate than current assets (assuming that this ratio is greater than 1.0 and that a portion of the cash generated by the reduction in inventory would be applied to lowering current liabilities).
Cash and Short-Term Investments Plus Accounts Receivable to Current Liabilities (Quick Ratio)	*Increase:* Greater coverage of current liabilities from liquid assets because of lower current liabilities (assuming that current liabilities would be lowered by a portion of the reduction in inventory).
Net Sales to Working Capital	*No change* (assuming that a portion of the reduction in inventory would be applied to lowering current liabilities).
Total Noncurrent Assets to Net Worth	*No change.*
Long-Term Liabilities to Working Capital	*No change.*
Net Profit to Total Assets	*Increase:* Greater return on assets (assuming a net profit) because of lower asset base.

CAUSAL RATIO 5: NET SALES TO FIXED ASSETS

If the other causal ratios remain unchanged at the same sales volume, an *increase* in *Net Sales to Fixed Assets* will have the following impact on the secondary ratios:

Net Profit to Net Worth	*Increase:* Greater return on equity (assuming a net profit) because less owners' equity is required to support a lower level of assets; interest-bearing debt may be reduced, increasing net profit.

Total Liabilities to Net Worth	*Decrease:* Lower financial leverage because reduced assets require less borrowing; decrease based on assumption that total liabilities would be paid down at a faster rate than net worth would be reduced through dividends or other distribution of equity.
Current Liabilities to Net Worth	*Decrease:* Lower current liabilities in relation to net worth because of (1) smaller current maturities of long-term debt used to finance fixed assets and/or (2) reduction of short-term debt.
Current Assets to Current Liabilities	*Increase:* Greater cushion between current assets and current liabilities because of lower current debt.
Cash and Short-Term Investments plus Accounts Receivable to Current Liabilities (Quick Ratio)	*Increase:* Greater coverage of current liabilities from liquid assets because of lower current debt.
Net Sales to Working Capital	*Decrease:* Greater working capital sufficiency in relation to net sales because of reduction in amount of funds shifted from working capital to fixed assets.
Total Noncurrent Assets to Net Worth	*Decrease:* Lower proportion of net worth used to support fixed assets because of reduction in fixed assets.
Long-Term Liabilities to Working Capital	*Decrease:* Lower dependence of working capital on long-term liabilities because of (1) greater working capital, due to reduction of funds shifted from working capital to fixed assets and (2) lower long-term debt used to support fixed assets.
Net Profit to Total Assets	*Increase:* Greater return on assets (assuming net profit) because of lower asset base.

CAUSAL RATIO 6: NET SALES TO NET WORTH

If the other causal ratios remain unchanged at the same sales volume, a *decrease* in *Net Sales to Net Worth* will have the following impact on the secondary ratios:

Net Profit to Net Worth	*Decrease:* Lower return on equity (assuming a net profit) because of greater owners' equity (net worth).*
Total Liabilities to Net Worth	*Decrease:* Lower financial leverage because of the rise in net worth.
Current Liabilities to Net Worth	*Decrease:* Lower current liabilities in relation to net worth because of the rise in net worth.

Current Assets to Current Liabilities	*Increase:* Greater cushion between current assets and current liabilities because of lower current liabilities.*
Cash and Short-Term Investments plus Accounts Receivable to Current Liabilities (Quick Ratio)	*Increase:* Greater coverage of current liabilities from liquid assets because of lower current liabilities.*
Net Sales to Working Capital	*Decrease:* Greater working capital sufficiency in relation to net sales because of lower current liabilities.*
Total Noncurrent Assets to Net Worth	*No change.**
Long-Term Liabilities to Working Capital	*Depends* whether the ratio is greater or less than 1.0: Increase (proportionately greater dependence of working capital on long-term liabilities) will result if the ratio is less than 1.0, because long-term liabilities would be increased at a faster rate than working capital; decrease (proportionately less dependence of working capital on long-term liabilities) will result if the ratio is grater than 1.0, because long-term liabilities would be increased at a slower rate than working capital.
Net Profit to Total Assets	*Indeterminate:* Depends on the substitution of liabilities (interest-bearing debt for interest-free funds, such as accounts payable).

* Unless the increase in net worth is used to pay off liabilities with an effective interest rate greater than pre-interest and pre-tax return on assets.

CAUSAL RATIO 7: LONG-TERM LIABILITIES TO TOTAL NONCURRENT ASSETS

Finance fixed assets and other noncurrent assets with long-term liabilities. High *Long-Term Liabilities to Total Noncurrent Assets* may increase interest expense (depending on the availability of "free" money such as accounts payable, and on long-term versus short-term interest rates). A high ratio, however, exerts a favorable influence on the secondary ratios by improving working capital sufficiency and strengthening working capital balance.

If all seven causal ratios are equal to their respective industry medians, the nine secondary ratios will also be in line with the industry norms. (Exhibits 4.1 through 4.4 follow.)

EXHIBIT 4.1   EROI Method

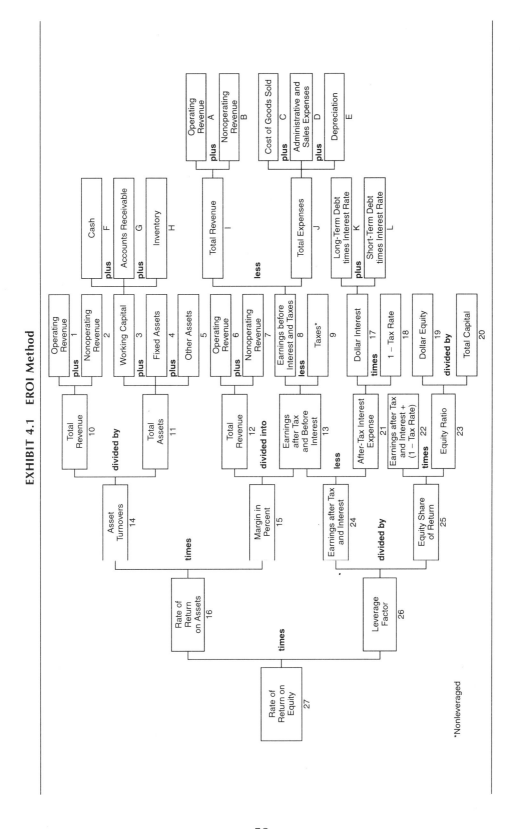

EXHIBIT 4.2   Simple ROI Method

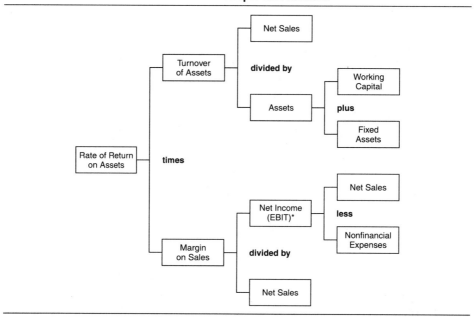

EXHIBIT 4.3   Sample Statements for an EROI Analysis

Income Statement

Operating revenue (sales)	$ 3,000,000
Less cost of goods sold	(1,420,000)
Less administrative expenses	(400,000)
Less sales expenses	(900,000)
Less depreciation	(100,000)
Total Earnings from Operations	180,000
Nonoperating income	20,000
Total Earnings before Interest and Tax	200,000
Less long-term debt (8%)	(20,000)
Less short-term debt (10%)	(5,000)
Total Earnings after Interest and before Tax	175,000
Less taxes (48%)	(84,000)
Total Earnings after Interest and Tax	$ 91,000

Balance Sheet

Assets

Cash	$ 50,000
Accounts receivable	100,000
Inventory	250,000
Fixed assets	500,000
Investments	100,000
Total Assets	$ 1,000,000

Capital sources

Short-term debt	$ 50,000
Long-term debt	250,000
Common stock at par	300,000
Retained earnings	400,000
Total Capital	$ 1,000,000
Rate of Return on Assets	10.4%
Rate of Return on Equity	13.0%

EXHIBIT 4.4 Sample Application of EROI Analysis

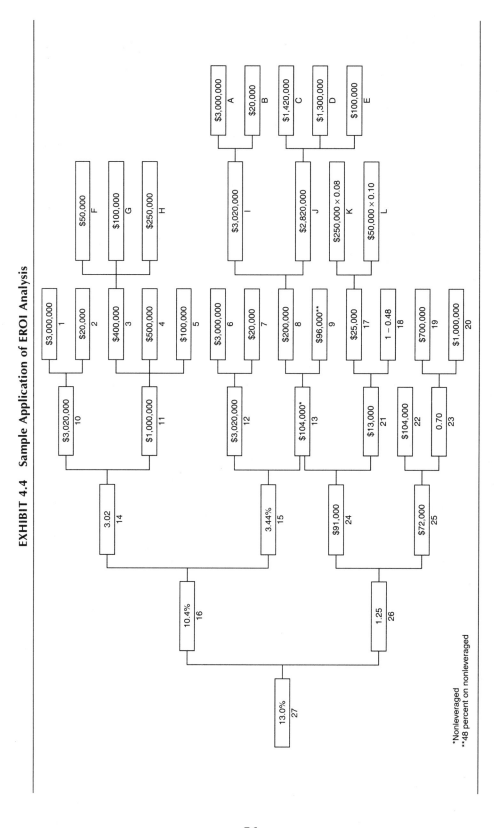

*Nonleveraged
**48 percent on nonleveraged

5

CASH FLOW AND
BREAK-EVEN ANALYSIS

CASH FLOW ANALYSIS

Cash flow analysis has become an increasingly important tool for determining a company's ability to meet its future operating requirements while servicing its actual or contemplated debt. In this area of financial management and bank relations, cause-and-effect ratio analysis can be especially useful. Unfortunately, many business owners and managers assume that the various tools of financial management are mutually exclusive, that one method is old-fashioned and another is very modern. The fact is that cash flow analysis and ratio analysis are closely linked.

Net Cash Flow

In discussing cash flow, a clear agreement on terminology is critical. The term, *net cash flow*—net profit after taxes plus depreciation (and any other non-cash charges)—was referenced earlier in connection with the *Debt Coverage Ratio*. Net cash flow (or *cash throw-off*), in theory, provided funds to service debt or replace fixed assets. This net amount, however, does not represent actual additions to cash or a bundle of money sitting idle at the end of the year. A substantial portion of the funds provided by net profit and depreciation may, in fact, be channeled into increased accounts receivable and inventory as fast as those funds are generated by the company. In some cases, accounts receivable and inventory grow so rapidly—through sales expansion, lax asset management, or both—that the net increase in these assets exceeds net cash flow. When that situation occurs, additional borrowing will be required, regardless of profit performance. Projecting cash flow obviously involves more than making an estimate of net income and depreciation from the operating statement. An understanding of cause-and-effect ratio analysis is also required.

Cash Flow from Operations

You should evaluate the trend in the ratio of cash flow from operations to net income. High earnings quality is present when revenue and expenses are recorded close to cash recognition, since the transaction is more objective.

Example: The following condensed income statement appears for a company.

Sales		$1,300,000
Less cost of sales		400,000
		$ 900,000
Gross margin		
Less operating expenses		
Wages	$150,000	
Rent	80,000	
Electricity	50,000	
Depreciation expense	90,000	
Amortization expense	70,000	
Total Operating Expenses		$ 440,000
Income before other items		460,000
Other revenue and expenses		
Interest	$ 60,000	
Amortization of deffered revenue	20,000	
Total Other Items		$ 40,000
Net Income		$ 420,000

The ratio of cash flow from operations to net income is:

Net income		$ 420,000
Plus non-cash expenses		
Depreciation expense	$ 90,000	
Amortization expense	70,000	
		160,000
Less non-cash revenue		
Amortization of deferred revenue		(20,000)
Cash Flow from Operations		$ 560,000

$$\frac{\text{Cash flow from operations}}{\text{Net income}} = \frac{\$560,000}{\$420,000} = 1.33$$

BREAK-EVEN ANALYSIS

Break-even analysis—also known as *analysis of contribution to overhead and profit*—is a basic management tool particularly useful to companies that have the option of acquiring capital equipment (fixed assets) as a means of reducing variable expenses.

Personnel, material, subcontracting, and other cost elements that tend to vary with business activity may be decreased as a percentage of net sales through automation, computerization, or more efficient facilities. But how will the realignment of costs affect the company's profit picture as sales rise or fall from their present levels? Break-even analysis is designed to answer that question. This analytical tool can also provide useful strategic insights for managing companies that face the decision of substituting highly specialized technical personnel (who become essentially fixed costs, because of the substantial recruitment and training commitment) for more readily available individuals (who represent variable costs, because their number might be reduced in the event of a business downturn). As expenses shift from variable to fixed, or vice versa, the equation that determines business survival and profitable growth is also changed.

Role of Fixed Costs

The basic concept underlying break-even analysis is simple: As a company makes increasing commitments to meet *fixed costs* (in the form of depreciation, interest, or payroll for highly skilled employees), it needs to make a reduction in variable costs, or increase its level of net sales. Otherwise, net profit will drop. A major investment in equipment, computer software, or high-tech personnel may enable a company to lower other labor, material, or subcontracting expenses, but it will raise the level of fixed costs, costs that must be met regardless of sales volume.

That is the key issue: Fixed costs come due month after month, whether or not the company meets its sales projections. Whereas variable costs are incurred gradually as sales increase, and can be reduced when sales decline, fixed costs represent an ongoing commitment. One major fixed cost, depreciation, is not actually a cash expense, but it ordinarily parallels the repayment schedule for loans incurred to purchase fixed assets. In any case, depreciation expense reduces net profit. Immediately following a major acquisition of fixed assets, a company often experiences a decline in profit, or even a few months of outright losses, owing to the larger amount of fixed costs. These costs will tend to depress profit until sales rise to a higher level (and thereby spread fixed costs over a larger sales base), or until the full reduction in variable costs can be achieved.

The ability to support higher fixed costs over the long run depends on either of two conditions:

1. More stable, and usually greater, sales volume, which permits the orderly substitution of fixed costs for variable costs, resulting in a net profit gain.
2. A higher profit in good economic times plus the financial structure to absorb reduced profit or outright losses during the down cycle.

An understanding of break-even analysis will enable management to assess the financial risk involved in the acquisition of equipment and computer software, or the hiring and training of specialized employees for sales expansion or cost reduction. At the same time, it is important to recognize that there is a significant (although difficult to quantify) risk in failing to respond to customer demands for increased technological capability, or to keep pace with the growing capabilities of competitors.

Need to Distinguish Fixed from Variable Costs

Break-even analysis involves only a few simple calculations. The critical factor is not the arithmetic; it is management's ability to separate costs (with reasonable accuracy) into fixed and variable components—and to maintain sufficient control of costs and pricing so that actual expenses will bear a predictable relationship to sales activity.

Five factors are involved in the break-even equation:

1. NS = net sales (in dollars);
2. VC = variable costs (in dollars);
3. FC = fixed costs (in dollars);
4. CM = contribution margin (as ratio); and
5. BE = break-even point (in dollars).

The difference between net sales and the total amount of variable costs is known as *contribution to overhead and profit* (COP). If COP is greater than fixed costs, the company will earn a profit. If not, the business will incur a loss. The break-even point is the level of net sales at which the contribution to overhead and profit is exactly equal to fixed costs. Above the break-even point, every additional dollar of COP goes directly to net profit.

The break-even point can be found in three simple steps. First, determine the *Contribution Margin:*

1. $CM = \dfrac{NS - VC}{NS}$

Contribution Margin (CM) represents the proportion of each dollar of net sales available to meet fixed expenses. This ratio is an important element in basic strategic planning, as well as a key factor in break-even analysis. The calculation of Contribution Margin may be based on historical records or future projections. If major changes in cost structure are anticipated, future projections should be made.

The exact dollar amounts of *net sales* (NS) and *variable costs* (VC) are not usually critical, since the proportion will ordinarily remain essentially the same through a fairly broad sales range. Proportionate change is the characteristic that makes certain costs variable. To find the Contribution Margin for a company that reports net sales of $1 million and variable costs of $750,000, you must first subtract variable costs of $750,000 from net sales of $1 million, to obtain $250,000, which represents the contribution to overhead and profit from those sales. Then simply divide the contribution amount, $250,000, by net sales, $1 million, for the result of 0.250. For break-even analysis, this ratio should be carried to three decimal places.

2. BE = FC divided by CM

Finding the *break-even point* (BE) (see Exhibit 5.1) depends on knowing *fixed costs* (FC) and relating this dollar amount to the Contribution Margin. Specifically, dividing fixed costs by the Contribution Margin will reveal the break-even point. If the company with a Contribution Margin of 0.250 has fixed costs of $200,000, the break-even point is $800,000 ($200,000 divided by 0.250). As the Contribution Margin rises, the break-even point falls, assuming that fixed costs remain the same. A company with

EXHIBIT 5.1   Break-Even Point: Effects of 25 Percent Increase in Sales Volume

	No Acquisition	Additional Sales with Reduced Total Sales Variable Costs	After Acquisition
Net Sales	$14,000,000	$3,500,000	$17,500,000
Fixed costs	2,800,000	784,000	3,584,000
Variable costs	10,500,000	2,362,500	12,862,500
Net profit before taxes	700,000	353,500	1,053,500
Contribution to fixed costs and profit	3,500,000	1,137,500	4,637,500
Contribution margin	0.250 ×	0.325 ×	0.265 ×
Break-even point (FC divided by CM)	$11,200,000*	$2,412,308*	$13,524,528*

*The sum of the break-even point is based on existing work plus the break-even point (which assumes that all net sales in the future will consist of 20% new sales at the new margin and 80% old sales at the old margin). When one set of relationships between fixed costs, Contribution Margin, and break-even point is blended with a second set of relationships, the resulting break-even point will not be a simple sum of the two previous amounts. The new break-even point reflects both the relative proportion of fixed assets and the relative proportion of Contribution Margin, and also incorporates the assumed relative proportion of net sales.

fixed costs of $200,000 and a Contribution Margin of 0.400 would, for example, have a break-even point of only $500,000.

Once fixed costs and the Contribution Margin have been identified, the first two calculations can be combined into a single formula:

3. $BE = FC$ divided by $\dfrac{(NS - VC)}{NS}$

This is a more concise expression, but the steps involved in its calculation are essentially the same as those we have just completed.

Fixed Costs

Some costs are clearly fixed: They do not decline with a decrease in sales activity. Other costs, such as personnel expenses, are often regarded as entirely variable, because they increase as sales activity grows. In reality, many of these expenses are variable when sales expand, but become essentially fixed costs during a business downturn. They often do not decline as sales activity decreases, because management may decide to retain employees for many reasons—the cost of training, unemployment compensation, difficulty in finding replacements during a business upturn, and other personnel factors. To the extent that management can distinguish essentially fixed personnel costs from those that are truly variable, break-even analysis can be successfully applied to distributorships, retailing companies, and service concerns, as well as manufacturers and capital-intensive wholesalers.

Variable Costs

Variable costs increase and decrease in general proportion to sales activity. The ability to maintain a consistent relationship between variable costs and net sales requires knowledge of actual costs, control of those costs, and adequate pricing policies. Semi-variable costs involve both fixed charges and a variable component. They increase and decrease as sales rise and fall, but their rate of change is lower than that of net sales, because they have a fixed element. Telephone service is typically a semi-variable cost: The basic fee is normally a fixed amount, but long distance and other activity charges generally vary with sales volume.

6

INVENTORY

GROSS MARGIN RETURN ON INVENTORY

Inventory is ordinarily the single most important financial factor affecting the financial structure of wholesaling/distribution and retailing companies. Inventory management, in the broadest sense, from anticipation of customer demand, through purchasing, marketing, and selling, is the essence of successful wholesaling and retailing. Other key factors, such as credit and collections, facilities management, and investment adequacy, can also exert a highly important influence on these companies, just as these factors determine the survival and growth of manufacturing and service companies. Nevertheless, inventory management is the foremost element in enterprises formed for the purpose of buying and selling.

As a result, many wholesalers and retailers direct particular attention to a special financial formula, *Gross Margin Return on Inventory* (also known as the *Inventory Turn and Earn Ratio*). It is derived by multiplying one of the causal measures, *Cost of Sales to Inventory* by *Gross Margin to Net Sales*. Some industries prefer to express *Gross Margin to Net Sales* as a percentage, leading to a *Gross Margin Return on Inventory* of approximately 100 to 200; others prefer to use a decimal fraction, which results in a ratio in the neighborhood of 1.0 to 2.0.

Company B (see Exhibit 6.1) reports net sales of $5 million and cost of sales of $3,775,000. Subtracting $3,775,000 from $5 million results in gross margin of $1,225,000. Dividing that amount by $5 million shows that Company B's *Gross Margin to Net Sales* is 24.5 percent (after converting the decimal fraction .245 to a percentage). When the cost of sales amount, $3,775,000, is divided by inventory of $750,000, *Cost of Sales to Inventory* is found to be 5.0. Multiplying *Gross Margin to Net Sales* of 24.5 percent by *Cost of Sales to Inventory* of 5.0 yields *Gross Margin Return on Inventory* of 122.5. Because this derived value does not relate to a specific denominator, it is neither considered a percentage nor properly designated in times; it is simply a reference value.

When High Gross Margin Is Needed

Gross Margin Return on Inventory illustrates the concept that a company needs to achieve a relatively high gross margin if it carries a comparatively high level of inventory in relation to sales activity. In general terms, this is certainly true. A retailer of

EXHIBIT 6.1 Gross Margin Return on Inventory for Four Companies

	Company A	Company B	Company C	Company D
Net sales	$1,500,000	$5,000,000	$12,500,000	$50,000,000
Cost of sales	1,100,000	3,775,000	9,750,000	40,000,000
Gross margin	390,000	1,225,000	2,750,000	10,000,000
Inventory	170,000	750,000	2,500,000	4,900,000
Cost of Sales to Inventory				
Company	6.5 times	5.0 times	3.9 times	8.2 times
Industry standard	5.1 times	5.1 times	5.1 times	5.1 times
Gross Margin to Net Sales				
Company	26.0%	24.5%	22.0%	20.0%
Industry standard	21.5%	21.5%	21.5%	21.5%
Gross Margin Return on Inventory				
Company	169.0*	122.5*	85.8*	165.0*
Industry standard	109.7	109.7	109.7	109.7

*This derived value is, strictly speaking, neither a percentage nor a ratio that can be readily expressed as times, since it has no clearly defined denominator. It is simply a reference value, which relates inventory turnover to gross margin. As inventory turnover declines (as inventory rises in relation to net sales), a higher gross margin percentage is ordinarily required, in order to achieve an adequate net profit percentage.

furs or jewelry with *Cost of Sales to Inventory* in the area of 1.5 will surely require higher *Gross Margin to Net Sales* than will a convenience food store with *Cost of Sales to Inventory* of 17.5. Similarly, a meat wholesaler with *Cost of Sales to Inventory* of 25.0 would not expect to earn the same *Gross Margin to Net Sales* as an auto parts distributor with *Cost of Sales to Inventory* of 3.5.

THE EFFECT OF VALUE ADDED

The term "value added," which is occasionally found in industry ratio studies, appears in a variety of business contexts, ranging from financial analysis, to marketing, to taxation. Value added, in its least specific sense, is the sum of special characteristics (such as exclusive design, reliability, style, or reputation) that enable a company to gain a pricing and profit advantage. In a more narrow context, a so-called value-added tax is essentially a tax on sales generated by a company, with credit given for the tax paid on purchases. As applied to ratio analysis, value added is calculated by subtracting purchases of goods and services from net sales. The difference—value added—includes the activities performed by personnel and facilities within the company plus the firm's net profit. Various ratios can be calculated using value added as the numerator (for example, *Value Added to Net Sales* and *Value Added per Employee*), or as the common denominator. The components of value added, such as direct labor and facilities expense, are ordinarily expressed as percentages of the denominator (value added).

A company (see Exhibit 6.2) with net sales of $1 million and outside purchases—including goods for conversion or resale, subcontracting, utilities, supplies, services

EXHIBIT 6.2   Value Added and Net Profit for Two Companies

	Company I	Company J
Net sales	$1,000,000	$1,000,000
Engineering*	100,000[†]	100,000[†]
Production:		
Subcontractor cost	500,000	0
Materials cost	0[†]	100,000
Subcontractor profit	50,000	0
Internal cost*	0[†]	400,000[†]
Assembly	150,000[†]	150,000[†]
Sales and Administration:		
Outside purchases	50,000	50,000
Internal purchases*	100,000[†]	100,000[†]
Net profit before interest expense	50,000	100,000
Interest expense	10,000	35,000
Net Profit before Taxes	$ 40,000[†]	$ 65,000[†]
Net Profit to Net Sales	4.0%	6.5%
Value Added to Net Sales	39.0%	81.5%

*Expenses attributable to the company's employees and facilities.

[†]Value added. Components of value added:

	Company I	Company J
Engineering	$100,000	$100,000
Production: Internal Cost	0	400,000
Assembly	150,000	150,000
Sales and Administration		
Internal	100,000	100,000
Net Profit before Taxes	40,000	65,000
	$390,000	$815,000

It is important, therefore, to ensure that the values of inventory at the start and at the end of the fiscal period are stated correctly. An understatement or an overstatement of inventory values leads to inaccurate results on financial statements.

An error in the ending inventory (see Exhibit 6.3) for one fiscal period will be transferred as an error in the beginning inventory for the succeeding fiscal period. This, in turn, will cause incorrect computation of results similar to that displayed in Exhibit 6.3.

(from accounting and legal services to repair and maintenance by other parties), rent, and interest—of $610,000 contributes value added of $390,000 through the firm's employees and physical facilities. If the expenses attributable to those employees and facilities are $350,000, then the company's net profit before taxes is $40,000. Value added, at $390,000, is the sum of internal costs and net profit. Although in most industry studies, profit-related measures are calculated on a pre-tax basis, an alternative approach is to consider income taxes as representing outside purchases of services and calculate value added as the sum of internal expenses and after-tax net profit. Using pre-tax net profit as a component of value added in this example, we find that the company's value added of $390,000, divided by net sales of $1 million, yields *Value Added to Net Sales of 39.0%* (after converting the decimal fraction, .390, to a percentage).

Higher Value Added in Relation to Sales

Every few years, the idea circulates throughout the business community that higher value added in proportion to sales volume leads to greater profitability. When value added is defined in its most general sense—as the ability to gain a pricing and profit advantage—the link between value added and profitability leads to a self-fulfilling prophecy. But, when the more specific definition of value added is used, does high *Value Added to Net Sales* actually lead to high *Net Profit to Net Sales?* Because net profit is a component of value added, a certain connection necessarily exists. Even beyond that, there appears to be a logical basis for concluding that increasing value added would boost net profit. If the profit earned by subcontractors and suppliers could be incorporated in the company's operations, profit per dollar of net sales would necessarily increase.

INVENTORY MANAGEMENT

One of the major responsibilities of the financial manager is to develop, implement, and maintain an effective *inventory management system* within a company. Development of such a system is particularly important, since the company often commits a substantial part of its capital to inventory.

Many companies frequently experience serious problems related to inventory management. Some typical inventory problems are as follows:

- The value of inventories is increasing at a faster rate than the level of sales.
- There is a disparity between the actual value of inventories in the stores and in relevant accounting records.
- There is a substantial quantity of slow-moving and obsolete inventories in the stores.
- There is a frequent shortage of fast-moving items, which results in a loss of sales.
- Shortage of certain inventories creates an unnecessary burden on production planning efforts and causes an increase in machine set-up times.
- Inventory turnover rate is below the norm acceptable in a particular industry.

Different types of inventory may be used by the company depending upon the nature of its activities. In an earlier discussion about the financial statements, all inventories have been classified as follows:

- *Merchandise inventory.* This represents all spare parts used by a service company and all goods purchased for resale by a merchandising company.
- *Direct materials inventory.* This represents all raw materials purchased by a manufacturing company. These materials, used in a manufacturing process, are converted into *work-in-process inventory* and, subsequently, into *finished goods inventory.*

Inventory is usually converted into cash during an accounting period not exceeding one year and, for this reason, it is considered a current asset. Inventory consists of all goods that are owned by the company at any point in time, and their value must be measured on a regular basis. The AICPA states that, "a major objective of accounting for inventories is the proper determination of income through the process of matching appropriate costs against revenues." Hence, inventory management plays an important role in determining the final results of the company's activities during a specific accounting period.

Inventory owned by the company at the start of an accounting period is termed *beginning inventory*, while inventory that remains at the end of the accounting period is termed *ending inventory*. The determination of inventory costs is essential in calculating such values as cost of goods manufactured, cost of goods available for sale, cost of goods sold, gross margin from sales, and net income.

It is important, therefore, to ensure that the values of inventory at the start and at the end of the fiscal period are stated correctly. An understatement or an overstatement of inventory values leads to inaccurate results on financial statements.

An error in the ending inventory (see Exhibit 6.3) for one fiscal period will be transferred as an error in the beginning inventory for the succeeding fiscal period. This, in turn, will cause incorrect computation of results similar to that displayed in Exhibit 6.3.

The cost assigned to inventory depends on two basic measurements: *Quantity* and *Unit Cost*. Quantity is determined by a systematic physical count of inventory, or simply *taking inventory*, at the end of the fiscal year. When taking inventory, all materials should be arranged in a suitable order, to ensure that items are neither counted twice nor omitted altogether. Furthermore, it is essential to establish correct ownership of

EXHIBIT 6.3   Effect of an Error on Results Specified in the Income Statement in Ending Inventory

	Income Statement For Period: January 1, 19XX–December 31, 19XX			
Description of Account	Correct Statement of Ending Inventory		Incorrect Statement of Ending Inventory	
(+) Revenue from sales		$200,000		$200,000
Cost of goods sold				
Merchandise Inventory				
(+) January 1, 1989	$ 25,000		$ 25,000	
(+) Net purchases	100,000		100,000	
(=) Cost of goods available for sale	125,000		125,000	
Merchandise inventory				
(−) December 31, 1989	15,000		20,000	
(−) (=) Cost of goods sold		110,000		105,000
(=) Gross margin from sales		90,000		95,000
(−) Total operating expenses		60,000		60,000
(=) Income from operations		$ 30,000		$ 35,000

materials at the inventory-taking date or a predetermined *cut-off point.* Only inventory that is the property of the company should be included in the count. All other materials that may have been sold but not yet dispatched to customers or materials received on consignment from suppliers (not yet purchased) must be excluded from the inventory count.

The AICPA states that, "the primary basis of accounting for inventory is cost, which has been defined generally as the price paid or consideration given to acquire an asset. As applied to inventories, cost means, in principle, the sum of applicable expenditures and charges directly or indirectly incurred in bringing an article to its existing condition and location." Thus, inventory should be recorded at its cost, which includes not only the net purchase price, but also all additional expenses in acquiring the material such as freight or transportation costs, transit insurance, custom and excise duties or tariffs, and handling charges.

Since the company's investment in inventory often constitutes a significant part of the total assets, it is very important to ensure accurate valuation of inventory. There are several general accepted methods of costing inventory, each based on a different assumption:

- *Specific identification method.* This method is based on the assumption that the cost of each inventory items can be identified.

- *Average cost method.* This method is based on the assumption that the cost of ending inventory is the average cost of beginning inventory plus the net cost of all purchases during the period.

- *First-in, first out (FIFO) method.* This method is based on the assumption that the first merchandise purchased is the first merchandise sold. As a result, the ending inventory consists of the most recently purchased merchandise.

- *Last-in, first-out (LIFO) method.* This method is based on the assumption that the most recently purchased merchandise is the first merchandise sold. As a result, the ending inventory consists of the merchandise purchased during the earlier period.

Each of these inventory-costing methods can be adopted by the company, regardless of whether or not the actual flow of merchandise corresponds with the relevant assumption. But once a particular method is selected, it must be used consistently from one year to the next, in order to meet the requirements of the IRS. Hence, the final selection of the most suitable method rests with the financial manager. Selection of a specific inventory-costing method often entails comparison of results pertaining to the application of each method.

It is apparent, from the comparison of inventory-costing methods, that there is a significant variation in the value of ending inventory, cost of goods sold and, subsequently, in the gross margin from sales. Hence, such variation may affect the costing of finished goods, as well as the tax liability of the company. All four methods are regarded as acceptable accounting practice and are used in determining taxable income.

The LIFO method appears to be the most popular, for several reasons. First, this method most accurately represents the measurement of net income based on the current costs. Second, this method helps to produce lower taxable income, thereby reducing the tax liability.

The FIFO method is used less frequently, because many accountants believe that, as a result of applying this method, the company's taxable profit is overstated. This leads to increased tax liability and, subsequently, lower net income.

The average cost method is becoming less popular, since it has an effect similar to the FIFO method. An additional disadvantage of the average cost method is that it conceals changes in current replacement costs of inventory, since these costs are averaged with the older ones. As a result of cost averaging, the reported taxable income may not reflect true market conditions.

INVENTORY-VALUATION METHODS

This is a very simplistic explanation of the process. The techniques that are used to accomplish this matching process become the basis for valuation strategies. There are, however, a number of alternative techniques from which an organization can choose. It seems appropriate at this point to review the various approaches to inventory valuation that are commonly employed for financial statement purposes. Exhibit 6.4 highlights the various techniques and the resulting inventory valuation using each approach.

From Exhibit 6.4 it can be seen that the various costing techniques can cause the gross valuation of physical inventory quantities to fluctuate from $4,950 to $10,350, depending on the technique and management philosophy employed in valuing the inventory. Although this is an exaggerated example, it does illustrate the potentially different results that can be encountered using various valuation techniques.

Exhibit 6.5 demonstrates that, for financial statement purposes, LIFO, weighted average, and FIFO are acceptable techniques for inventory valuation. The use of standard costs is not an acceptable method of inventory valuation, unless it approximates the results that would be obtained by using one of the conventional methods.

EXHIBIT 6.4 Comparison of Four Methods of Inventory Costing

Description of Account	Specific Identification Method	Average Cost Method	First-In, First-Out Method (FIFO)	Last-In, First-Out Method (LIFO)
(+) Revenue from sales	$1,000	$1,000	$1,000	$1,000
Cost of goods sold:				
(+) Beginning inventory	100	100	100	100
(+) Net purchases	500	500	500	500
(=) Cost of goods available for sale	600	600	600	600
(−) Ending inventory	250	230	300	200
(−) (=) Cost of goods sold	350	370	300	400
(=) Gross margin from sales	650	630	700	600

EXHIBIT 6.5   Inventory Valuation Example

		Inventory Units		
Facts		Add	Delete	On-Hand Balance
Purchase 200 units July 1	@ $10 each	200		200
Purchase 200 units August 1	@ $11 each	200		400
Purchase 200 units September 1	@ $15 each	200		600
Sale 150 units September 15		200	150	450

On September 18, the purchasing agent ordered an additional quantity for delivery in November at $18 each. The price for deliveries from December through March is expected to be $21 each, and the price for subsequent deliveries is expected to be $23 each. What is the current dollar value for the 450 units left in the physical inventory on September 30? Using conventional costing techniques, the following options are available:

- LIFO (last-in, first-out):

$$200 \text{ @ } \$10 = \$2,000$$
$$200 \text{ @ } \$11 = 2,200$$
$$50 \text{ @ } \$15 = 750$$
$$450 \$4,950$$

- Weighted or moving average:

$$200 \text{ @ } \$10 = \$2,000$$
$$200 \text{ @ } \$11 = 2,200$$
$$200 \text{ @ } \$15 = 3,000$$
$$\$7,200 = \$12 \text{ each}$$

less $150 \text{ @ } \$12 = 1,800$

$$450 \$5,400$$

- FIFO (first-in, first-out):

$$50 \text{ @ } \$10 = 500$$
$$200 \text{ @ } \$11 = 2,200$$
$$200 \text{ @ } \$15 = 3,000$$
$$450 \$5,700$$

Using a standard cost approach, the following additional values might be possible depending on management's philosophy in setting standards:

- Last invoice price:

$$450 \times \$15 = \$6,750$$

- Current replacement cost:

$$450 \times \$18 = \$8,100$$

- Average annual price for coming year:

$$2 \text{ months @ } \$18 \text{ each} = \$36$$
$$4 \text{ months @ } \$21 \text{ each} = 84$$
$$6 \text{ months @ } \$23 \text{ each} = 138$$
$$\$258 = \$21.50 \text{ each}$$
$$450 \times \$21.50 = \$9,675$$

- Long-term replacement cost (cost at next revaluation):

$$450 \times 23 = \$10,350$$

This is often accomplished through the use of reserve accounts, in conjunction with the standard cost method.

LIFO: ADVANTAGES AND DISADVANTAGES

With the substantially different results that can be obtained by using alternate approaches, it seems appropriate to review the basic advantages and disadvantages of each. Summarized briefly, the basic advantages of using LIFO for inventory valuation purposes are:

1. It matches current cost with current revenues during times of changing price levels. This results in reported net income more closely approximating distributable net income.
2. It removes from taxable income the increased cost of replacement inventory until it is realized as profit through future price declines or reductions in inventory quantities.
3. It improves cash flow and reduces the need for borrowing, by decreasing a company's tax liability.
4. It protects a company's earnings from the impact of substantial commodity price declines.
5. Improves long-term return on stockholders equity, through cumulative impact of the LIFO reserve.

Some of the basic disadvantages of LIFO include:

1. The inventory value shown on the balance sheet is unrealistic. There is no relationship between the reported inventory value and the cost actually paid for that inventory. The further away from the date of implementing LIFO in an inflationary economy, the greater the distortion on the balance sheet. This causes a worsening of a company's reported working capital position, which can affect its ability to obtain credit.
2. LIFO depresses reported current period earnings, which may cause potential investors to shy away from a company's stock. It can also affect existing dividend policies, bonus and profit-sharing plans, the market value of a company's securities, and restrictive loan covenants tied to corporate profits.
3. If a company uses LIFO for tax purposes, the tax law requires that it also be used for financial statement purposes, and places disclosure restrictions on identifying the impact of LIFO on current period earnings. Recently there has been some easing of these disclosure restrictions.
4. Once LIFO is adopted, the LIFO cost acts as a floor for future taxable income determination. However, generally accepted accounting principles require the use of the lower of cost or market concept for financial statement purposes. If

the material price should drop below the LIFO base level, a reserve to market would be required for financial statements purposes that is not tax deductible.

5. LIFO provides a tax deferral, not a tax savings. If adopted when on-hand inventory is higher than normal, or if raw material or other product shortages develop in future periods, a company may be forced to liquidate base-year inventory stocks involuntarily and end up paying higher income taxes in periods when they can least afford them.

6. Earnings can be manipulated, to some extent, through the international expansion or contraction of inventory levels.

7. Depending on the approach employed, LIFO accounting can result in a more complicated record-keeping system.

FIFO: ADVANTAGES AND DISADVANTAGES

The basic advantages of using the FIFO method of inventory valuation are the following:

1. Recorded current period earnings reflect actual transaction profits, which will be higher in an inflationary economy, thereby making the company's stock more attractive to potential investors. Using the FIFO approach to valuation increases income by matching old costs against current selling prices, and has a leveraged effect on ROI (return on investment).

2. Inventory on the balance sheet is more realistically stated with FIFO. The FIFO concept of inventory valuation assumes that the ending inventory consists of the items most recently purchased. Therefore, ending inventory is carried at current actual cost.

3. FIFO improves the reported working capital position of a company, thereby increasing its ability to obtain credit.

4. Both LIFO and FIFO pertain to the flow of costs, not the flow of goods. However, FIFO more closely approximates the actual physical flow of goods.

Some of the disadvantages of using FIFO are these:

1. It results in the payment of income tax on the cost of business maintenance during periods of rising prices. Inventory units purchased at old prices are sold and must be replaced with new units at the prevailing price level, if the company is to continue in business. Under FIFO, this difference is treated as a transaction profit and is subject to income tax.

2. Cash flow is reduced because of the higher income tax liability, creating an increased need for borrowing to finance continued operations and business expansion.

3. It delays recognition, through financial statements, of the impact of changing cost levels on operating profits. Current selling prices are matched against old

costs, indicating a higher level of profitability than actually exists based on prevailing cost levels.

4. It indicates a level of profitability for the business that does not recognize the continued reinvestment needed to maintain the existing operating level. This can result in increased demands for higher dividends by stockholders, and greater demands by union and other employee groups.

IMPACT ON INCOME STATEMENT AND BALANCE SHEET

From an income statement standpoint, the difference between LIFO and FIFO can be summarized as follows:

- FIFO recognizes profit on an individual transaction basis and incorporates inventory profits with the company's operating profits for financial statement and tax purposes.
- LIFO, on the other hand, determines profits on a going-concern basis and only recognizes the portion of income that will not have to be reinvested in inventory to continue operating the business at the existing volume and inventory level.

From a balance sheet standpoint, the difference between LIFO and FIFO can be summarized as follows:

- With FIFO, ending inventory is carried at a current actual cost and consists of the items most recently purchased.
- With LIFO, the portion of the ending inventory quantity equaling the beginning inventory is valued at beginning inventory prices. Any increase in ending inventory quantity over beginning inventory quantity is valued at current cost.
- With standard costs, the gross inventory value reflects a predetermined cost level incorporating management philosophy and operating considerations into standards. Since standard costs are not an acceptable method of inventory valuation, unless they approximate a LIFO and FIFO method of valuation, an inventory valuation reserve is often required for proper financial statement presentation.

Exhibit 6.6, an example of a Monthly Management Report, depicts monthly and year-to-date inventory purchases and costs, as well as direct labor costs and subcontracted service costs, as well as the spectrum of other costs and purchases.

EXHIBIT 6.6 Monthly Management Report
Page 1

Account Description	Month: June 19XX			Year-to-Date: 19XX			Percentage of Actual YTD Net Sales
	Budget ($)	Actual ($)	Variance ($)-(F/U)	Budget ($)	Actual ($)	Variance ($)-(F/U)	
Direct materials inventory							
+ (beginning)	67,500	67,000	500 F	60,000	60,000	— F	10.0
Direct materials purchases							
+ (net)	29,000	30,000	1,000 U	174,000	169,000	5,000 F	28.0
Cost of direct materials							
= available for use	96,500	97,000	500 U	234,000	229,000	5,000 F	38.0
− Direct materials inventory (ending)	69,000	68,000	1,000 U	69,000	68,000	1,000 U	11.3
Cost of direct materials							
+ = used	27,500	29,000	1,500 U	165,000	161,000	4,000 F	26.7
+ Direct labor costs	13,000	12,400	600 F	78,000	77,000	1,000 F	12.8
Direct subcontracting							
+ service costs	400	600	200 U	2,400	2,200	200 F	0.4

EXHIBIT 6.6 (Continued)
Page 2

Account Description	Month: June 19XX			Year-to-Date: 19XX			Percentage of Actual YTD Net Sales
	Budget ($)	Actual ($)	Variance ($)-(F/U)	Budget ($)	Actual ($)	Variance ($)-(F/U)	
Depreciation, production + equipment	1,200	1,200	—F	7,200	7,200	—F	1.2
Indirect labor and + supervision costs	5,400	5,000	400 F	32,400	32,200	200 F	5.3
Indirect materials + purchases (net)	300	400	100 U	1,800	2,500	700 U	0.4
Insurance, production + equipment	300	300	—F	1,800	1,700	100 F	0.3
Maintenance, production + equipment	400	900	500 U	2,400	2,300	100 F	0.4
+ Property taxes	100	100	—F	600	600	—F	0.1
+ Rent	2,400	2,400	—F	14,400	14,400	—F	2.4
Rental expense, production + equipment	100	—	100 F	600	—	600 F	—
+ Utilities	700	600	100 F	4,200	4,300	100 U	0.7
+ = Total Plant Overhead Costs	10,900	10,900	—F	65,400	65,200	200 F	10.8

(continued)

75

EXHIBIT 6.6 *(Continued)*
Page 3

Account Description	Month: June 19XX			Year-to-Date: 19XX			Percentage of Actual YTD Net Sales
	Budget ($)	Actual ($)	Variance ($)-(F/U)	Budget ($)	Actual ($)	Variance ($)-(F/U)	
= Total Manufacturing Costs	51,800	52,900	1,100 U	310,800	305,400	5,400 F	50.6
+ Work-in-process inventory (beginning)	77,500	77,000	500 F	70,000	70,000	— F	11.6
= Total cost of work-in-process	129,300	129,000	600 U	380,800	375,400	5,400 F	62.3
= Work-in-process inventory (ending)	79,000	78,000	1,000 U	79,000	78,000	1,000 U	12.9
= Cost of goods manufactured*	50,300	51,900	1,600 U	301,800	297,400	4,400 F	49.3
+ Gross sales	103,000	101,000	2,000 U	618,000	621,000	3,000 F	103.0
− Sales returns and allowances	2,000	1,500	500 F	12,000	13,000	1,000 U	2.2
− Sales discounts	1,000	500	500 F	6,000	5,000	1,000 F	0.8
+ = Net Sales	100,000	99,000	1,000 U	600,000	603,000	3,000 F	100.0

EXHIBIT 6.6 (Continued)
Page 4

Account Description	Month: June 19XX			Year-to-Date: 19XX			Percentage of Actual YTD Net Sales
	Budget ($)	Actual ($)	Variance ($)-(F/U)	Budget ($)	Actual ($)	Variance ($)-(F/U)	
Finished goods inventory							
+ (beginning)	75,000	76,000	1,000 U	80,000	80,000	— F	13.3
Cost of goods manufactured							
+ (from page 3)	50,300	51,900	1,600 U	301,800	297,400	4,400 F	49.3
Cost of goods available							
= for sale	125,300	127,900	2,600 U	381,800	377,400	4,400 F	62.6
Finished good inventory							
− (ending)	74,000	75,000	1,000 F	74,000	75,000	1,000 F	12.4
− = Cost of goods sold	51,300	52,900	1,600 U	307,800	302,400	5,400 F	50.1
= Gross Margin from Sales	48,700	46,100	2,600 U	292,200	300,600	8,400 F	49.9
+ Advertising expenses	200	400	200 U	1,200	1,600	400 U	0.3
+ Audit and secretarial fees	300	—	300 F	1,800	1,600	200 F	0.3
+ Communication expenses	600	700	100 U	3,600	3,800	200 U	0.6
Depreciation, office							
+ equipment and vehicles	200	200	— F	1,200	1,200	— F	0.2
+ Freight out expenses	600	500	100 F	3,600	3,500	100 F	0.6

(continued)

EXHIBIT 6.6 (Continued)
Page 5

Account Description	Month: June 19XX			Year-to-Date: 19XX			Percentage of Actual YTD Net Sales
	Budget ($)	Actual ($)	Variance ($)-(F/U)	Budget ($)	Actual ($)	Variance ($)-(F/U)	
+ Insurance, vehicles Office supplies and	400	400	— F	2,400	2,500	100 U	0.4
+ expenses Salaries and wages,	400	200	200 F	2,400	2,300	100 F	0.4
+ administration and sales	2,500	2,100	400 F	15,000	14,600	400 F	2.4
+ Salaries, officers	5,000	4,200	800 F	30,000	30,000	— F	5.0
+ Traveling and entertainment	400	600	200 U	2,400	2,900	500 U	0.5
− = Total operating expenses	10,600	9,300	1,300 F	63,600	64,000	400 U	10.6
= Income from Operations	38,100	36,800	1,300 U	228,600	236,600	8,000 F	39.2
− Interest expense	1,500	1,400	100 F	9,000	10,500	1,500 U	1.7
= Net miscellaneous revenue	400	200	200 U	2,400	1,600	800 U	0.3
= Income before taxes	37,000	35,600	1,400 U	222,000	227,700	5,700 F	37.8
− Income taxes expense	12,000	12,000	— F	72,000	73,000	1,000 U	12.1
= Net Income	25,000	23,600	1,400 U	150,000	154,700	4,700 F	25.7

Note: F = Favorable   U = Unfavorable
*Transfer this cost to page 4 of Monthly Management Report.

7

OPERATIONS

EFFICIENCY MEASURES

Almost every discussion of competitiveness revolves around the concept of productivity improvement. How to measure that concept, unfortunately, remains a matter of controversy. In today's relatively unforgiving business environment, a company that enjoys a clear productivity advantage usually finds that fact reflected in a comparatively high *Net Profit to Net Sales,* a relatively high *Net Profit to Net Worth,* and a list of satisfied customers. Likewise, most companies with low productivity already understand the consequences. There is, however, no universal measure of company productivity, although this concept is often defined *as the number of units of output produced per unit of input.*

Some economist attempt to use financial ratios as substitutes for actual physical measures in productivity analysis. All evidence suggests that the conclusions drawn from such studies are, at best, confusing and, at worst, utterly misleading. *Net Sales to Fixed Assets* is, for example, not a good productivity measure, since the book value of fixed assets is greatly affected by the depreciation period allowed and by the age of the assets. *Net Sales of Fixed Assets* is an important causal ratio with respect to a company's operating results and its fundamental financial structure, but it is not intended to measure the productivity of physical facilities.

As a compromise between broad generalities and unreasonably detailed approaches, a simple ratio, *Units Per Man-Hour* (person-hours), would seem to be a basic measure of employee productivity and is often employed. As a company acquires new technology, there is often a shift in the balance between direct-labor employees (who work directly on the product) and indirect-labor employees (who are involved in estimating, software support, supervision/coordination, and maintenance). With increased automation, indirect labor tends to rise rapidly, leading to an artificially great increase in reported productivity if management continues to use direct labor man-hours as the denominator for this ratio. Should *Units Per Man-Hour* be based on the hours of all employees, including sales, general, and administrative personnel? The answer depends on the purpose of the analysis.

A somewhat more narrowly focused ratio, designed to measure labor productivity, is *Value Added Per Man-Hour,* which involves subtracting all outside purchases (such as utilities, supplies, and services), as well as direct material, from net sales before dividing by total man-hours for the year. If, for example, the company had purchased $200,000 of such utilities, supplies, and services during the year, its value added would be $600,000: net sales of $1 million minus total outside purchases of $400,000 (direct material of $200,000 plus other outside purchases of $200,000). Value added of $600,000 divided by 20,000 man-hours yields *Value Added Per Man-Hour* of $30.

In any process in which work must flow from one operation to another, from one work station to another, the capacities of each work station must match. Just as the chain is only as strong as its weakest link, so too is the work output as great as the smallest capacity. In an examination of more than five-hundred operations, in which work flow depended upon matched capacities, it has been found that, in the majority of cases, mismatches were the order of the day.

Myths and Realities

Tough competition worldwide is forcing service center executives to reconsider their conceptions about productivity. As we look closely at these beliefs, we find that many of them are simply myths. Companies that base productivity programs on such myths may actually achieve gains, but these gains will fall far short of their potential and come at too high a cost.

Everyone's view of productivity is different. To one, it is making labor work faster. To another, it is the development of systems. To another, it is the use of capital. To others, it is new equipment, a new organization, a computer system, only to name a few. Companies tend to deal with each of these elements in isolation, assuming that, by upgrading each separately, they will gain a full measure of improvement. That is a myth. This piecemeal approach fails, because it ignores the fact that all of these elements are interconnected and affect each other in a myriad of ways. The real productivity payoff comes from dealing with all of the related elements at the same time so that everything is made to happen as planned, in the right quantity and quality, with the right work effort, in the right amount of time, and in the right place.

At first glance, most service center operations appear to have this kind of synchronization, with an incredible number of things happening with amazing precision. This synchronization seems very impressive, until you look behind it. Then you discover that it actually involves the calculated use of a large amount of waste. Companies, for instance, meet their schedules by building excess time and a certain number of rejects into them. This kind of waste, in terms of manpower, material, inventory, equipment, and facilities, riddles virtually every facet of every kind of organization.

The total amount of waste, once identified, can be dismaying. Yet, identifying such waste is the first step toward eliminating it. The resultant gains in productivity can be enormous, and the savings are almost pure profit, dropping straight to the bottom line.

Myths about Middle Management.   When management attacks waste across the board, it obtains far greater gains in a far shorter time than expected. It also uncovers several more myths about productivity. A major myth is the belief that someone with the title "manager" or "supervisor" actually knows how to manage or supervise. Middle managers, in fact, are generally named to their positions without their having a clear understanding of their new responsibilities or adequate training in how to carry them out. Studies show that the training of middle management is almost universally neglected. This neglect can be enormously wasteful, since it is the middle manager who has the mission of implementing senior management's directives and accomplishing its goals.

Diagnostic attitude and perception studies show that senior and middle management are often pursuing different, even conflicting goals. While senior management's goal may be to improve profits, middle management may be directing its main efforts toward keeping the work force happy, or the equipment running. Diagnosing each individual manager's attitudes, perceptions, and goals can be a first step toward building an effective management team—one that knows where it is going and how to get there.

When things go wrong, the blame generally falls not on the managers, but on the workers. The typical complaint is that workers don't really want to work or improve, or that they take no pride in their jobs or their companies. Attitude studies, however, refute these charges. They show that the vast majority of workers want to work much closer to their capabilities, but are kept from doing so by inadequate and uninspired management and supervision.

Myths about Systems. In recent years companies have tried to manage their operations more effectively through the use of systems such as production control, strategic planning, human resources, billing control, and management by objectives. Here the myth is that, by simply imposing a new system and giving it an impressive-sounding name, you're actually going to get improved results. The reality is that such systems are no better than the people running them. If those people lack the proper skills and supervision, they will simply degrade the system. Too often the system is never properly implemented in the first place. What's needed is someone who understands the system, with all its potential imperfections, who can put it in place, adjust it, and, as conditions change, continue to upgrade it. The goal must be to make the system work as planned, with everyone involved knowing their function and carrying it out correctly. Only then does the system truly work and repay the company with increased productivity.

Myths about Computers. Another increasingly prevalent myth is the idea that computers in themselves are the answer to all problems. The reality is that computers can represent a huge uncontrolled cost, with results that fall far short of expectations. An analysis of a typical computer system uncovers a large amount of incompatibility and redundancy, a dearth of software for operational or training functions, a lack of adequate training and communications, and an inadequate measurement of costs and results. Costs are generally understated, ignoring the user cost, while results are often unknown.

In most companies, senior management has effectively abdicated its control over the computer area, by leaving key decisions to the data-processing experts. Left to set their own goals, most data-processing experts design a system that may be technically correct, but which, as a practical matter, may not help management in achieving its goals and objectives.

To regain control over its computer systems, management must first begin communicating its needs to the data-processing experts and, perhaps, even retraining those experts so that they can better understand and support management's objectives. Once management succeeds in harnessing its computers to its objectives, it is well on its way to creating a more manageable, more productive, and more profitable operation.

The failure of computers to live up to expectations should not be surprising. Business has developed a great many ingenious systems for improving productivity, all of which, in practice, have been disappointments. The fault, though, is not with the computers or the systems, but with the people running, supervising, and managing them. Computers and systems are just tools. The human beings using those tools must be skilled in their use and capable of applying them to the proper objectives. Accomplishing this is not easy, nor does it lend itself to a piecemeal approach.

The Myth That "We Can Do It Ourselves."   With regard to installing productivity-improvement programs, one fundamental myth stands out time and again; company managements believe they can make the necessary changes themselves. What these managers fail to realize is the incredible resistance to change that exists in every type of business.

Experience shows that, by far, the greatest difficulty encountered in trying to improve productivity isn't in finding large areas of waste, or even developing prescriptions and solutions to break down the barriers to productivity and allow people to achieve their full potential. By far, the greatest difficulty is overcoming resistance to change, in order to get the process started. It requires dedication and tenacity to overcome such resistance.

Summary

The most effective approach, as stated earlier, is to seek productivity improvements, on a simultaneous basis, throughout the entire organization. In this way, as management upgrades systems and equipment, it also upgrades the people who make those systems and equipment work, thus making everything more responsive to management's goals.

When implemented properly by management that truly wants to increase productivity, such changes can create a synergistic effect—an operation where the total productive result really does exceed the sum of the separate parts.

Exhibits 7.1 through 7.4 provide an experienced based review of how to meet nonuniform production demands that will help contradict productivity improvement myths. Exhibit 7.5 provides you with an analysis form for the purpose of analyzing your own operational improvement methods.

After review of the analysis results, go back and review Exhibits 7.1 through 7.4 and pick which operational planning strategy is right for you.

EXHIBIT 7.1 Operational Planning and Control Strategies for Meeting Nonuniform Demands

Methods	Costs	Remarks
Strategy: Absorb demand fluctuation by shifting manpower capacity.		
Move employees from one position to another, where the demand is higher	No additional cost is involved, except perhaps the cost of additional training of employees	The motivation level of some employees may decrease as a result of a frequent shifting to different positions
Strategy: Use part-time employees.		
Hire part-time employees, when the demand increases	Additional cost of searching for and compensating part-time employees	Part-time employees may not perform effectively enough if they do not get sufficient training
Strategy: Use existing employees for overtime.		
Work overtime, to accommodate peak demands	Additional cost of overtime	Additional compensation may enhance motivation of employees
Strategy: Reschedule the vacation period of employees.		
Reschedule the vacation period to accommodate peak demands	No additional cost, except perhaps an "appreciation" bonus	Occasionally employees may get dissatisfied for not having vacations when they want them
Strategy: Use variable work shifts.		
Assign employees to various work shifts to meet specific operational goals	No additional costs, except perhaps increased pay rate for night shifts	Sometimes employees may be discouraged from the lack of constant work schedules
Strategy: Stabilize demand pattern for services.		
Offer special price reductions or discounts during a period of low demand	Cost of discounts only	Stabilizing demand pattern may create a more uniform operational procedure
Strategy: Use an appointment procedure.		
Develop and maintain an appointment schedule for specialized services	No additional cost	Stabilizing the equipment and human resource capacity utilization
Strategy: Use a priority procedure.		
Develop and maintain a priority procedure to accommodate the operational demands	No additional cost	Stabilizing the equipment and human resource capacity utilization
Strategy: Use a delayed delivery procedure.		
Develop and maintain a delayed delivery schedule, to meet operational requirements	No additional cost	Stabilizing the equipment and human resource capacity utilization
Strategy: Maintain a fixed operational schedule.		
Develop and maintain a fixed operational schedule for standard service	Cost per unit service is reduced to a minimum	This is one of the most popular methods of rendering a standard service

EXHIBIT 7.2   Production Planning Strategies for Meeting Nonuniform Demands

Methods	Costs	Remarks
Strategy: Absorb demand fluctuations by varying inventory level, back-ordering, or shifting demand.		
Produce in earlier period and hold until product is demanded	Cost of holding inventory	Service operations cannot hold service inventory. They must staff for peak levels or shift demand
Offer to deliver the product or service later when capacity is available	Causes a delay in the receipt of revenue at the minimum. May result in lost customers	Manufacturing companies with perishable products often are restrained in the use of this method
Special marketing efforts to shift the demand to slack periods	Costs of advertising, discounts, or promotional programs	This is another example of the interrelationship between functions within a business
Strategy: Change only the production rate in accordance with the nonuniform demand pattern.		
Work additional hours without changing the work-force size	Requires overtime premium pay	Reduces the time available for maintenance work without interrupting production
Staff for high production levels, so that overtime is not required	Excess personnel wages during periods of slack demand	Sometimes work force can be utilized for deferred maintenance during periods of low demand
Subcontract work to other firms	The company must still pay its own overhead plus the overhead and profit for the subcontractors	Utilizes the capacity of other firms, but provides less control of schedules and quality levels
Revise make-or-buy decisions to purchase items when capacity is fully loaded	The company must have skills, tooling, and equipment that will be unutilized in slack periods	All of these methods require capital investments sufficient for the peak production rate, which will be underutilized in slack periods
Strategy: Change the size of the workforce to vary the production level in accordance with demand.		
Hire additional personnel as demand increases	Employment costs for advertising, travel, interviewing, training, etc. Shift premium costs if an additional shift is added.	Skilled workers might not be available when needed, since they are more likely to be employed elsewhere

EXHIBIT 7.2   *(Continued)*

Methods	Costs	Remarks
Lay off personnel as demand subsides	Cost of severance pay and increases in unemployment insurance costs. Loss of efficiency because of decreased moral and higher-seniority workers being moved into jobs for which they are inexperienced as they move into ("bump") jobs of workers with less seniority	The company must have adequate capital investment in equipment for peak workforce level

EXHIBIT 7.3   **Classification of Operational Activities**

Manufacturing Activities		
Job Shop Production	**Batch Production**	**Flow Production**
Custom-designed products	Bakery	Appliances
Special purpose machinery	Clothing	Brewery
Tool-making manufacturing	Electrical products	Brick and tile
General engineering shop	Fasteners	Cable and wire
Model manufacturing	Footwear	Chemicals
Handmade products	Furniture	Cement
	Jewelry	Cosmetics
	Machinery	Food
	Metal products	Glass
	Plastic products	Newspapers
	Printing	Paint
	Sheet metal products	Paper mill
		Pharmaceutical
		Refinery
		Soft drinks
		Textile mill
		Tobacco products
		Vehicles

EXHIBIT 7.4   Comparative Evaluation of Manufacturing Methods

Description	Manufacturing Methods		
	Job Shop	**Batch Production**	**Flow Production**
Manufacturing	To customer's orders only	To customer's orders only	To stock and sometimes to order
Type of order	Most orders are unique and nonrepetitive	Most orders are not unique and repetitive	All orders are standard and repetitive
Product range	There is no standard range of products	There is a broad range of standard and non-standard products	There is a limited range of standard products
Product unit cost	Very high	Average	Very low
Production volume	Very low, usually one or few items	Average, in batches of tens, hundreds, or even thousands	Very high
Production method	Very diversified and sometimes repetitive	Diversified, but usually repetitive	Standardized and repetitive (e.g., conveyor line)
Equipment application	Very general application to various manufacturing processes	General and semispecialized; approximately one week in manufacturing processes	Very specialized application to a limited number of tasks
Operational capacity planning	Can be scheduled at short notice only	Can be planned and scheduled approximately one week in advance	Must be planned and scheduled well in advance
Raw material inventory	Should be purchased for every order on an individual basis	Should be purchased in advance in optimal quantities	Must be repurchased in advance in optimal quantities
Work-in-process and components inventory	No need	Buffer stocks should be kept in optimal quantities for selected products	Buffer stocks should be kept in optimal quantities for all products
Finished goods inventory	No need	Optimal quantities should be kept for selected products	Optimal quantities should be kept for all finished goods
Subcontracting services	Should be used on an individual order basis	Should be preplanned and used on an individual batch basis	Must be planned well in advance for every production run
Personnel skills, requirements	Very high level for a general application	Average level for semi-standardized application	Average level for a highly standardized application

EXHIBIT 7.5   Job Sequence Outline

Date: _____

Staff: _____

Area: _____

Reviewed by: _____

1. *Organization Chart:* (See Attachment A*)
   a. Prepare organizational chart for areas in similar manner as shown on Attachment A.

2. *Department Functions:*
   a. Brief description of department's function: _____
   _____
   _____

   b. Supervisors and foremen's names and their normal working hours:

Name	Position	Hours
_____	_____	_____
_____	_____	_____
_____	_____	_____
_____	_____	_____
_____	_____	_____
_____	_____	_____
_____	_____	_____
_____	_____	_____

   c. Prepare the 'Employee Flexibility and Training Needs Status' data:

   (See Attachment B)

   d. Identify normal working hours of department, shifts, breaks, and lunch times.

Name	Position	Hours
_____	_____	_____
_____	_____	_____
_____	_____	_____
_____	_____	_____
_____	_____	_____
_____	_____	_____
_____	_____	_____
_____	_____	_____

   e. How are vacations and absenteeism covered in the department? Are employees borrowed from other areas to cover these situations? Which departments are people drawn from normally? Can and do they shift people out of the area due to major breakdowns? How is this time reported? What is the absentee percentage in department in last twelve months?
   _____
   _____
   _____
   _____

* Attachments are not included.

(continued)

EXHIBIT 7.5 *(Continued)*

f. What is the relationship of this department to others?

_____

_____

_____

_____

_____

g. Are there any repetitive problems in such relationships that need attention, in order to make interfacing of work flow more effective? What are they?

_____

_____

_____

_____

_____

3. *Department Scheduling:*
   a. Where do production schedules originate?

   _____

   _____

   How soon does the department receive the schedules? Are they timely?

   _____

   _____

   When do the people involved in the flow, line supervisors, actually get the schedules?

   _____

   _____

   Does the supervisor think the schedules are adequate?

   _____

   _____

   b. Does the schedule tie in materials and personnel requirements effectively? If not, who determines this date and when?

   _____

   _____

   c. How is production stated on schedules and reports? In terms of units per hour, shift, day, week, etc?

   _____

   _____

   Are due dates or completion times reflected on these schedules?

   _____

   _____

   Who establishes times of completion? Are they realistic?

   _____

   _____

EXHIBIT 7.5   *(Continued)*

d. What is the frequency of schedule changes?

Is this a formal (written) or a verbal change?

e. Do any schedules exist for support personnel functions?

Who prepares these schedules?

How are major clean-ups handled?

What type of checklist/reports are used for supporting functions?

(1) In any given area of the department, how are work assignments made? Verbal, Written?

(2) How is work laid out in the department? Is it planned a day ahead, one week prior? How?

(3) Does a line supervisor shift personnel on need-priority during the day? How is this done? How is different work tracked?

(4) What happens, particularly in production areas, when product mix changes? How is this handled? By whom? What types of schedules or controls are used for making changes and reporting changes?

(5) How is nonscheduled work, e.g., cleaning (minor), or other small tasks, requiring shift of employees, handled? How is this work scheduled? If not scheduled, how does supervisor plan these support functions?

(6) Does the supervisor experience problems due to inadequate planning? What does he feel would prevent these situations from recurring?

(continued)

EXHIBIT 7.5 *(Continued)*

f. Do backlogs exist in the department?
How are the backlogs expressed in hours, units, work orders, etc.?

What is the normal backlog in the department?

_____

_____

_____

g. In *maintenance-type areas,* where does work input originate?

_____

_____

Who receives input and what is done with it?

_____

_____

Does a work order system exist in the department? How does it function?

_____

How are work schedules prepared? By whom?

_____

Are schedules prepared in terms of person-hours per job? If not, how is it done?

_____

_____

Are only actual person-hours reported for work after work is completed? Why?

_____

How are these hours reported? By whom?

_____

How are work priorities established for the department? By whom?

_____

Does this system of setting priorities work?

_____

h. Describe peak workload periods experienced by the department. When do they occur? Hourly, daily, weekly, monthly?

_____

_____

What are the reasons for these peaks and valleys in the department workload?

_____

_____

Does the supervisor think this fluctuation is necessary? Could it be reduced? How?

_____

_____

EXHIBIT 7.5   *(Continued)*

---

i. In clerical areas, list *key* documents processed. Describe purpose, where documents originate, how often received, what is done with them, who handles them, and where they go when they are completed:

Document	Purpose	Originator	Frequency Received	What Is Done to Them?	By Whom?	Where Are They Sent?

j. What types/categories of historical data are maintained in the department?

Are these records/logs updated on a routine basis? By whom?

What is the purpose of maintaining data/logs?

Note: Obtain live samples of each type volume log/record maintained in department or sketch of column heading for each type identifying data covered and purpose of each.

k. What standards are used in the department?

Are these standards used for scheduling purposes? If not, why not?

Are supervisors' estimates used for scheduling work?

List estimates used in the department and units of measure, work-to-time relationships:

4. *Physical Layout:*
   a. Draw physical layout of area. Indicate area designations, major pieces of equipment, furniture, etc. Denote names of areas surrounding this department as they exist.

5. *Personnel Roster:*
   a. Complete personnel roster, indicating employees names, hire dates, shifts, job classifications, and positions, as well as appropriate pay rates and vacations, in weeks, for total department. Employees' names should be arranged in alphabetical order.

6. *Flexibility Chart:*
   a. Flexibility charts are used to identify employee's skills. How could they be used in the department where he/she now works?

(continued)

EXHIBIT 7.5   *(Continued)*

---

7. *Equipment List and Location within the Department:*
   a. List all major machines and equipment located in the department. Their limitations
      and normal operating output speeds in units/hour:

   (Production Areas Only)

Quanity	Name of Equipment of Machine	Limitations Maximum Output/Hour	Normal Operating Speed-Output/ Hour
_____	_____	_____	_____
_____	_____	_____	_____
_____	_____	_____	_____
_____	_____	_____	_____
_____	_____	_____	_____
_____	_____	_____	_____

   b. Draw equipment layout as shown on Attachment G. (Sample)

8. *Current System:*
   a. Prepare paper/work flow of existing system in force as per sample. Break system
      down from input (planning) to execution (implementation of plan) to reporting
      stage (what was accomplished and when).
   b. Obtain live copies of all controls/documents used in area and write purpose of
      each on reverse side of controls and number each control to identify position in
      flow cycle of existing system.

9. *Product Flow:*
   a. Indicate flow of finished product/materials through area, starting with first stage
      of activity, moving through area, routing movement through department through
      final output from area.

10. *Major Operating Problems:*
    a. What are the major *operating* problems existing in the department as described by
       the supervisor?

	Problems	Reasons
1.	_____	_____
2.	_____	_____
3.	_____	_____
4.	_____	_____
5.	_____	_____
6.	_____	_____
7.	_____	_____
8.	_____	_____
9.	_____	_____
10.	_____	_____

11. *Method Changes Anticipated in the Future:*
    a. What changes are contemplated for the department? When will they take place?
       What effect will they have on the department's functions/workload.

Definition of Change	Time Table	Effect of Change
_____	_____	_____
_____	_____	_____
_____	_____	_____
_____	_____	_____

EXHIBIT 7.5 *(Continued)*

b. What is the relationship of these plans/changes to the planned installation of the pending system?

_____

_____

_____

12. *Supervisory Points:*
   a. What is the supervisor looking to us to provide, to assist him in better control and scheduling of his/her department?

_____

_____

_____

_____

13. *Training:*
   a. Do you have any formal or special training for your people?

_____

_____

_____

_____

   b. If no, how do you train your people?

_____

_____

_____

_____

   c. Do you feel this is adequate?

_____

_____

   d. What do you feel are its shortcomings?

_____

_____

   e. How much time during a month do you spend on training?

_____

   f. How do you know when a person needs training? (By new person to job, by error rates, by performance, etc.)

_____

_____

   g. What type of historical data are maintained on training needs and results?

_____

_____

_____

ANALYSIS AND EVALUATION

Productivity Defined

Productivity, in its simplest form, is a ratio of the products and services of an organization to the inputs consumed to generate them. Looked at a little differently, it is a measure of the efficient use of a company's resources. For the mathematically oriented:

$$\text{Productivity} = \frac{\text{Total outputs of the firm}}{\text{Total inputs used by the firm}}$$

Thus, if a company generates the same output with less input, the ratio gets larger, and it can be said that the organization has been more productive. This increase, then, is at the heart of productivity-improvement efforts. It is insufficient to measure the ratio of output to input, unless something is done to increase that ratio overtime. To do this, management and the organization, as a whole, have only five options to making the ratio bigger.

1. Make the output larger for the same input.

2. Make the input smaller for the same output.

3. Increase the output while decreasing the input.

4. Increase output faster than the input increases.

5. Decrease the output less than the inputs decrease.

The following representations may help to visualize these five possibilities:

```
                --
    ----      ----      ----      ----      ----
     --
    (1)       (2)       (3)       (4)       (5)
```

Story of the Pipeline

Many years ago, it is told, a farmer in a Midwest community decided to pipe water from a stream on his property to a corner of his farm, which was given over to grazing his cows. He bought one-hundred feet of three-inch-diameter pipe and, when he had it all laid out and connected, he found he was about twelve feet short of the trough to which the water was to be piped. When he went to the store for additional pipe he found that they were out of three-inch pipe, so he bought two reducers and twelve feet of one-inch pipe, and got his twelve additional feet. The output of water to the trough was insufficient to keep the cows supplied with water. Explaining the problem to a neighbor, he expressed perplexity at his problem and showed him how well the water pumped into the beginning of the line at maximum pressure; but at the delivery end, he had hardly a trickle. The neighbor explained to him that the output at the end of the pipe was controlled by the capacity of the twelve-foot length of one-inch pipe. No more water could pass through the line in a given period than could pass through the smaller diameter pipe.

This story may seem exaggerated, but, in many service center flows, the mismatching of capacities is a very serious situation.

Aspects of Financial Statements Most Critical to Management

Although the statement of income (Exhibit 7.6) and statement of financial position (Exhibit 7.7) reflect the financial health of the entire business, certain portions of both statements pertain directly to the manager's area of direct control.

Cost of goods sold represents the cost of manufacturing the company's products, and consists of direct materials, direct labor, and manufacturing overhead, which are covered in the following section.

The cost of materials used directly in the company's products, will be: (1) raw material and (2) purchased parts.

Direct labor costs are those associated with processing. Machine operators and assemblers, who work directly on the product itself, are classified as direct labor, as opposed to such people as inspectors, material handlers, and maintenance people (called indirect labor), who provide essential services, but who do not work on or change the configuration themselves.

The final cost (costs included in overhead) consists of all other costs not considered direct materials or direct labor costs. Overhead includes such costs as indirect labor, taxes and insurance, heat, light, and power, depreciation, and indirect materials and supplies (tooling, janitorial supplies, lubricating oils, paperwork expenses).

EXHIBIT 7.6   Statement of Income

Statement of Income
For Year Ended Dec. 31, 19XX

Gross sales		$45,750,525
Less: Returns and allowances	$ 732,561	
Cash discounts	683,228	
		1,415,789
Net sales		$44,334,736
Cost of goods sold		25,110,706
Gross Margins		$19,224,134
Sales administration	700,335	
Sales commissions	652,079	
General and administrative	1,632,994	
Total		$ 2,895,408
Operating Profit		$16,238,726
Gain on assets sold	950	
Rental and interest income	25,245	
Total		$ 26,195
Net income before taxes		$16,264,921
Federal income tax		7,807,162
Net Income		$ 8,457,759

EXHIBIT 7.7   Statement of Financial Position

Statement of Financial Position
December 31, 19XX

Current assets		
Cash		$ 658,007
Securities (at cost)		525,362
Accounts receivable	$ 7,894,210	
Minus reserve for bad debts	24,000	
Net accounts receivable		7,870,210
Inventories		
Houston	12,003,865	
Pittsburgh	2,833,529	
Los Angeles	1,702,058	
Total inventories		$16,539,452
Prepaid expenses		9,406
Total Current Assets		$25,602,437
Plant and equipment	25,876,254	
Less depreciation	12,325,976	
Total plant and equipment		13,550,278
Total Assets		$39,152,715
Current liabilities		
Accounts payable		$ 1,823,151
Accrued liabilities		1,602,252
Payroll deductions		87,155
Total Current Liabilities		$ 3,512,558
Equity		
Corporate clearing account		$ 8,592,891
Divisional control		17,335,627
Retained earnings		9,711,639
Total equity		$35,640,157
Total Liabilities and Equity		$39,152,715

Gross margins, then, reflect profits before other company costs such as sales and administrative expenses are subtracted from gross margins. When they are subtracted, net income is the final result.

Those accounts concerning the manager directly are inventories and plant and equipment. The inventories account represents the different stages of processing: (1) raw materials and purchased parts; (2) work-in-process, which denotes the former raw materials and purchased parts somewhere in the process of being manufactured; and (3) finished goods inventory—the stock of completely processed products ready for sale.

Plant and equipment includes buildings, machinery, and equipment. This subject will be discussed in more detail later. For the moment, just remember that plant and equipment represents an investment that must be made to yield attractive profits for the business. When a manager seeks to add new plants and equipment, profitability must be carefully determined and actual results monitored to assure that the investments are paying off.

Calculating Return on Assets.   If you, as a person, invest money, your very first concern is "How much will I earn?" A business asks exactly the same question when it invests its money. Return on assets is the measurement of success ("How much did I earn in relation to my investment?") that corporate management burdens its divisions with. Return on assets (ROA) is the ratio of net income to sales, multiplied by asset turnover, as seen here:

$$\text{ROA} = \frac{\text{Income before taxes}}{\text{Net sales}} \times \frac{\text{Net sales}}{\text{Total assets}}$$

By canceling out the net sales (in true arithmetical form), ROA then becomes:

$$\text{ROA} = \frac{\text{Income before taxes}}{\text{Total assets}}$$

Return on assets is the prime measurement of how well each division performs financially. It is the best way of answering the question, "How well did this division perform in relation to the assets it had at its disposal?"

Below are the steps involved in calculating Return On Assets:

1. Add total assets. These numbers are taken directly from the balance sheet (Statement of Financial Position). They are added together to form the total assets shown to the immediate right of the left-hand column.

2. Divide net sales by total assets, to show asset turnover, that is, how many sales dollars were generated with the assets.

3. Determine net income before taxes, by subtracting sales administration expenses, sales commissions, and general (administrative) expenses from gross margins. Then, add miscellaneous income to gross margins.

4. Divide net income before taxes by net sales, to derive return on sales.

5. Multiply asset turnover by return on sales to get ROA.

Capacity Utilization Calculation

Exhibit 7.8 displays a nine-month summary showing a total of 21,424.5 tons processed, using .69 hours, or 1.44 hours per ton.

At a rate of .69 tons per hour, from the number of hours worked for that entire period, it can be determined that the department functioned at only 88% of its capacity (see Exhibit 7.9).

Regardless of the service center, most companies keep records of production in an identifiable unit of measure. They also keep records of hours worked. *What few service centers do is to actually compare the units and hours to determine the consistency or variances in the output.*

The higher the variances, the more indication of the lack of good operational tools to control costs and, therefore, the greater potential for improvement.

EXHIBIT 7.8 Utilization Analysis Report

Month	Jan.	Feb.	Mar.	Apr.	May	June	July	Aug.	Sep.	Oct.	Nov.	Dec.	Total
Number of work days													
Gross hours—eight people													
Vacation, absent hours													
Actual hours worked	3895.75	3855.5	4619.75	3310.25	4439.2	3651.25	3336.25	4202.25	3511.50				
Tons processed	2424	2457	2608	2297	2808	2428	1946	2304.5	2152				
Tons per hour	0.62	0.63	0.56	0.69	0.63	0.66	0.58	0.54	0.61				
Hours per ton	1.61	1.56	1.77	1.44	1.58	1.50	1.71	1.82	1.63				
Variance low to high				1.44				1.82					
Percent utilization	.895	.917	.812	.999	.910	.957	.839	.789	.882				

Hours .38 = 26%

EXHIBIT 7.9   Capacity Utilization Calculation

Percent capacity $= \dfrac{\text{Hours per ton} \times \text{Tons processed}}{\text{Actual hours worked}} \times 100$

Percent capacity $= \dfrac{1.44 \times 21424.5}{34821.75} = \dfrac{30851.28}{34821.75} = 88\%$

(The best hours per ton (1.44) becomes the standard for the calculation in the other months.)

The best performance was in the month of April, when production reached 99% of its capacity.

Percent capacity for April $= \dfrac{1.44 \times 2297}{3310.25} = 99\%$

The worst month was August, at 78.9% of its capacity.

There is a variance of 25% of its capacity. These figures go straight to the bottom line: (.26 $\times$ Total labor costs = Savings)

Operating Performance Ratios

Operating Performance Ratios are listed below:

- Percent Productivity is the percentage indicator that measures the output (earned hours) versus input (available hours).

$$\text{Percent productivity} = \dfrac{\text{Earned hours*}}{\text{Available hours}} \times 100$$

- Percent Performance is the *output* of measured work in relationship to total hours worked. It also measures how *productive* the area is.

$$\text{Percent performance} = \dfrac{\text{Earned hours}}{\text{Total hours worked}^{\dagger}} \times 100$$

- Percent Efficiency represents how *well* an employee has *performed* on measured work.

$$\text{Percent efficiency} = \dfrac{\text{Earned hours}}{\text{Hours on measured work}^{\ddagger} \text{ (actual hours)}} \times 100$$

---

*Earned hours are the output of measured hours of work produced (real work accomplished) in the department.
†Hours on measured work represent those hours actually spent by employees on measured or estimated work.
‡Total hours worked are the total clock hours for which an employee works in the department.

- Percent Utilization represents the percentage of time employees are working against measured activities and is determined by:

$$\text{Percent utilization} = \frac{\text{Measured hours worked}}{\text{Total hours worked}} \times 100$$

- Percent Scheduled attainment is the successful completion of planned volume, at a controlled reasonable cost, and on schedule (this is the goal of the service center).

$$\text{Percent scheduled attainment} = \frac{\text{Operations completed}}{\text{Total operations}} \times 100$$

Other Direct Labor Control Measures

Many other measurements of direct labor can be made to control and correct costs. Some of the more prevalent are as follows:

Utilization

$$\text{Utilization} = \frac{\text{Time on standards}}{\text{Total time available}} \times 100$$

Example: A processing department with twenty direct-labor employees shows the following statistics for one eight-hour production:

$$\text{Total time available} = 20 \times 8 = 160 \text{ Person-hours}$$

$$\text{Time on standards} = 120 \text{ Person-hours}$$

$$\text{Time off standards} = 40 \text{ Person-hours}$$

$$\text{Utilization} = \frac{120}{160} \times 100\% = 75\%$$

Direct-Labor Productivity

$$\text{Productivity} = \text{Performance} \times \text{Utilization} \times 100\%$$

Example: In the same department cited in the example on utilization, performance (percent efficiency of direct labor) was 95 percent for that shift:

$$\text{Productivity} = 95.0\% \times 75.0\% \times 100\% = 71.3\%$$

Labor productivity is a more encompassing index than separate measures of performance and utilization. It provides a ready measurement of direct labor productivity in a single ratio.

Direct-Labor Cost per Unit

$$\text{Direct labor cost per unit} = \frac{\text{Total direct labor costs}}{\text{Number}} \text{ of units produced}$$

Example: If the twenty direct-labor employees each were paid $10 per hour, then

$$\text{Direct labor cost per unit} = \frac{20 \times \$10 \times 8 \text{ Hours}}{1{,}000} = \frac{\$1{,}600}{1{,}000} = \$1.60$$

Average Earnings.   Average earnings is defined as those earnings derived from operations not on standard. In most union shops, average earnings is a negotiable issue, and payment resulting from average earnings is based on what each individual operator averaged on incentive for the past week. If a sheer operator, for example, ran several jobs not yet measured on incentive (usually new jobs), his incentive pay for those jobs would be the average incentive pay he earned during the previous week.

Average earnings is payment of something for nothing. Since unmeasured work is looked upon as a fault of management, unions are generally successful in their demands for average earnings. In that case, the measurement of average earnings becomes a significant ratio for management.

$$\text{Average earnings} = \frac{\text{Average earnings}}{\text{Total incentive earnings}} \times 100\%$$

The service center had the following average earnings for one calendar year:

$$\text{Average earnings} = \frac{\$241{,}632}{\$1{,}550{,}750} \times 100 = 15.6\%$$

No matter how you look at it, either 15.6 percent, or $241,632 is too much. Most average earnings are better held to maximums of five to seven percent.

Percent Performance to Standard.   This ratio is the most significant one in measuring the results of incentive coverage. It shows increases in performance that can be directly related to increases in production. The service center, before incentives, had the following annual performance:

$$\text{Performance} = \frac{\text{Earned hours}}{\text{Standard hours}} \times 100$$

$$\text{Performance} = \frac{398{,}140}{563{,}178} = 100 = 70.7\%$$

After installation of the incentive system for one year, their performance had improved 25 percent (despite their average earnings), as seen here:

$$\text{Performance} = \frac{506{,}442}{571{,}280} \times 100 = 88.7\%$$

In terms of actual improvement in performance:

$$\text{Percent improvement} = \frac{88.7\% - 70.7\%}{70.7\%} \times 100 = 25.5\%$$

The 25.5-percent improvement in performance represented a real gain of equal amount in production output.

Exhibit 7.10 charts a report on efficiency, utilization, and productivity.

EXHIBIT 7.10 Efficiency, Utilization, and Productivity Report

Week No.	Dept.	(1) Actual Hours	(2) Quantity Processed	(3) Earned Hours	(4) Available Hours [(1) 1(8)]	(5) Percent Efficiency [(3)/(1)]	(6) Percent Utilization [(1)/(4)]	(7) Percent Productivity [(3)/(4)]	(8) Total	Indirect Hours					
										Training	Meetings	Down Time	Waiting Parts	Medical	Other
1	64122	854.50	155347	1391.49	913.70	162.84	93.52	.152.29	59.20	2.00	1.70	0.00	0.00	0.00	55.50
2	64122	1258.00	79326	921.50	1316.50	73.25	95.56	70.00	58.50	3.20	7.60	0.00	4.80	0.00	42.90
3	64122	1211.60	160031	1562.86	1306.00	128.99	92.77	119.67	94.40	20.00	4.90	3.40	0.00	0.00	66.10
4	64122	1064.90	110948	1132.24	1139.60	106.32	93.45	99.35	74.70	7.00	0.00	5.70	0.00	4.00	58.00
Monthly Totals		4389.00	503652	5008.09	4675.80	114.11	93.87	107.11	286.80	32.20	14.20	9.10	4.80	4.00	222.50
1	64126	396.00	337	502.83	409.20	126.98	96.77	122.88	13.20	0.00	0.00	0.00	13.20	0.00	0.00
2	64126	445.80	282	503.33	466.90	112.90	95.48	107.80	21.10	0.00	2.20	6.00	7.90	0.00	5.00
3	64126	434.30	271	469.42	469.50	108.09	92.50	99.98	35.20	0.00	1.82	2.10	22.30	0.00	9.00
4	64126	447.90	401	572.33	464.00	127.78	96.53	123.35	16.10	0.00	0.00	2.50	10.60	0.00	3.00
Monthly Totals		1724.00	1291	2047.91	1809.60	118.79	95.27	113.17	85.60	0.00	4.00	10.60	54.00	0.00	17.00
1	64134	383.70	298	234.00	429.00	60.99	89.44	54.55	45.30	0.00	10.70	0.40	2.00	0.00	32.20
2	64134	474.30	761	628.50	522.50	132.51	90.78	120.29	48.20	0.00	13.80	0.10	6.10	0.00	28.20
3	64134	515.10	586	478.67	580.00	92.93	80.81	82.53	64.90	0.00	3.50	2.60	7.70	0.00	51.10
4	64134	573.50	650	528.58	623.90	92.17	91.92	84.72	50.40	1.50	0.00	4.00	7.60	0.00	37.30
Monthly Totals		1946.60	2295	1869.75	2155.40	96.05	90.31	86.75	208.80	1.50	28.00	7.10	23.40	0.00	148.80
						Weekly Plant Composite									
1	All	1634.20	153982	2128.32	1751.90	130.24	93.28	121.49	117.70	2.00	12.40	0.40	15.20	0.00	87.70
2	All	2178.10	80369	2053.33	2305.90	94.27	94.46	89.05	127.80	3.20	23.60	6.10	18.80	0.00	76.10
3	All	2161.00	160888	2510.95	2355.50	116.19	91.74	106.60	194.50	20.00	10.20	8.10	30.00	0.00	126.20
4	All	2086.30	111999	2233.15	2227.50	107.04	93.66	100.25	141.20	8.50	0.00	12.20	18.20	4.00	98.30
Monthly Totals		8059.60	507238	8925.75	8640.80	110.75	93.27	103.30	581.20	33.70	46.20	26.80	82.20	4.00	388.30

EXHIBIT 7.11   Operations to Return on Assets

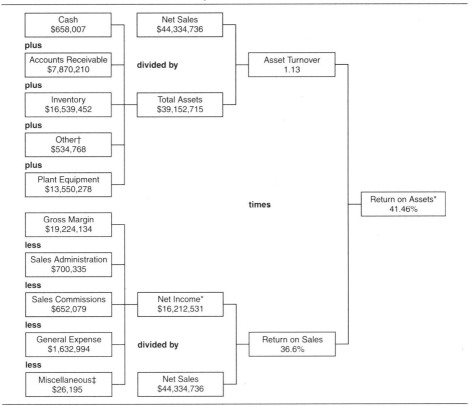

*Before taxes.

†Securities plus prepaid expenses.

‡Gain on assets sold plus rental and interest income.

Return on Assets.   While ROA is a picture of overall divisional performance (see Exhibit 7.11), the chief contributor to results, either good or bad, is the operations function.

Control of ROA, therefore, is *the paramount concern* for the manager.

Cost of Goods Sold Analysis.   Return on Assets, while being the yardstick of divisional financial status, is only one of the several measures used by corporate management to control divisional performance. There are several additional measures that you should know to help monitor progress to achievement of ROA goals. A description of the more popular of these follows.

Analyzing Gross Margins.   Gross margins reflect that portion of money left over after operations cost of goods sold is subtracted from net sales. Gross margins, as a percentage of net sales, is a basic indicator of how good a job is being done to control operating costs.

(Thousands Omitted)

	19X0	19X9	19X8	19X7	19X6
Net sales	$44,334	$42,105	$39,634	$30,912	$30,027
Cost of goods sold	25,110	25,263	28,536	22,878	23,727
Gross Margins	$19,224	$16,842	$11,098	$ 8,034	$ 6,300
$\dfrac{\text{Gross margins}}{\text{Net sales}} \times 100 =$ 43.4%		40.0%	28.0%	25.9%	20.9%

Note: Gross margins divided by net sales, as shown above, is multiplied by 100 to obtain a percentage. All three can be analyzed by breaking down cost of goods sold for the five-year period under study:

(Thousands Omitted)

	19X0	19X9	19X8	19X7	19X6
Net sales	$44,334	$42,105	$39,634	$30,912	$30,027
Cost of goods sold					
Material	$10,322	$ 9,004	$ 8,225	$ 7,195	$ 7,248
Direct labor	4,379	4,980	5,163	5,632	5,465
Overhead	10,409	11,079	15,148	10,051	11,014
Total Costs	$25,110	$25,163	$28,536	$22,878	$23,727

To break down those costs, we will take each of the cost categories (material, direct labor, overhead) individually, and divide them by net sales for the year, and multiply the result by 100 to obtain the percentage of costs to sales:

	199X	*198X*
Material	23.3%	23.3%
Direct labor	9.9%	18.2%
Overhead	23.5%	35.6%

Example: Material costs for 199X were $10,332 and sales were $44,334. Then, dividing material costs by sales, and multiplying the result by 100 provides the 23.3%.

$$\frac{\$10,332}{\$44,334} \times 100 = 23.3\%$$

Material costs as a percentage of net sales have held steady over the last five years.

Inventory Turnover

Inventory turnover is an indication of how efficiently an organization is using materials that comprise the products. A low inventory turnover rate could indicate excessively high levels of usable inventory, or high levels of obsolete inventory.

Too high an inventory turnover rate, conversely, could indicate that not enough inventory is on hand to satisfy customer demands—a condition that results almost invariably in lost sales. This same condition can also be an indication of short machine run times, with its consequent higher costs resulting from excessive machine set-ups and higher material handling costs.

How to Calculate Inventory Turnover. Inventory turnover is computed as follows:

$$\frac{\text{Manufacturing cost of goods sold}}{\text{Average inventory levels during the year}} = \text{Inventory turnover}$$

Inventory turnover, however, is not a measure that stands alone. It must be analyzed in relation to company objectives. If you will recall the ROA formula, it is just as important to determine how much profit is being generated per turnover.

Overhead as a Yardstick of Performance

As explained earlier, overhead is composed of all operating costs other than direct material and direct labor.

Example: $10,655,000 for one million machine hours:

	Budget	Actual
Manufacturing overhead	$10,655,000	$10,051,000
Machine hours	1,000,000	800,000
Overhead rate	$ 10.65	$ 12.56

Computing Fixed and Variable Costs

While direct material and direct labor dollars are relatively accessible for purposes of measurement and control, overhead costs are not. Overhead is composed of a variety of costs, both fixed and variable, which need to be separated and measured to control overhead performance.

Fixed Costs are those costs that do not change in response to a change in product volume. Typical fixed costs are depreciation, management salaries and benefits, taxes, rent, heat, light, and some power costs. From the viewpoint of the manufacturing manager, costs should *never* be considered fixed.

Variable costs are those costs that move, more or less, proportionately with product volume. Direct materials and direct labor are the prime examples. Others include indirect supplies, most power costs, and maintenance costs.

How Overhead Is Measured and Controlled

It is necessary to define the ways in which manufacturing overhead is measured and controlled. Variances for overhead are classically divided into three categories: *spending, efficiency,* and *capacity.*

Calculating Spending Variance. This is found by comparing overhead costs of budgeted machine hours to overhead costs of actual machine hours. It is a measure of efficiency of machine hours used.

Budget at 800,000 machine hours	$10,003,000
Actual at 700,000 machine hours	− 9,676,000
Unfavorable efficiency variance	$ 327,000

Calculating Capacity Variance. This measures the variance derived from performance attributable to operating the plants at below-normal capacity. Normal capacity can be defined as *average* use of facilities over the past several years.

Normal capacity	1,000,000	Machine hours
Actual hours used	− 800,000	Machine hours
Underabsorbed capacity	200,000	Machine hours

Now that machine hours have been determined in the capacity variance calculation, costs must be applied. Since capacity variance measures the overabsorption or underabsorption of *fixed* overhead, variable costs are not considered (because they change with changes in product volume, while fixed costs do not). Using the fixed overhead rate shown, $7.39 per machine hour, the capacity variance is calculated:

Fixed overhead rate × Underabsorbed machine hours

$7.39 × 200,000 = Capacity variance $1,478,000

Combining Variances. Exhibit 7.12 allows the pulling together of all three variances to observe their cumulative impact on costs. The chart that follows summarizes this impact.

Actual overhead	$10,051,000		
		Spending variance $48,000	
Flexible budget for 800,000 hours actually used	$10,003,000		Controllable variance $375,000
		Efficiency variance $327,000	
Flexible budget for 700,000 hours required	$ 9,676,000		

The $375,000 represents that portion of the overhead that could have been avoided, had manufacturing management done a better job. It is an unfavorable variance that is strictly controllable.

Capacity variance, on the other hand, is related to product volume attributable to sales, and, as such, is beyond the control of the manufacturing manager.

EXHIBIT 7.12   Flexible Budget

					19XX Actual Results
Number of parts produced	5,000,000	4,500,000	4,000,000	3,500,000	3,500,000
Machine hours of operation	1,000,000	900,000	800,000	700,000	800,000
Variable overhead:					
Indirect materials and supplies	$ 1,116,000	$ 1,004,000	$ 893,000	$ 781,000	$ 946,000
Maintenance	810,000	729,000	648,000	567,000	648,000
Power	1,277,000	1,149,000	1,022,000	894,000	1,022,000
Other	60,000	54,000	48,000	42,000	50,000
Total Variable Costs	$ 3,263,000	$ 2,936,000	$ 2,611,000	$2,284,000	$ 2,666,000
Fixed Overhead:					
Supervision	$ 3,003,000	$ 3,003,000	$ 3,003,000	$3,003,000	$ 3,003,000
Taxes and insurance	2,370,000	2,370,000	2,370,000	2,370,000	2,349,000
Heat and light	792,000	792,000	792,000	792,000	805,000
Depreciation	1,177,000	1,177,000	1,177,000	1,177,000	1,177,000
Other	50,000	50,000	50,000	50,000	51,000
Total Fixed Costs	7,392,000	7,392,000	7,392,000	7,392,000	7,385,000
Total Overhead	$10,655,000	$10,328,000	$10,003,000	$9,676,000	$10,051,000

Note: Variable overhead rate per machine hour $ 3.26
       Fixed overhead rate per machine hour   7.39

       Total overhead rate per machine hour $10.65

Both controllable and uncontrollable variances, when put together, look like this:

Unfavorable spending and efficiency variances	$ 375,000
Capacity variance	1,478,000
Total variances	$1,853,000

Overhead costs are important to the manager. Through use of a flexible budget and monthly reports of the variances indicated, you can keep the manufacturing overhead rate in line and hold costs to a minimum.

8

OPERATIONS EFFICIENCY MEASURES

CAPACITY ANALYSIS

Every manager needs to be aware of what the capacity of his plants is. Having this knowledge assures that realistic workloads are scheduled. Too heavy a workload in relation to capacity leads to missed customer promises, and high in-process inventory levels. Too light a workload causes high capacity variances.

Capacity is the amount of product the facilities are capable of producing within a given time period. Capacity is generally expressed in terms of standard direct labor hours. Normal capacity refers to *average* use of the facilities over a number of years, while manufacturing capacity, as discussed here, signifies capability of the facilities to manufacture the most product possible or the most product schedules.

Generally, capacity is calculated, by product line, for each production machine in the plant.

Determination of capacity is basically a three-step process:

1. *Determination of weekly raw capacity.* This assumes that all machines run seven days per week on three shifts, at eight hours per shift, with no allowances for downtime. It is a starting point only, and the purpose is to make management

EXHIBIT 8.1   Determination of Weekly Raw Capacity

Department	Available Machines	Crew Size	Total Crew ×	Days Available ×	Shifts per Day ×	Hours per Shift =	Raw Capacity Standard Direct Labor Hours
Chuckers	14	.5	7	7	3	8	1,176
Grinders	12	.5	6	7	3	8	1,008
Millers	12	1	12	7	3	8	2,016
Drills	12	1	12	7	3	8	2,016
Heat treat	4	.5	2	7	3	8	336
Plating line	4	1	4	7	3	8	672
Paint booths	5	1	5	7	3	8	840
Assembly lines	3	4	12	7	3	8	2,018
Total Plant			60				10,082

EXHIBIT 8.2   Determination of Weekly Planned Capacity

Department	Available Machines	Planned Machines	Total Crew	×	Days Planned	×	Shifts Planned	Hours per Shift	=	Planned Capacity Standard Direct Labor Hours
Chuckers	14	12	7		5		1	10		350
Grinders	12	10	6		5		1	10		300
Millers	12	12	8		5		1	10		400
Drills	12	10	8		5		1	10		400
Heat treat	4	4	2		5		1	10		100
Plating line	4	2	2		5		1	10		100
Paint booths	5	4	4		5		1	10		200
Assembly lines	3	3	3		5		1	10		150
Total Plant			40							2,000

aware of the full capability of equipment, were it to be employed in its most productive state. (See Exhibit 8.1.)

2. *Determination of weekly planned capacity.* This calculation is based on the number of days per week the machinery is scheduled to operate, along with the number of shifts and the number of hours per shift. (See Exhibit 8.2.)

3. *Determination of weekly available capacity.* Using planned capacity as a base figure, available capacity realistically subtracts standard hours lost because of downtime and yields. Yields include direct labor hours for producing both avoidable and unavoidable scrap. Unavoidable scrap examples are chips and shavings removed during machining operations, skeleton scrap from stamping operations, and gates and risers out from castings. (See Exhibit 8.3.)

EXHIBIT 8.3   Determination of Weekly Available Capacity

Department	Planned Standard Hours	×	Uptime Objective Percent	×	Yield Percent	=	Available Capacity Standard Direct Labor Hours
Chuckers	350		80		90		252
Grinders	300		75		85		191
Millers	400		80		90		288
Drills	400		90		94		338
Heat treat	100		80		90		72
Plating line	100		80		95		76
Paint booths	200		95		97		184
Assembly lines	150		75		85		96
Total Plant	2,000						1,497

EXHIBIT 8.4   Capacity Analysis Summary

| | Standard Direct Labor Hours—Weekly | | |
Department	Raw Capacity	Planned Capacity	Available Capacity
Chuckers	1,008	250	158
Grinders	840	250	180
Millers	1,680	400	288
Drills	1,680	400	285
Heat treat	168	50	44
Plating line	336	100	87
Paint booths	504	150	138
Assembly lines	1,344	400	304
Total Plant	7,560	2,000	1,484

Note: Planned capacity is based on one shift, five days per week, ten hours per day.

Capacity Summary

It is helpful at this stage to put raw capacity, planned capacity, and available capacity together and to compare them. The first, and most obvious conclusion (see Exhibit 8.4) is that available capacity of 1,484 standard hours is but a small percentage of the 7,560 standard hours of raw capacity. That is true, but it must be remembered that Los Angeles is a new plant, and that available capacity will expand to more closely approximate raw capacity, given time. Shifts will be added to increase available capacity. Additionally, as time progresses and the learning curve extends, uptime and yields will improve as management and operators refine production operations.

Division: Capacity Analysis Summary

Capacity planning allows management to marry production forecasts with available capacity. Through knowledge of what plant capacity is, management can more effectively make plans for future workloads. As sales levels grow, management will have a base upon which to ask for additional facilities.

EMPLOYEE TURNOVER ANALYSIS

Exhibit 8.5 depicts a turnover analysis. If the manager knows what to expect in the way of employee turnover, he can better control his staffing and on-the-job training, either formal or informal, and will know much better what to expect from a standpoint of permanency of the employees. An examination of the attitudes of long-term and new employees is shown in Exhibit 8.6.

Another service that can help the manager in his analysis of his workforce is a listing, or marked map, of locations of employees' residence areas. This enables him to better judge possibilities of absenteeism due to weather disturbances or problems with traffic.

EXHIBIT 8.5 Turnover Analysis

	Month	YTD	Prior YTD	Prior Year Total
Job Group				
Hours				
Travel too far			2	2
Better job	2	2	1	11
Dissatisfied with job				3
Family	2	3	2	8
Other	1	3	1	2
Not qualified (term)			2	3
Not dependable				4
Permanent force reduction			1	1
Violation of rules	1	1		
Other		1		
Organization				
Production	5	9	9	39
Materials	2	3	3	9
Engineering	1	1		2
Management		1	1	1
Average Years of Service	2.2	2.0	1.5	2.2
Percent Turnover	3.7	6.6	5.8	23.3
Job Group				
Managers		1	1	1
Supervisors				
Buyers				1
Engineers				1
Technicians	3	5	1	10
Clerks	1	1	1	1
Secretaries				
Analysts				1
Group leaders		1	1	1
Assemblers	3	5	8	27
Material handlers				5
Machine operators				
Custodial workers				1
Schedulers	1	1		2
Total	8	14	12	51
Reasons				
Wages (Quit)				
School				4
Leaving locality	2	4	4	12
Health				1

EXHIBIT 8.6   Long-Service Interviews: Then and Now Comparisons

No.	Statement	Long-Term Then	Long-Term Now	New Employees Now
1.	People were (are) important.	9.0	5.6	8.3
2.	Experience was (is) respected.	7.2	5.6	7.2
3.	The company was (is) a nice place to work.	9.4	7.3	8.2
4.	Employees had (have) an opportunity to get ahead.	7.4	6.3	7.4
5.	The benefit package was (is) good.	8.6	8.6	8.4
6.	Salary was (is) fair.	7.5	6.3	6.4
7.	The work environment was (is) pleasant.	8.7	7.1	7.6
8.	There was (is) too much red tape.	2.0	3.6	3.7
9.	The company was (is) responsive to employees' needs.	8.4	6.1	8.1
10.	Employee questions were (are) answered quickly.	7.6	6.1	7.0
11.	People were (are) proud of their work.	9.2	6.0	7.2
12.	Employees were (are) competent.	9.0	7.0	7.5
13.	Solutions to problems made (make) sense.	7.5	7.1	7.2
14.	Employees had (have) job security.	8.6	6.5	7.7
15.	Pay was (is) related directly to performance.	4.2	3.4	4.7
16.	Top managers talked (talk) to employees.	9.5	4.6	7.9
17.	The company was (is) better than other companies.	8.8	8.1	7.5
18.	Employees helped (help) run the business.	7.8	6.6	6.4
19.	We had (have) a team spirit.	9.4	5.4	8.0
20.	Supervisors listened (listen) to their employees.	7.6	6.7	7.0
21.	The company had (has) a bright future.	9.3	7.7	8.5

1 = Strongly disagree; 10 = Strongly agree.

DOWNTIME ANALYSIS

One of the very useful by-products of both direct and indirect labor control is the realization that downtime must be quantified and categorized so that it can be reduced. Exhibit 8.7 is an example of a downtime summary by company division. Exhibit 8.8 analyzes by operation. The report is presented in two sections: (a) Summary, and (b) Detail Analysis. The summary describes, by total division and individual plant, the number of direct labor hours used on production, and the number of direct labor hours wasted on downtime.

In Exhibit 8.7, under "Detail Analysis," general categories of downtime are listed. Notice the relatively large amount of direct labor hours Los Angeles lost on machine repairs. In fact, the amount of time Los Angeles lost for set-up, machine adjustments, and tooling repairs are very high in comparison to its sister plants, when you consider that Los Angeles' total number of direct labor hours worked are smaller.

Tooling repairs for the three plants, for example, when considered as a percentage of their direct labor hours worked, looks like this:

$$\text{Houston} = \frac{153 \text{ Hours}}{8,163 \text{ Hours}} \times 100 = 1.9\%$$

$$\text{Pittsburgh} = \frac{116 \text{ Hours}}{4,015 \text{ Hours}} \times 100 = 2.9\%$$

$$\text{Los Angeles} = \frac{312 \text{ Hours}}{2,725 \text{ Hours}} \times 100 = 5.0\%$$

Los Angeles, most obviously, is experiencing more than its share of machine repair downtime. Now let's look at machine repairs:

$$\text{Houston} = \frac{253 \text{ Hours}}{8,163 \text{ Hours}} \times 100 = 3.1\%$$

$$\text{Pittsburgh} = \frac{285 \text{ Hours}}{4,015 \text{ Hours}} \times 100 = 7.1\%$$

$$\text{Los Angeles} = \frac{312 \text{ Hours}}{2,725 \text{ Hours}} \times 100 = 11.4\%$$

Here again, Los Angeles is in far worse shape than Houston and Pittsburgh.

Total machine repair hours, for example, constitute almost 27 percent of all downtime experienced (850 Hours/3,199 Hours × 100 = 26.5%). To the practiced eye, that is quite a bit: Machine repair in most manufacturing operations will probably be among the highest of downtime categories, but it should not amount to 27 percent. In like fashion, rework is a hefty 746 hours. To a large extent, rework can always be reduced and, as a guide, should not exceed 10–15 percent of downtime hours. In this case it's 23.3 percent (746 Hours/3,199 Hours × 100 = 23.3%), and can readily be reduced.

EXHIBIT 8.7   Downtime Analysis Summary

	Houston	Pittsburgh	Los Angeles	Total Plants
A. Summary				
Total direct labor hours worked	8,163	4,015	2,725	14,903
Direct labor hours on production	7,018	2,996	1,690	11,704
Direct labor hours on downtime	1,145	1,019	1,035	3,199
Downtime (percent)	14.0	25.4	38.0	21.5
B. Detail Analysis (in Direct Labor Person-Hours)				
Set-up	215	139	181	535
Machine adjustments	190	112	131	433
Rework	306	265	175	746
Wait time-materials	28	94	60	182
Machine repairs	253	285	312	850
Tooling repairs	153	116	136	405
Training	0	8	40	48
Totals	1,145	1,019	1,035	3,199

EXHIBIT 8.8 Downtime Analysis

A. Summary

	Person-Hours	Percent
Direct Labor Hours on Production	1,690	62.0
Direct Labor Hours on Downtime	1,035	38.0
Total Direct Labor Hours Worked	2,725	100.0

B. Detail Analysis

Direct Labor Person-Hours

	Chuckers	Grinders	Milling	Drilling	Heat Treat	Plate	Paint	Assembly	Total
Set-up	42	20	28	46	23	0	5	17	181
Machine adjustments	25	17	11	33	0	9	11	25	131
Rework	56	22	8	27	33	8	21	0	175
Wait-time-materials	0	0	15	0	0	0	0	45	60
Machine repairs	64	38	41	109	18	29	0	13	312
Tooling repairs	27	43	26	20	0	0	0	20	136
Training	0	0	0	0	0	0	0	40	40
Totals	214	140	129	235	74	46	37	160	1,035
Percent of Total	20.7	13.5	12.5	22.7	7.1	4.4	3.6	15.5	100.0

114

The Pareto Principle

After carefully analyzing the downtime percentages, the manager is then able more effectively to focus the organization's attention on problem correction. Inherent in that statement is the assumption that just a few of the many problems that confront a manufacturing business at any given time generate the lion's share of lost dollars.

If, for example, the manufacturing manager were able to dissect the 850 machine-repair labor hours lost during the week, he might find this distribution:

Machine Repair Category	Direct-Labor Hours Lost
Electrical repairs	574
Mechanical repairs	105
Hydraulic repairs	93
Air system repairs	78
Total	850

Electrical repairs are the main problem. If the manager had not made this subsequent breakdown, that fact might never have emerged. Having done so, he is in a much better position to take corrective action.

In similar fashion, had he asked *where* the electrical problems were located, these facts might have surfaced:

Plant	Department	Hours Lost
Houston	Equipment	160
Pittsburgh	Equipment	94
Los Angeles	Equipment	256
Total		510

Therefore, 510 of the 574 direct-labor hours lost to electrical repairs were attributable to problems found in equipment in all three plants.

At this stage, the manager is in an excellent position to focus corrective actions where they will do the most good. The type of analysis this represents is referred to as the "Pareto Principle." Pareto was an Italian economist who discovered, early in the twentieth century, that a relatively large amount of money was concentrated in a relatively small proportion of the problems that make up the population. The application of the Pareto Principle to manufacturing problems remains a viable tool in the resolution of those problems.

COST REDUCTION/PRODUCTIVITY IMPROVEMENT ANALYSIS

The program for cost reduction/productivity improvement will be most successful if all areas are subjected to an analysis that will define the potential, and enable a schedule to be made and goals to be set. The analysis will be similar to a physician's examination of a patient. It will be designed to assess those systems that indicate the need for remedial action. The methodology will basically be a threefold approach, as follows:

1. Interviews with those people closest to each operation;
2. Review of historical records; and
3. Observations of current activities.

From these three simple steps, it is possible to develop enough symptomatic data upon which to base decisions relative to developing the program.

It is best to begin analysis in those areas that are labor intensive. An examination of the organizational structure and payroll records can usually reveal which areas incur the highest costs. Once these are defined in terms of size, the analysis can be started.

Interviews with Department Managers and Supervisors

The interview technique (see Exhibits 8.9 and 8.10) is designed to determine just how much information the manager and the supervisor have at their command, which enables them to manage the resources for which they are responsible. It will further develop how they use the data in the day-by-day function of control. The results will go a long way toward revealing the potential degree of improvement that is available through the development of productivity-improvement techniques. The interview will also develop information on the managers' or supervisors' attitudes, how they perceive their problems, and, indeed, what some of the problems are that detract from the department's ability to produce.

Interview the Manager

An overall picture of a department, that has supervisor between management and the workforce, should be obtained from the manager. The following information should be sought:

- An overview of the department and its functions;
- How the department is organized to accomplish the function (full details on the structure of the department, down to the last person in it);
- Knowledge of the work input, flow-through, and output of the department and subsections; and
- Deadline requirements for work output.

The key to the management interview, as it relates to the potential for cost savings, is how much knowledge the manager has of the volume of work and how well he has related to it the workforce, equipment, and other necessary resources. Are records of input available? Records of output? Records of hours worked? Are the volume records

EXHIBIT 8.9   Management Interview Summary

	Yes	No
Does manager have accurate records of:		
Work input?	_____	_____
Work output?	_____	_____
Hours worked?	_____	_____
Backlog?	_____	_____
Does manager have established goals to accomplish		
Weekly?	_____	_____
Daily?	_____	_____
Hourly?	_____	_____
Does manager relate hours worked to units produced?	_____	_____
Does manager know how the number of people in his department was established?	_____	_____
Does manager receive reports from his supervisors		
Weekly?	_____	_____
Daily?	_____	_____
Does manager know his schedule status at all times?	_____	_____
Does manager have objective criteria by which to rate his supervisors?	_____	_____

Each yes answer has a point value of 1

Rating

Excellent	Good	Fair	Poor
12–14	9–11	7–10	under 7

compared to the hours worked? Is there a goal(s) of accomplishments based on some kind of unit of work production? How well are the goals met? How were they established? Are the goals monthly, weekly, daily? Are records kept? Pick up samples of available records.

How was the staffing in the department established? Are there *specific* yardsticks by which to relate the number of people to the work volume? What are they? Again, pick up samples of any records.

Does the manager receive reports directly from the supervisors on work output, backlogs, schedule conditions, problems? Are these formal reports with documentation? How often are they received? Are they kept in a file? Ask for copies of reports for at least the past several weeks.

How does the manager rate the supervisors? Does he have clear-cut, objective yardsticks related to the performance that is measurable? Are these ongoing? How are they used to improve supervisory performance? Ask for a specific example and copies of any documentation.

EXHIBIT 8.10   Supervisor's Interview Summary

	Yes	No
Does supervisor know how many people are in the department?	_____	_____
Does supervisor know how many people are actually at work on the day interview?	_____	_____
Could supervisor locate each person in his department?	_____	_____
Did supervisor know each person's specific assignment?	_____	_____
Did supervisor know when each person's current assignment		
Started?	_____	_____
Would be completed?	_____	_____
Did supervisor have each one's next assignment planned?	_____	_____
Did supervisor have a departmental work plan?	_____	_____
Does supervisor know if the plan is on schedule?	_____	_____
Does supervisor assign work directly to each person or work group?	_____	_____
Does supervisor relate each person or group assignment to a time requirement?	_____	_____
Does supervisor inform the person or group of the time requirement?	_____	_____
Does supervisor maintain ongoing records of:		
Work input?	_____	_____
Work output?	_____	_____
Backlog?	_____	_____
Productivity?	_____	_____
Does supervisor adjust the workforce to fluctuating volumes?	_____	_____
Does supervisor formally document operational problems?	_____	_____
Does supervisor follow-up on work assignments		
Daily?	_____	_____
Hourly?	_____	_____

Each yes answer has a point value of 1

Rating

Excellent	Good	Fair	Poor
17–19	14–16	10–13	under 10

Interview the Supervisor

The supervisor should have the most intimate knowledge of the workings of his or her department or section. The line of questioning involved is designed to determine just how much knowledge he or she has of the productive output of the people, and how well their time is utilized on a day-to-day or even hour-to-hour basis. The less knowledge demonstrated by the supervisor, the higher the probability that there is room for increasing the productivity of the work area.

When the answers to these questions are positive, the interviewer must follow up and request further data, or, with the supervisor, verify the accuracy of the information. For example:

1. *How many people are at work today?* Get an actual head count, verify that the answer is correct or not, and mark the chart accordingly.

2. *Do you know if your department is on schedule as of now?* Determine what the schedule is and how the actual schedule is measured against the planned schedule. Is there a true means of determining the schedule position, or is the supervisor just making an assumption?

3. *Do you have a method of measuring the productivity of the department?* What is the method? Does it measure output in terms of units per hour? Per day? Get copies of productivity records.

Evaluating the Interview Results

With both the manager's and supervisor's interview forms, the evaluation is one of summing-up positives and negatives. Each negative answer demonstrates a decided weakness. Each positive answer demonstrates a strength.

It will be found that the majority of supervisors will not have positive answers to many of the questions. For those that do, the examination of the facts will reveal that the answers have no real basis in fact. The reason that this is true is not a reflection on the supervisor, but the result of a lack of training and a lack of management tools that might enable the supervisor properly to manage the time of the people and the other resources under his or her control.

Review of Historical Records

The purpose of a review of historical records will primarily be to investigate the consistency, or, more likely, the inconsistency of performance. The company may or may not have the information available in the format that this portion of the analysis requires. If it does not, it will be necessary to go to several different sources to get it. Charting this information is the best way to demonstrate the impact of actual practices and to reveal the potential for improvement. On the basis of the information given in Exhibit 8.11, and a cost of $7.00 per hour, the order-processing labor cost in October was $2,448 higher than in August (2,690 $\times$ .13 $\times$ $7.00). This is a considerable cost variance and strongly indicates a cost-reduction potential.

EXHIBIT 8.11   Example of Performance Record

Month	June	July	Aug.	Sept.	Oct.
Number of work days	22	22	21	21	22
Gross hours—eight people	1,320	1,260	1,260	1,320	1,320
Vacation, absent hours	150	165	255	90	105
Actual hours worked	1,170	1,155	1,005	1,170	1,215
Orders processed	3,461	2,640	3,192	2,859	2,690
Orders per hour	2.96	2.28	3.17	2.44	2.21
Hours per order	.34	.44	.32	.41	.45
Variance low to high	.13 Hours = 40%				

Hours versus Production Units

The example seen in Exhibit 8.10 can be developed in various forms. The elements required are simple; units of work produced and the hours required to produce them. In the exhibit, we find a monthly record, and monthly records tend to have a flattening effect. Though they reveal a strong variance, this variance will become more dramatic as the time span is shortened. For example, in Exhibit 8.11, an actual case, the month of June was broken down into 22 working days. On a day-by-day basis, variances as high as 230 percent became evident.

Regardless of the type of business, most companies keep records of production in an identifiable *unit of measure*. They also have records of hours worked. What few do is to actually compare the units and hours to determine the consistency or variances in the output. The higher the variances, the more indication of lack of good operational tools to control costs, and, therefore, greater potential for improvement.

In-Process Time versus Time in Process

Another technique of analysis is to compare in-process time to the time in process. In any company or department within a company, two elements of information are required.

1. How long it takes, from start to finish, to produce an item in process time.
2. The *actual* time applied to the item at each stage of production time in process.

Standard versus Actual Performance Records

In any organization that works with engineered time standards, records are available to show actual performance against the standard. These reports normally will reveal worker productivity on a weekly basis, or actual versus standard performance on each job completed or some combination of the two. Careful analysis is required, particularly when performance is rated close to 100 percent and the reports create the impression that everything is close to or on schedule.

Observations as the Key to Analysis

Interviews with management and supervision and looking for variances and problems within company records are usually very revealing, and will alert the analyst to the degree of improvement potential from a probability standpoint. Actual observations of the people at work are even more revealing. This portion of the chapter will explain the types of observations that should be made, how to make them, and how to chart results. (See Exhibits 8.12 and 8.13.)

Near–Far Observations.   The near–far observation is perhaps the simplest one to make and can be done in several different ways. It can be applied to a variety of work activities. Basically it involves observing a worker or workers performing their normal activities at close range, with full knowledge on their part that they are being observed. Count the result of their effort. The observation time can be relatively short, say, 15 minutes to a half-hour.

Move away from the work station to a point where the worker believes that he or she is no longer being observed and continue the observation. Again, count the number of "pieces" produced. For simplicity, use the same length of time for the *far* observation.

Convert both observations into pieces per hour. The results will often be very startling.

Another method of the same theme would be to take several *near* observations of the same activity at different times, even on different days. There will probably be slight variances in units per hour from one observation to the other. Then, secure the actual production and the actual time spent by the person observed on that particular activity, for a complete day or week. Again, the contrast will be quite startling.

EXHIBIT 8.12   Near–Far Observation—Invoice Processing

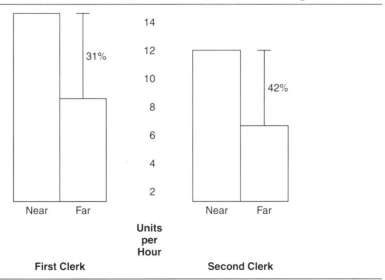

EXHIBIT 8.13   Near–Far Observation—Filling Number 3 Size Tubes

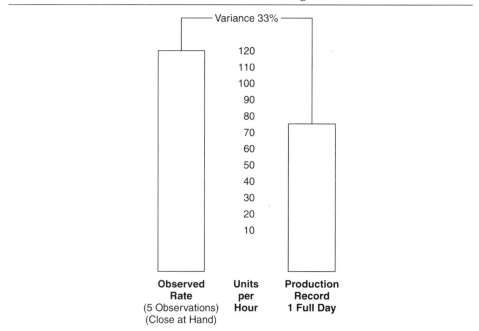

Ratio Delay Studies.   A ratio delay study can best be applied to groups of work-ers. It is designed to determine what percentage of the time at work is actually produc-tive and what percentage represents delay or lost time. A number of observations are required. (See Exhibit 8.14.)

The observer records the date, department, and name of the supervisor on a work-sheet. The observer must know, in advance, the number of people that are at work in the area. This can be the number of people in an office, on a shipping platform, in a manufacturing department, and so forth.

The observer goes into the area and quickly counts the number of people actually present in the department, noting how many people are actively working and how many people are not. It's like taking a flash picture, quick and simple. Some people will be found busily at work, some will be idle, and others will not be in evidence.

Record each observation on a ratio delay format. A line will be filled out for each observation, noting the time that the observation was made, how many people were supposed to be in the department (crew size), how many were observed working, and the number that were idle. These are recorded under **W** (working) and **I** (idle). The difference between the sum of W and I and the crew size is recorded under **A** (away). For each observation, then, we know that, out of a group of a given number of people, a certain number were actually working, others were idle, and some were not at their work stations.

EXHIBIT 8.14   Ratio Delay Study

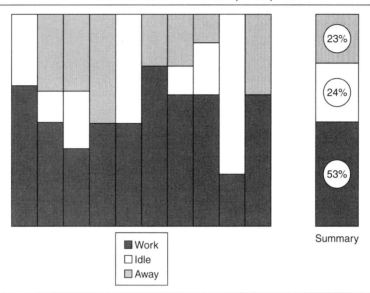

Work
Idle
Away

Summary

It is important to note on the form the shift (if applicable), start time, break times, lunch times, and stop time. Any observations taken within five minutes of start and stop times or during break periods should be discounted, because of the normal delays and inaccuracies that could exist.

It is rare that the observer will find *less than 20 percent* outright lost time. Very often it will exceed *30 percent.*

Time Diaries.   A time diary (see Exhibits 8.15 and 8.16) is the result of a continuing observation of a person, or group of people, for a specified period of time. Observations of 20 minutes to several hours in duration can be made. The observer must be in a position to distinguish actual work being done from idle time that exists. The record is kept in blocks of time, distinguishing between the two. The observations can then be charted as observed and can be charted in summary. These observations are usually very revealing and reflect direct lost time, much of which can be captured and put back to work.

Performance versus Ability to Perform.   A five-month summary showed a total of 14,842 orders processed, using 5,715 hours or 2.6 hours per order. Observations were taken on several different occasions, which showed an ability on the part of the department to produce at a rate of 3.5 orders per hour. From the number of hours worked for that entire period, it can be determined that the department functioned at only 74 percent of its capacity.

14,842 divided by (5,715 × 3.5)

EXHIBIT 8.15   Time Diary—Repair of Solar Gear Box

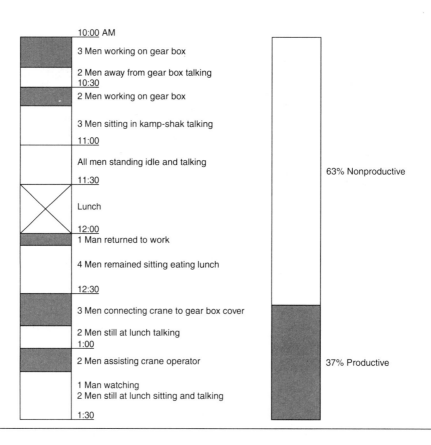

Assignment: Repair Solar Gear Box
Crew–2 Contract Workers
–3 Company Workers

Maintenance
Platform 41-B

Time Diary

10:00 AM
3 Men working on gear box
2 Men away from gear box talking
10:30
2 Men working on gear box
3 Men sitting in kamp-shak talking
11:00
All men standing idle and talking
11:30
Lunch
12:00
1 Man returned to work
4 Men remained sitting eating lunch
12:30
3 Men connecting crane to gear box cover
2 Men still at lunch talking
1:00
2 Men assisting crane operator
1 Man watching
2 Men still at lunch sitting and talking
1:30

63% Nonproductive

37% Productive

The best performance was in the month of August, when production reached 91 percent of capacity

$$3192 \text{ divided by } (1{,}005 \times 3.5)$$

The worst was the month of October, with a performance of 63 percent. This type of performance is not unusual. Though it may take considerable time and effort to research and make the observations, the results, most often, will be quite startling. This type of analysis can be applied to any operation where a defined unit for measuring productive output is available.

EXHIBIT 8.16   Time Diary—Replace Valve on Heater #2

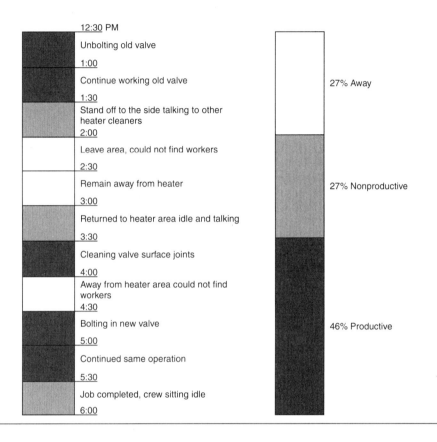

Assignment: Replace Valve on Heater #2
Crew–2 Contract Workers

12:30 PM
Unbolting old valve
1:00
Continue working old valve   27% Away
1:30
Stand off to the side talking to other
heater cleaners
2:00
Leave area, could not find workers
2:30
Remain away from heater   27% Nonproductive
3:00
Returned to heater area idle and talking
3:30
Cleaning valve surface joints
4:00
Away from heater area could not find
workers
4:30
Bolting in new valve   46% Productive
5:00
Continued same operation
5:30
Job completed, crew sitting idle
6:00

Calculating the Dollar Improvement Potential.   In order to determine the priority of a department's position in the program, the real potential for dollar improvement should be determined. Recognize that, at this point, it is not necessary to determine *how* this improvement will be brought about. That will be determined in the actual program development. Exhibit 8.17 demonstrates the potential for dollar recovery.

Once the analysis reveals that enough symptoms exist to indicate a strong potential for improvement, the degree of that potential can be figured out and a goal established—a 53.6 percent lost-time factor for a crew of 27 people with an annual wage of $16,250 each. It has been determined that 46.4 percent of their time is productive and has a value of $203,580. The remaining 53.6 percent represents lost time of $235,170. Consideration has been given that 25 percent of the lost time is, most likely, not recoverable. This gives a recoverable factor of $175,500, representing 40 percent of the total payroll.

EXHIBIT 8.17   Dollar Improvement Potential

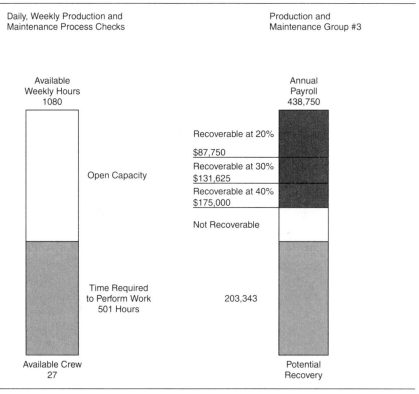

Targets can be set lower than the 40 percent, and a judicious application of common sense may dictate that a target of 20 or 30 percent would be more practical and achievable. It is better to set a lower target and achieve more than to set one too high and fall short. During the application of the program, the objective will be to achieve the highest practical figure.

In assuring that all departments receive their proper priority, the recovery percentage should be uniform throughout. The target, though established on the basis of the payroll, does not necessarily mean that payroll will be reduced by the target amount. It means that the cost of doing business in a given department will be reduced when measured against the department output. This could mean an increase in production, reduction of rework, better quality, or any combination of measurable factors. The payroll approach is usually the simplest to apply in arriving at a potential, and is normally quite accurate, regardless of the way the final results are measured.

9

REDUCING OPERATING COSTS

Once action plans have been established, and once the organization is in place to achieve those action plans, some method of measurement and control is needed, to assure the plans are being completed according to established timetables. Controls are the proven method of accomplishing that goal.

USING PROCESSING CONTROLS TO REDUCE COSTS

Effective controls are superb tools for reducing costs and holding them down at lower levels. But they must first possess certain attributes in order to make them successful. They need these three characteristics:

1. *Controls must be simple.* A control measurement must be both easily applied and understood.
2. *Controls must be expressed quantitatively.* An old management expression is "if you can't reduce it to numbers, it ain't worth a darn." Controls that are not measurable in numbers are too easily misinterpreted. Subjective judgments and opinions substitute for objective measurements. Progress, or lack of it, cannot be readily determined.
3. *Controls must be timely.* What happened last quarter is of historical interest only. It is too late to do anything about it. If it is too late to take effective corrective action, then reporting is not timely. Measurements of operations need to be geared to the events being measured. Such important events as production and direct labor, for example, need to be measured *at least* daily, if not every few hours. The short interval of time between the event and its feedback to management permits corrective action to bring the plan back into schedule before it is too late. In operations, almost all events need to be reported weekly or daily, seldom at longer intervals.

CUTTING DIRECT-LABOR COSTS

Daily Labor Report

The first control tool installed was the direct-labor control report. (See Exhibit 9.1.) The left-hand column of Exhibit 9.1 lists each of the plant's operating departments.

EXHIBIT 9.1   Daily Labor Report—8/16/XX

	Direct-Labor Measurements				
Department	Standard Hours	Earned Hours	Percent Efficiency	Time Off-Standard	Percent Off-Standard
Pre-heat	260.0	260.0	100.0	20.0	7.1
Hot roll	232.4	216.6	93.2	63.6	21.5
Pre-heat	248.0	258.4	104.2	0	0
Cold roll	231.5	217.6	94.0	48.5	17.3
Slitters	574.7	471.6	82.1	201.3	25.9
Anneal	148.0	148.0	100.0	0	0
Packing	470.0	456.4	97.1	50.0	9.6
Totals	2164.6	2028.6	93.7	383.4	15.0

The next column to the right displays Standard Hours. These numbers reflect the total standard hours for the work performed in each department for the time period being measured, in this case, one day.

Earned Hours, the next column, shows actual performance measured in labor-hours. This example explains how earned hours are derived:

Operation	*Standard Hours*
Slit 6″ Coils	.5 Per Coil

In the plant, the operator would be required to slit sixteen six-inch coils in an eight-hour shift to meet standard. Following are earned hours an operator will be awarded for different production levels of six-inch coils.

No. of 6″ Coils Slit	*Percent Efficiency*	*Earned Hours*
4	25.0%	2.0
8	50.0	4.0
12	75.0	6.0
16	100.0	8.0
20	125.0	10.0
24	150.0	12.0

Earned hours for the day are accumulated for all direct-labor operations for each department and posted to the report shown. For the day in question, the plant averaged 95.2 Percent Efficiency.

Percent Off-Standard displays the total time that direct labor employees are performing jobs not measured by standard hours. These hours can be caused either by time spent on direct-labor jobs, which have not yet been measured, or by downtime. In the case above, the percent of time off-standard for the day amounted to 18.6 percent.

Daily Downtime Analysis

This report, shown in Exhibit 9.2, also issued daily, expands information taken from the "Percent Off-Standard" section of the Direct Labor Control Report. It describes reasons for the occurrences of off-standard time. In essence, it is a downtime report.

The first column in Exhibit 9.2 lists the same production departments found in the Daily Labor Report. The second column shows the Percentage of Off-Standard Time also contained in the former report. The following column shows year-to-date results (YTD), and the next column displays last year's averages. The final column, Downtime Reasons, describes reasons for the current day's downtime.

Notice that downtime for the plant has been reduced from 9.8 percent in 19X1 to the current year's average of 7.2 percent through August 16.

The Daily Downtime Analysis is a useful tool for analysis of downtime, where it occurred, how extensive it is, and reasons for the downtime.

Monthly Direct-Labor Control Report

The final report used by the aluminum plant to reduce costs is historical in nature but useful, nevertheless, to compare direct labor performance over a period of time. (See Exhibit 9.3.)

The columns in Exhibit 9.3 are arranged the same as for the Daily Downtime Report, but the results for the current period are monthly, not the daily period of the Daily Downtime Report.

Notice in Exhibit 9.3 that, while results for the current month and year exceed levels of the previous year, the slitter department's performance is depressed, and the reason given is electrical problems. A careful analysis of both daily performance and downtime reports by plant management should yield clues about reasons for the lackluster performance. Corrective action can then occur.

EXHIBIT 9.2 Daily Downtime Report—8/16/X2

Department	Percent Time Off-Standard			Downtime Reasons
	Today	YTD	19X1	
Pre-heat	7.1	4.5	6.4	Thermostat Failure
Hot roll	21.5	6.8	9.5	Roll Crack 3
Pre-heat	0	3.1	2.9	—
Cold roll	17.3	10.7	8.9	Electrical Failure
Slitters	25.9	8.5	10.3	Electrical Failure
Anneal	0	3.1	16.4	—
Packing	9.6	1.8	2.1	Interleave Quality Problem
Totals	15.0	7.2	9.8	

EXHIBIT 9.3   Monthly Labor Report—8/X2

Department	Percent Efficiency			
	This Month	YTD	19X1	
Pre-heat	95.2	93.8	85.4	—
Hot roll	90.7	91.4	82.8	—
Pre-heat	98.5	97.0	95.3	—
Cold roll	97.3	98.1	104.1	—
Slitters	80.1	82.5	93.2	Electrical Problems
Anneal	102.1	100.8	70.1	—
Packing	93.2	90.6	93.4	—
Totals	96.0	96.8	89.2	

Calculating Savings by Monitoring Direct-Labor Costs

A plant that doesn't have direct-labor control reports can generally realize a savings of 10 to 20 percent when the reports are published and used for corrective action. The savings are generated basically through reduced downtime, but some increases in direct-labor performance can be anticipated. In the case of the plant that employed 320 direct-labor people, the equivalent of 35 employees was eliminated over a period of eighteen months, through implementation of direct-labor controls. The breakdown is seen in Exhibit 9.4.

Four Ways to Measure Direct-Labor Control

Many other measurements of direct labor can be made to control and correct costs. Some of the more prevalent are as follows:

1. *Calculate Labor Utilization*

$$\text{Utilization} = \frac{\text{Time off standards}}{\text{Total time available}} \times 100\%$$

Example: A production department with twenty direct-labor employees shows the following statistics for one eight-hour day.

$$\text{Total time available} = 20 \times 8 = 160 \text{ Labor hours}$$

$$\text{Time on standards} = 120 \text{ Labor hours}$$

$$\text{Time off standards} = 40 \text{ Labor hours}$$

$$\text{Utilization} = \frac{40}{160} \times 100\% = 25\%$$

2. *Calculate Direct Labor Productivity*

$$\text{Productivity} = \text{Performance} \times \text{Utilization} \times 100\%$$

Example: In the same department cited in the example on utilization, performance (percent efficiency of direct labor) was 95 percent for that shift.

$$\text{Productivity} = 95.0\% \times 75.0\% \times 100\% = 71.3\%$$

Labor productivity is a more encompassing index than separate measures of performance and utilization. It provides a ready measurement of direct-labor productivity in a single ratio.

EXHIBIT 9.4 Savings through Monitoring of Direct-Labor Costs

Downtime Savings

Department	Hours/Years Saved	Dollars per Year Saved at $10/Hour*
Pre-heat	4,150	$ 41,500
Hot roll	6,670	66,700
Pre-heat	6,830	68,300
Cold roll	4,060	40,600
Slitters	14,190	141,900
Anneal	5,350	53,500
Packing	8,170	81,700
TOTALS	49,420	$494,200

Performance Savings

Department	Hours/Years Saved	Dollars per Year Saved at $10/Hour*
Pre-heat	8,990	$ 89,900
Hot roll	6,350	63,500
Pre-heat	2,280	22,800
Cold roll	(1,672)	(16,720)
Slitters	(3,830)	(38,300)
Anneal	10,150	101,500
Packing	Even	Even
TOTAL	22,268	$222,680

Total Direct Labor Savings

	Dollars	Percent
Downtime savings	$494,200	68.9
Performance savings	222,680	31.1
Total	$716,880	100.0%

*The $10 per hour is based on an average hourly rate of $8, and a fringe level of $2 per hour (25 percent).

Notice that downtime savings are approximately double performance savings, and that performance savings are somewhat erratic with both the cold roll and slitter departments showing decreases in performance. Nevertheless, total direct labor savings amounted to over $700,000 for the entire plant.

3. *Measure Units per Employee*

$$\text{Units per employee} = \frac{\text{No. of units produced (output)}}{\text{No. of direct labor employees}}$$

Example: Continuing with the same department example, if twenty workers had produced 1000 valves during their shift, then:

$$\text{Units per employee} = \frac{1,000}{20} = 50$$

This ratio is used only when high production volumes of discrete units are produced. If the same twenty workers assembled two tractors during one shift, use of the "units per employee" ratio would be meaningless.

4. *Calculate Direct Labor Costs Per Unit*

$$\text{Direct labor cost per unit} = \frac{\text{Total direct labor costs}}{\text{No. of units produced}}$$

Example: If the twenty direct-labor employees each were paid $10 per hour, then:

$$\text{Direct labor cost per unit} = \frac{20 \times \$10 \times 8 \text{ Hrs.}}{1,000} = \frac{\$1,600}{1,000} = \$1.60$$

Incentive Coverage to Increase Production

Every organization must decide on whether or not it wants to use incentive systems to stimulate production output. Generally, incentive coverage yields more results in proportion to the amount of manual work involved. One-hundred-percent manual work, such as hand assembly of small components, is a natural for incentive coverage; a numerically controlled (NC) machine tool, where the machine controls the cycle, is at the other end of the spectrum. Also, short-cycle, highly repetitive work is amenable to incentive coverage, while long-cycle, highly technical, nonrepetitive work, such as missile assembly, is not.

Measuring Incentive Coverage

The first control tool when measuring incentive operations is the degree of coverage. This measurement is made in two parts:

1. Percent employees covered; and
2. Percent operations on incentive.

In the first case, it is relatively simple to measure the number of direct-labor employees on incentive. Here, 550 employees were classified as direct labor. Of these, 490 were on incentive. Therefore:

$$\text{Percent employees covered} = \frac{490}{550} \times 100\% = 89.1\%$$

For most operations, it is not necessary to have all direct-labor employees on incentive. There are always instances when to do so would not be practical. A good example is a small section of direct-labor employees doing all nonrepetitive miscellaneous operations. Standards here would be difficult to establish.

The latter measurement, "Percent Operations on Incentive," is an index that is somewhat better than "Percent Employees Covered," simply because *all* employees could be on incentive, but have only 25 percent of their work on incentive.

$$\text{Percentage operations on incentive} = \frac{\text{Operations on incentive}}{\text{Total plant operations}} \times 100\%$$

Total plant operations, of course, refers only to direct-labor work. The company had 312 operations (counting all variations as measured by production routings), and 249 of those were on incentive. Therefore,

$$\text{Percentage operations on incentive} = \frac{249}{312} \times 100 = 79.8\%$$

Generally speaking, incentive coverage of 80 percent to 90 percent is considered acceptable, but each company must make its own determination, and that is usually done by measuring production increases generated by the incentive system.

Calculating Average Earnings

Average earnings is defined as those earnings derived from operations not on standard. In most union shops, average earnings is a negotiable issue, and payment resulting from average earnings is based on what each individual operator averaged on incentive for the past week. If an operator, for example, ran several jobs not yet measured on incentive (usually new jobs), his *incentive* pay for those jobs would be the average incentive pay he earned during the previous week.

Average earnings is payment of something for nothing. Since unmeasured work is looked upon as a fault of management, unions are generally successful in their demands for average earnings. In that case, the measurement of average earnings becomes a significant ratio for management.

$$\text{Average earnings} = \frac{\text{Average earnings}}{\text{Total incentive earnings}} \times 100\%$$

A company had the following average earnings for one calendar year:

$$\text{Average earnings} = \frac{\$241,632}{\$1,550,750} \times 100 = 15.6\%$$

No matter how you look at it, either 15.6 percent or $241,632 is too much. Most average earnings are better held to maximums of 5 percent to 7 percent.

Measuring the Results of Incentive Coverage: Percent Performance to Standard

This ratio is the most significant one in measuring the results of incentive coverage. It shows increases in performance that can be directly related to increases in production. The company, before incentives, had the following annual performance.

$$\text{Performance} = \frac{\text{Earned hours}}{\text{Standard hours}} \times 100$$

$$\text{Performance} = \frac{398,140}{563,178} \times 100 = 70.7\%$$

After installation of the incentive system for one year, their performance had improved 25 percent (despite their large average earnings) as seen here:

$$\text{Performance} = \frac{506,442}{571,280} \times 100 = 88.7\%$$

In terms of actual improvement in performance,

$$\text{Percent improvement} = \frac{88.7\% - 70.7\%}{70.7\%} \times 100 = 25.5\%$$

The 25.5 percent improvement in performance represented a real gain of equal amount in production output.

Reducing Indirect-Labor Costs

Indirect-labor costs constitute a significant portion of overhead, and overhead is that type of cost that must be constantly pruned to keep it from growing. An operation that ignores those costs will soon find its costs escalating beyond control. Typical indirect labor costs are:

Material handlers   Warehouse personnel

Truckers   Inspectors

Pipefitters   Machinists

Electricians   Tool grinders

Tool crib attendants   Sweepers

Janitors   Clerks

Supervisors   Managers

Comparing Direct to Indirect Labor

Section "A" of Exhibit 9.5 displays the total number of direct and indirect employees on the books for 19X0, 19X1, and the first four months of 19X2.

A ratio of direct labor divided by indirect labor is then developed. Notice that this ratio was 3.90 in 19X0 and 4.92 to 4.95 for the first four months of 19X2. This represents an improvement of 26.4 percent, as seen here:

$$\frac{4.93\% - 3.90\%}{3.90\%} \times 100 = 26.4\%$$

Section "B" of Exhibit 9.5 shows the actual number of indirect employees by classification, and reveals reductions made in each classification of indirect labor.

Measuring Indirect Labor as a Percentage of Cost of Sales

The second measurement used by the company was the ratio of indirect-labor costs to cost of sales. Use of that ratio permitted an unbiased and objective look at progress—or lack of it—in controlling indirect-labor costs. The ratio is:

$$\text{Indirect-labor costs ratio} = \frac{\text{Indirect-labor costs}}{\text{Total cost of sales}}$$

For the company being studied, his 19X0 and January–April 19X2 ratios are seen here:

$$\text{19X0 Indirect-labor costs} = \frac{\$1,963,520}{62,073,985} \times 100 = 3.16\%$$

$$\text{Jan.–April 19X2 Indirect-labor costs} = \frac{\$478,515}{21,173,228} \times 100 = 2.26\%$$

Change

$$3.16\% - 2.26\% \times 100 = 28.5\% \text{ Improvement}$$

The 28.5 percent represents real-dollar improvement adjusted for inflation, in terms of today's dollars.

EXHIBIT 9.5	Indirect-Labor Control—4/X2					
	19X0	**19X1**	**1/X2**	**2/X2**	**3/X2**	**4/X2**
A. *Direct to Indirect*						
Direct	460	495	483	485	485	482
Indirect	118	118	98	98	98	98
Direct/Indirect	3.90	4.19	4.93	4.95	4.95	4.92
B. *Indirect Classification*						
Inspectors	29	29	22	22	22	22
Attendants	4	4	2	2	2	2
Sweepers	6	6	3	3	3	3
Maintenance	28	28	24	24	24	24
Warehouse	30	30	29	29	29	29
Truck drivers	21	21	18	18	18	18
Totals	118	118	98	98	98	98

Reducing Operating Overhead

Overhead costs are composed of the following types of accounts in operations:

- Salaries;
- Travel and entertainment expenses;
- Overtime;
- Dues and subscriptions;
- Heat, light, and power;
- Rent;
- Insurance;
- Supplies;
- Training;
- Rework and scrap;
- Depreciation;
- Downtime; and
- Recruiting expenses.

The spending variance is the difference between the actual overhead and budgeted overhead for actual standard hours of operation. The company had forecast a monthly rate of 70,000 standard hours at a total overhead cost of $280,000, as shown here:

Budgeted overhead costs:	$280,000
Actual overhead costs:	255,000
Favorable spending variance:	$ 25,000

Since actual costs were $25,000 less than anticipated, a favorable spending variance occurred. An annual rate of savings was then $300,000 ($25,000 per month × 12 months), as actually happened during the course of the year.

The company had been forecast to produce 1,200 tons during the year, and to consume 70,000 standard hours per month, or an annual rate of 840,000 standard hours (70,000 standard hours × 12 months). Instead, 760,000 standard hours were used to process those same 1,200 tons. A favorable efficiency variance resulted:

Budget for 840,000 std. hrs:	$3,360,000
Actual for 760,000 std. hrs:	3,040,000
Favorable efficiency variance:	$ 320,000
Total savings:	
Favorable spending variance:	$ 300,000
Favorable efficiency variance:	320,000
Total favorable variances:	$ 620,000

The very nature of budgeting overhead costs to departments, then measuring and reporting them by area of responsibility, soon produces cost savings. Supervisors and

EXHIBIT 9.6   Material Burden Analysis—1/X3

	This Month		Year-to-Date	
Price Variances	**Standard**	**Actual**	**Standard**	**Actual**
Soluble materials	$20,500	$18,550	$20,500	$18,550
Dry materials	16,800	17,200	16,800	17,200
Liquids	2,500	2,400	2,500	2,400
Packaging	18,900	17,500	18,900	17,500
Totals	$58,700	$55,650	$58,700	$55,650
Quality Variances	**Standard**	**Actual**	**Standard**	**Actual**
Weigh, screen, mix	12,500	10,660	12,500	10,660
Absorption and mixing	13,100	12,770	13,100	12,770
Packaging	10,000	10,000	10,000	10,000
Boxing	3,000	3,200	3,000	3,200
Totals	38,600	36,630	38,600	36,630

Quantity variances in material burden reflect the difference between specified and actual usage.

managers, when aware of *where* costs are, and *how much* they are, are then in a position to apply their skills in cost reduction. The company was successful in reducing overhead because they intelligently applied those principles.

Reducing Material Burden

Materials, in this sense, means materials used in the sold product. It does not include supplies, tools, gauges, fixtures, or any other expense classified as overhead.

There are two measurable variances connected with material burden: price and quantity. This is seen in Exhibit 9.6. That amounted to a rather large savings since material costs are usually the largest single category of cost in a service center company.

Price variances in material burden measure the difference between actual purchased prices and standard costs.

Reducing Inventory

A company reduced inventory by $1 million through use of control measurements of its inventory turnover rate, as well as the size of its inventory during different stages of manufacture. (See Exhibit 9.7.)

Measuring Inventory Turnover

Inventory turnover is the annual number of times that a plant ships products equivalent in value to the average monthly costs of its inventory. A company, for example, reported the following turnover for 1990:

$$\text{Turnover} = \frac{\text{Cost of sales}}{\text{Average monthly inventory}}$$

$$\text{Turnover} = \frac{9,350,000}{3,230,000}$$

Turnover = 2.89 Times per year

Actual inventory turnover results are published monthly by the company and compared to the plan. (See Exhibit 9.8.)

Tracking Your Inventory Carrying Costs Carefully

In today's economy, inventory carrying costs of 30 percent of the value of the inventory are not uncommon. Therefore, the importance of keeping inventories to an absolute minimum to support delivery schedules is paramount. This annual cost includes such major segments as:

Space Costs

- Building and equipment depreciation;
- Heat, light, and power;
- Building equipment maintenance;
- Insurance;
- Fire systems; and
- Plant protection.

Inventory Costs

- Interest on capital invested (about 20 percent);
- Transportation and handling;
- Clerical costs;
- Physical inventory costs;

EXHIBIT 9.7   Inventory Turnover Rate

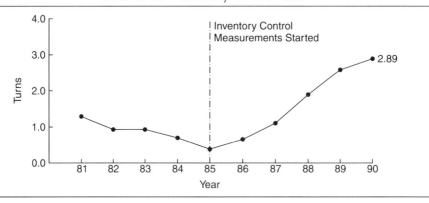

EXHIBIT 9.8 Inventory Turnover Plan—19X1

		Inventory			
	Cost-of-Sales	Raw Material	W.I.P.	Finished	Turnover
January	700,000	300,000	800,000	1,000,000	3.0
February	700,000	300,000	800,000	1,000,000	3.0
March	700,000	300,000	800,000	1,000,000	3.0
April	700,000	300,000	800,000	1,000,000	3.0
May	700,000	300,000	800,000	1,000,000	3.0
June	700,000	300,000	800,000	1,000,000	3.0
July	700,000	300,000	800,000	1,000,000	3.0
August	1,000,000	700,000	1,000,000	1,500,000	3.2
September	1,000,000	700,000	1,000,000	1,500,000	3.2
October	1,500,000	700,000	1,000,000	1,500,000	3.2
November	2,000,000	2,200,000	1,800,000	3,000,000	3.5
December	1,000,000	0	800,000	2,500,000	3.3
Total	10,700,000				

- Damage to inventory;
- Obsolescence; and
- Theft.

Maintaining Accurate Inventory Records

Accurate inventory records are of prime importance, because if they are not maintained properly, variances in purchasing materials and usage of materials in production can be expected. Shrink is caused by many different things, among them:

- Clerical errors;
- Failure to process paperwork quickly;
- Unreported scrap and rework;
- Misplaced inventory;
- Theft;
- Unauthorized material substitutions; and
- Inaccurate bills of material (see Method 8).

MONITORING SHRINKAGE THROUGH CYCLE COUNTING

A metal-working company in the South countered this problem through cycle counting. Cycle counting is a system of perpetual physical inventory-taking, conducted on selected inventory parts every day, normally after business hours. It emphasizes the

EXHIBIT 9.9   Cycle Count Report—Week of 9/7/19X1

	Part Nos. Checked	No. of Pieces
Number of Counts		
Cycle counter "A"	306	30,143
Cycle counter "B"	294	32,650
Total Counts	600	62,793
Number of Errors Found		
Cycle counter "A"	3.1%	
Cycle counter "B"	2.5%	
Total Errors	5.6%	

Errors in Dollars

$$\frac{\text{No. of pieces wrong}}{\text{Total inventory counted}} = \frac{1,633}{62,793} = 2.6\%$$

$$\frac{\text{Pieces wrong}}{\text{Inventory counted}} = \frac{\$21,528}{1,040,697} = 2.1\%$$

review of high-value inventory parts. In cycle counting, employees physically count and check location accuracy as well. Mistakes are reconciled to perpetual inventory records.

This report, displayed in Exhibit 9.9, provides the following information:

- The actual number of different numbers checked and the total number of counts.

- The number and percentage of errors found in actual pieces counted.

- A dollar amount on the errors found as well as a dollar and percentage figure based on the sample derived.

Use of this report (along with bills of material accuracy) enables managers to spot errors and take effective corrective action. It also gives a reliable picture of the estimated percentage of errors to be found in the inventory.

BILLS OF MATERIAL

A key function of product engineering is the creation of bills of material that accurately reflect the type and number of parts to be used in the product. Inaccurate or incomplete BOM (Bills of Material) directly affect the level of inventory accuracy. If a BOM is wrong, unauthorized parts may need to be substituted, and this generates additional costs if the substituted parts are of higher value. It then also creates quantity variances in the parts being substituted because of unplanned issues.

Typical BOM. The bill of material seen in Exhibit 9.10 is typical of bills originating in engineering departments. Listed in the body of the bill are all of the components that make up the part described on the top of the bill, in this case a tension bracket. The bill of material is used by all relevant departments—manufacturing, engineering, and accounting—to extract the information they need to do their jobs.

Engineering. Uses BOM to list and specify all components, materials, and parts in the product.

Manufacturing. Structures the bill according to sequence of manufacture (called a production routing), and specifies work methods and standards for each operation.

Accounting. Uses BOM to cost the product and obtain variances from standards.

BOM accuracy is then essentially a function of how well manufacturing and engineering have done their jobs. It is an audit of the correct parts to be used in manufacturing. In the typical BOM accuracy audit, literally hundreds of bills, such as those seen in Exhibit 9.10, are examined for errors, and a BOM accuracy rate is derived.

EXHIBIT 9.10   Bill of Material (BOM)

Part: Tension Bracket
Part Number: 136-72A

Parts Description	Part Number	Quantity Used
Bracket frame	136-72A1	1
Sprocket	136-72A2	1
Spring	136-72A3	2
Set screen	136-72A4	1
Holding screen	136-72A5	3

**BOM Audit
Week of Sept. 7, 19XX
Count**

Parts Audited	Specified	Actual	Comments
136-72A1	1	1	
136-72A2	1	1	Wrong part no. (should be 136-72AC)
136-72A3	2	2	
136-72A4	1	1	
136-72A5	3	2	Should be two parts

Summary of Results

$$\frac{\text{No. of parts incorrect}}{\text{No. of parts audited}} = \frac{4}{354} = 1.0\% \text{ error}$$

Summary of Errors

2	Excess parts specified
1	Insufficient parts specified
1	Wrong parts specified
4	

Exhibit 9.10 is a typical report on BOM accuracy. Both counts and correct part numbers are examined, as can be seen in the top half of the form. The bottom half lists the summary of results, along with the type of errors found.

CONTROLLING QUALITY COSTS

A plant in South Carolina was experiencing severe quality problems and high associated quality costs. In 1987 its COQ (Cost of Quality) was running about 8 percent with much of its costs deriving from warranty. Because of poor quality in customers' hands it was beginning to lose repeat sales.

Computing Quality Costs. A new quality manager was hired and installed a quality cost report. The quality cost report, shown in Exhibit 9.11, lists the following items:

- *Warranty*—Contractual costs arising from product failures in customers' hands.
- *Rework*—Product rejected by inspectors and salvaged in the plant.
- *Scrap*—Products rejected by inspectors and scrapped.
- *Inspection*—Cost in inspectors' salaries.
- *Support*—All other overhead expenses of the quality control department.

The bottom of the report compares total quality costs to total sales, with the derived ratio indicating that percentage of the sales dollar needed to support a quality effort. Notice that, from a high of 8 percent in 1987, COQ during 1990 is at 3 percent, a 63 percent improvement. The change from 8 to 3 percent generated a savings of over half a million dollars, based on January through October results:

$$5.0\% \times \$10,750,000 = \$537,500$$

The calculation of quality costs, along with its attendant pressure to closely examine its components, soon enabled the textile mill to achieve the significant savings shown in Exhibit 9.11.

EXHIBIT 9.11   Quality Costs—10/X0

	19X0 Oct.	19X0 YTD	19X9 Total
Warranty	$ 5,000	$ 62,000	$ 78,000
Rework	3,000	26,000	29,000
Scrap	1,000	7,000	16,000
Inspection	19,000	188,000	225,000
Support	7,000	39,000	41,000
Total	$35,000	$322,000	$389,000
Sales	1,110,000	10,750,000	8,061,000
Cost of Quality	3.2%	3.0%	4.8%

EXHIBIT 9.12   Cost-Reduction Results

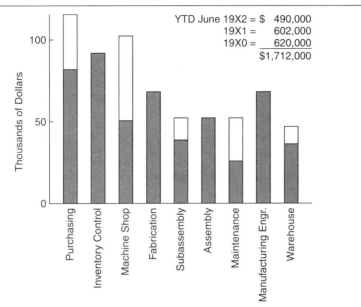

COST-REDUCTION MEASURES

Through assignment of cost-reduction goals to each segment of the organization, and with the agreement of key managers in each of those functional areas, a company was able to eliminate $1.7 million in costs from its operating budget. Each year, commitments were made and forecast, based on specific plans to reduce costs. A large board with posted results was hung outside of the plant cafeteria for everyone to see. This can be seen in Exhibit 9.12.

Typical areas of attack for cost reduction, as used by a distributor, are listed as follows:

- Opening up engineering tolerances;
- Low-cost designs;
- Increasing feeds and speeds;
- Cheaper materials;
- Standardized production methods;
- Reduction of paper work;
- Improved materials handling;
- Replacement of slow and obsolete equipment;
- Scrap and rework reduction;
- Reducing downtime;
- Selling scrap;

- Elimination of production operations;
- Mechanizing manual operations;
- Curtailing utilities usage (fuel, etc.);
- Damage and corrosion protection;
- Traffic rate reductions;
- Implementing work standards;
- Improved material flow;
- Employee training;
- Quality cost reduction;
- Reduction of indirect labor;
- Combining salaried jobs;
- Reducing overtime;
- Reducing supply usage;
- Reducing inventory balances;
- Shrinking lead times;
- Using economic lot sizes;
- Renegotiate vendor prices; and
- Control over obsolete blueprints.

MAINTENANCE COSTS

Maintenance costs are easily forgotten in operations. There is a tendency to bury them in the overhead account and focus instead on direct-labor costs for cost reduction.

The targeting of maintenance costs for reduction, however, is an imperative for a well-run company; otherwise, those costs will grow unimpeded year after year and could damage even the most productive program for reducing direct-labor costs in two ways. First, an ever increasing maintenance budget is a cost that offsets any gain made in other areas. Second, out-of-control maintenance costs reflect an out-of-control maintenance department. That hinders the cost-reduction efforts of production departments due to machine downtime.

There are six major ways to measure the effectiveness of the maintenance department. These are:

1. Maintenance labor ratio $= \dfrac{\text{No. of maintenance workers}}{\text{Total direct labor}} \times 100$

This demonstrates the control of the number of maintenance workers as a portion of all direct-labor workers. It is a key indicator.

2. Maintenance dollars $= \dfrac{\text{Total maintenance expenditures}}{\text{Cost of sales}} \times 100$

This is the same type of indicator as the first one, but uses dollars as the yardstick instead of number of people. It is a better reflection of the effectiveness of maintenance, because it takes into account the higher cost of maintenance workers as opposed to direct labor workers.

$$3. \ \text{Perishable tools} = \frac{\text{Perishable tool expense}}{\text{Cost of sales}} \times 100$$

This ratio shows how efficiently maintenance workers are using expendable tools in their everyday jobs. Perishable tools are expensive and must be controlled or else their costs can zoom out of sight.

$$4. \ \text{Machine uptime} = \frac{\text{Machine operating time}}{\text{Total operating time available}} \times 100$$

This measurement comes from the production department. It is a key indication of how maintenance is doing its job. What better indicator than the percentage of time production machines are actually being used? This ratio must be interpreted with some discretion. Obviously, it is possible that factors other than maintainability, factors such as high absenteeism or low production orders, may be affecting this ratio.

$$5. \ \text{Machine maintenance} = \frac{\text{Maintenance costs of machines}}{\text{Machine hours available}} \times 100$$

In this case, unit maintenance costs are based on machine hours available. This method is preferred over #2 or #4 only when delays other than maintenance have been subtracted from machine hours.

$$6. \ \text{Maintenance overtime} = \frac{\text{Maintenance overtime dollars}}{\text{Total maintenance labor costs}} = 100$$

Maintenance departments in most plants have worse records than other departments when it comes to overtime. Nowhere is it easier to lose control because of the normally nonrepetitive type of work maintenance does—work that is hard to measure. So nowhere is it more important to measure and control overtime than in maintenance. This ratio helps accomplish that.

CAPITAL EXPENDITURES

Although capital expenditures occur less frequently than other categories of plant costs, they must be controlled as closely as other costs, because each capital expenditure is generally high. There are two ratios in common use for that purpose:

$$1. \ \text{Capital intensity} = \frac{\text{Capital equipment costs}}{\text{No. of direct labor workers}} \times 100$$

This ratio is an indication of the relative expenditure made per worker. As such, its value is comparative. That is, there are no absolute good or bad ratios. Companies can observe whether or not capital expenditures are increasing proportionately from one financial period to another.

2. Capital replacement costs $= \dfrac{\text{Capital equipment costs}}{\text{Depreciation}} \times 100$

Here, the purpose is to determine how many times depreciation costs are covered by new capital expenditures. When the ratio is less than 100 percent, machinery productivity is lagging and is a sure sign that the company does not have an adequate capital expenditure program. A ratio greater than 100 percent indicates the company is investing in new equipment to keep machine productivity advancing.

EMPLOYEE CONCERNS

Keep Grievances and Disciplines to a Minimum

Grievances and workforce discipline, like other areas of concern in a plant, need to be adequately measured and controlled. In this area, particularly, trends can be discerned that will allow management to prevent serious labor problems before they occur. Four ratios are used. All of these ratios are self-explanatory and are best used as comparative measurements:

1. Grievances $= \dfrac{\text{Number of grievances}}{\text{Month}}$

2. Grievances $= \dfrac{\text{Number of grievances}}{\text{Employee}}$

3. Discipline $= \dfrac{\text{Number of disciplinary actions}}{\text{Month}}$

4. Discipline $= \dfrac{\text{Number of disciplinary actions}}{\text{Employee}}$

Control Absenteeism

Like grievances and discipline, absenteeism is a reflection of trouble brewing. Therefore, absenteeism trends need to be monitored carefully to avoid gradually slipping into a condition where absent employees disrupt the production schedule. There are three monitors in widespread use.

1. Absenteeism $= \dfrac{\text{No. of labor days lost}}{\text{Month}}$

2. Absenteeism cost $= \dfrac{\text{Cost of labor days lost}}{\text{Total labor costs}}$

3. *Reasons for labor days lost:* sickness, death in family, jury duty, other explained absences, or unexplained absences. Reasons for labor days lost must always accompany the two ratios provided.

Lower Accident Frequency

Accident frequency needs to be monitored carefully at all times. A rash of small accidents is often an indication of safety rules being ignored, which usually results in a catastrophic accident where a worker is seriously maimed. Managers and safety professionals watch these trends closely; as soon as a series of accidents is evident, you should quickly conduct a safety investigation of all the recent accidents and review whether safety rules are adhered to throughout the plant. This must be done periodically, since it is all too easy for supervisors and workers alike to gradually ignore safety precautions. There are two basic methods to monitor accident frequency. First, and foremost, is

$$\text{Accident frequency} = \frac{\text{Number of lost time accidents}}{\text{Total labor hours worked}}$$

This is the key monitor. The other way is to track workers' compensation costs. Although too far after the fact, it is a good way for financial managers to prevent their compensation rates from going through the roof.

To offset operational expenses and boost operational efficiency Exhibit 9.13 provides a model by which you can summarize, gauge and compare operational expense trends and operational efficiency patterns. The three key measurements for a well run operation are: percent efficiency, percent utilization, and percent productivity. The higher the percentages, the more effective the operation will be.

COST-CUTTING IDEAS FOR THE PLANT

The following is a list of ideas to spur the imagination of its salaried employees and to suggest productive areas of investigation for cost reduction. This list can be used by just about any operation to help stimulate ideas. Exhibits 9.14–9.18 demonstrate cost-cutting controls and reports.

Cut Costs in Product Engineering

1. Make tolerances more flexible.
2. Reduce surface finish requirements.
3. Eliminate need for a specific part.
4. Substitute a cheaper material.
5. Reduce the number of parts needed.
6. Combine part functions.
7. Design for low-cost tooling.
8. Design for high-speed production.
9. Increase feeds and speeds.
10. Improve the print control procedure.
11. Reduce the number of design changes.

EXHIBIT 9.13 Sample Production Evaluation Report

	Attendance Hours	Standard Hours Reported	Percent on Standard	Reported Hours	Nonstandard Hours Reported	Standard Hours Earned	Downtime	Exception Hours	Efficiency Percent	Utilization Percent	Productivity Percent
Henry Smith											
Johnson	357.80	237.14	66%	349.26	112.11	72.65	0.00	0.01	52.9%	97.6%	51.6%
Jones	369.00	252.36	68	367.53	58.57	203.93	56.60	0.00	84.4	84.3	71.1
White	598.00	523.20	87	591.43	36.89	586.69	28.29	3.05	111.3	9.37	104.3
Banks	1,022.70	865.81	85	1,012.92	105.81	745.78	38.04	3.25	87.6	95.0	83.3
Carmody	433.50	314.58	73	430.56	108.70	280.30	7.27	0.00	91.9	97.6	89.7
Snover	1,152.80	948.25	82	1,144.97	170.55	1,066.68	26.12	0.04	110.6	97.1	107.3
Total	3,933.80	3,141.34	80	3,896.67	592.63	2,956.03	156.32	6.35	95.0	94.9	90.2
Jim Maliet											
Menke	515.20	451.49	88	568.50	49.26	419.79	59.80	7.95	93.7	97.2	91.0
Clemons	658.20	444.98	68	645.15	136.30	365.56	63.37	0.50	86.3	88.3	76.2
Chamberlain	650.30	431.79	66	623.56	91.41	387.31	81.53	18.83	91.5	80.5	73.6
Conrad	402.10	296.78	74	364.52	40.71	352.01	26.00	1.02	116.4	83.9	97.7
Cox	964.10	761.48	79	978.05	89.54	721.53	102.78	24.25	95.3	88.3	84.1
Total	3,189.90	2,386.52	75	3,179.78	407.22	2,246.20	333.48	52.55	95.0	87.6	83.2
Ernest Cooper											
Swift	289.40	235.49	81	345.62	50.10	211.45	55.37	4.66	91.6	98.7	90.4
Stoffa	1,002.40	431.23	43	920.78	167.06	170.69	191.96	130.53	56.5	59.7	33.7
Total	1,291.80	666.72	52	1,266.40	217.16	382.14	247.33	135.19	67.8	68.4	46.4
John Taggart											
Templer	56.00	7.27	13	55.73	11.76	2.25	36.70	0.00	73.6	34.0	25.0
Total	56.00	7.27	13	55.73	11.76	2.25	36.70	0.00	73.6	34.0	25.0
Total Work Force	8,471.50	6,201.85	73	8,398.58	1,228.77	5,586.62	778.83	194.09	91.7	87.7	80.5

EXHIBIT 9.14 Manpower Requirement Summary

Department: _____

Manager: _____

Number of people on payroll	10
Potential hours available for work 10 people @ 40 hours	400
Less absenteeism and vacation 2% (MGMT-HISTORICAL)	8
Hours available for work	392
Less lost time hours 25% (unnecessary hours)	98
Current output level	294
Person-hours required at planned performance 85% 294/.85	51.9
Fixed hour allowance (added on, if necessary)	
Total hours required	345.9
Absentee allowance & vacation 2%	6.9
Total adjusted hours required	352.8
Total equivalent people required @ 40 hours	8.8
People variance	1

EXHIBIT 9.15 Person–Load Fabrication for Master Schedule

1. Take total estimated hours.
2. Times % factor (from management history).
3. Equals required hours to perform job.
4. Hours required to do job times % absentee—vacation, etc.
   Equals additional hours required to do job.
5. Take number working days in month times 8.0 hours per day.
   Equals number of hours required for each person.
6. Take total hours required divide by 1 person–load for month.
   Equals number people required for month.
7. Subtract total people available equals + / − crew required.

Sample:

1100	= Estimated hours (mo.)
× 19%	= Performance factor (from management history)
209	
1100	
− 209	
891	= Hours required
× 12.5%	= Absentee %
112	
+ 891	
1003	= Total hours required (mo.)
21	= Number days for month
× 8	= Person hours
168	= Hours 1 person per month

1003 divided by 168 = 6 people required for month.

Note: + / − People (crew) required—available.

EXHIBIT 9.16 Production Scheduling

Action Focus	N/A	Strong	Satisfactory	Needs Some Improvement	Weak: Needs Major Improvement	Action Plan, Responsibility
Improve accuracy of production forecasts						
Enhance delivery of small quantities of raw materials frequently						
Assure vendor compliance of wrapping in exact quantities						
Check conformity to raw material quantity specifications						
Encourage proximity of suppliers to plant						
Provide for quick, easy detection of defective products						
Be willing to make engineering changes when required						
Increase inventory control system's responsiveness to JIT (just-in-time)						
Assure production equipment is operating at maximum capacity						
Verify that equipment is running at rated speed						
Provide breakdown analysis of machines to isolate "losers"						
Do maintenance in advance of peak periods						
Have planned replacement program of automated manual equipment						
Intensify use of numerical control programs						
Use CAD/CAM						
Examine overall plant size versus "scaled down" installation						
Review tools, jigs, etc.						
Use standard parts for different types of equipment						
Employ air pressure, gravity feed and other natural aids						

Item							
Use automatic feed mechanisms rather than manual instruments							
Check accuracy of gauges and other measuring instruments							
Use advanced power tools (drills, hammers, etc.)							
Review degree of cross-training and flexibility to meet changing situations							
Evaluate quality of oral instructions by supervisors							
Evaluate quality of reference manuals for job procedures							
Monitor operators' current productivity, overall trend, and quality							
Determine whether operators are meeting prescribed schedules							
Examine job setups: Operator versus setup specialist							
Analyze strength of safety inspections (better morale, cost avoidance)							
Encourage production employee cost-reduction suggestions							
Use Quality Circles to address specific production problems							
Pinpoint exact production stations causing high number of rejects							
Determine precise reasons for parts breakdowns							
Ensure that customer returns can be traced to their production source							
Use computer-aided design (CAD) to maximize product performance							
Employ robots for moving materials along prescribed paths							
Consider numerically controlled (NC) machines for specific manufacturing functions							
Combine robots and NC machines to move and operate on materials							
Integrate design, manufacturing, information management (CIM)							

EXHIBIT 9.17 Production Engineering Survey

Action Focus	N/A	Strong	Satisfactory	Needs Some Improvement	Weak: Needs Major Improvement	Action Plan, Responsibility
Intensify long-range planning for new product development						
Improve short-term planning for product improvement						
Participate in setting quality standards						
Develop more accurate product unit costs						
Evaluate customer inquiries for clues to product failures						
Review appropriations for research and development						
Investigate budget versus actual variances for new product development						
Report on projects with schedule overruns						
Coordinate with cost-accounting function on analysis of reports						
Review procedures on treating costs as expenses or capital expenditures						
Automate system for estimating product costs						
Increase degree of component standardization as opposed to special design						
Improve accuracy of production time forecasts						
Clarify parts identification method						
Check staffing of product engineering and use of outside consultants						
Use microfilm for reducing records-management space and costs						
Make parts lighter through use of different materials						
Examine production tolerances for possible reduction						
Alter design to reduce scrap materials						

Check product for temperature and/or pressure specifications									
Substitute less expensive metals or plastics									
Attend vendor trade shows to save research money									
Visit key resources' plants to check facilities, quality control, distribution, financing									
Revitalize proven techniques that are not being used									
Intensify value analysis in product design									
Reduce special packages and/or labels without affecting aesthetics									
Question whether new products will add volume or detract from existing items									
Determine timing of new product introduction to consumers									
Check out economies in packaging, handling, distribution									
Have representative consumers field-test product									
Employ direct charges or allocation for data-processing services									
Pinpoint standard costs for products and component parts									
Assure that cost-accounting records agree with other financial items									
Maintain control over major expense and/or capital categories									
Report frequently on actions concerning controllable expenses									
Use cost-avoidance techniques to prevent expenditures									
Involve a steering committee on high-cost projects									
Have cost-accounting participate in production contract preparation									

153

EXHIBIT 9.18   Productivity Improvement and Cost Control

Action Focus	N/A	Strong	Satisfactory	Needs Some Improvement	Weak: Needs Major Improvement	Action Plan, Responsibility
Create a productivity-awareness culture at all levels						
Publish productivity goals in company media						
Establish a performance-measurement and improvement system						
Set up a research/exchange network to exchange information						
Select quality-assurance checkpoints and performance indicators						
Choose reliable volume figures, including sampling						
Calculate productivity performance and determine trends						
Define goals and "status" (on or off target)						
Use graphics and exception reporting to save time						
Isolate controllable from noncontrollable costs						
Distinguish between profit center and cost center						

12. Design-in quality.
13. Design to reduce scrap.
14. Design to standardize production processes.
15. Use standard hardware in place of custom hardware.
16. Design to reduce manual production operations.
17. Design to reduce material content.
18. Design to reduce number of fasteners required.
19. Specify alloys to enable faster machining.
20. Specify alloys to cut tool wear.
21. Design the cheapest finish feasible.

Cost-Reduction Ideas for Shipping, Receiving, and Warehousing

1. Use conveyors for moving operations.
2. Use reusable pallets and storage boxes.
3. Keep warehouse locked.
4. Minimize travel distances.
5. Group similar parts together in warehouse.
6. Use hydraulic lifts instead of ladders.
7. Ship and receive in unit loads.
8. Protect product from damage and corrosion.
9. Use maximum height for warehouse storage.
10. Speed handling by improving scheduling.
11. Use proper storage containers.
12. Prearrange movement of materials.
13. Replace obsolete equipment.
14. Combine clerical operations.
15. Place fastest-moving items near dock.
16. Mechanize all movement of material.
17. Keep aisle space down to minimum needs.
18. Practice first-in, first-out.
19. Properly identify all stock.
20. Check all freight rates.
21. Audit freight bills.
22. Use economical small package ship methods.
23. Keep less than truckload to a minimum.
24. Minimize demurrage costs—unload promptly.

25. Keep bills of lading legible.
26. Count number of parts received.

Slash Expenses in Production Planning and Control

Reduce inventories:

1. Reduce number of product lines.
2. Reduce size of purchased lots.
3. Reduce size of production lots.
4. Improve forecasting techniques.
5. Convert obsolete parts to current production.
6. Keep inventories organized.
7. Keep inventory records accurate.

Reduce number of salaried people needed:

8. Keep overtime low.
9. Keep warehouse space filled.
10. Reduce office space.
11. Reduce overhead expenses.
12. Improve package design.
13. Keep written procedures current.
14. Keep work standards up to date.
15. Shrink lead times.
16. Reduce emergency orders.
17. Keep product routings up to date.
18. Provide fast access to stock.
19. Use effective communication systems.
20. Minimize material flow.
21. Maintain fork trucks in good order.
22. Improve inspection techniques.
23. Improve vendor performance.
24. Guard against incorrect engineering drawings.
25. Provide for scrap/rework when planning.
26. Schedule to minimize waiting time.
27. Renegotiate vendor prices.
28. Keep production overruns to a minimum.
29. Recognize production bottlenecks, then eliminate them.
30. Keep accurate records.

31. Load work centers to minimize setups.
32. Minimize sales changes to master schedule.

Reducing Plant and Production Engineering Costs

1. Correct wrong bills of material.
2. Reduce average earnings.
3. Curtail use of fuel and electricity.
4. Correct loose work standards.
5. Keep 90 percent of all production jobs on standard.
6. Keep 80 percent of all indirect labor jobs on standard.
7. Use allowances in standards sparingly.
8. Ensure use of proper feeds and speeds.
9. Issue frequent labor performance reports.
10. Combine production operations.
11. Change standards to reflect improved methods.
12. Sample production counts for accuracy.
13. Analyze and reduce machine downtime.
14. Standardize equipment parts.
15. Combine or reduce machine setups.
16. Simplify tooling, jigs, and fixtures.
17. Keep accurate and up-to-date equipment records.
18. Lease rather than buy equipment.
19. Mechanize manual operations.

Improve Quality Control

1. Reduce scrap levels.
2. Reduce rework levels.
3. Reduce warranty.
4. Improve tool and gauge inspection.
5. Reduce vendor quality problems.
6. Calibrate testing equipment.
7. Prohibit use of marked-up prints.
8. Scrap all makeshift tooling.
9. Segregate defective stock.
10. Modernize inspection equipment.
11. Review packaging quality.
12. Investigate sales of plant scrap.

Backlog Data in Management Reporting

Many service center operations must be concerned with the amount of work in backlog. Most manufacturing companies keep careful account of the orders in their backlog. Many departments within a company want to see backlog in their staging areas. A given amount of backlog is healthy, and too little can cause interruptions in the work flow, with a resulting loss of person and machine time. *Too much backlog can mean delays in delivery promises or can extend delivery schedules beyond the point of customer acceptance, resulting in lost business.*

It is important, therefore, in many service center operations, that the backlog be reported as part of the management reporting system. Maintenance operations present a good example of this need, as do many clerical operations. *Backlog information must be translated into the hours required to handle the backlog, so that decisions can be made to ensure that the facility is adequately equipped.*

For example: In a department consisting of 10 people with 375 hours available per week, a backlog of 3750 hours would represent 10 weeks of work. Is this an acceptable backlog? *This is a question that can only be answered by management, which therefore has a need to know.*

Conversely, if a department loses time waiting for work, then a backlog should exist to run the department in an economic fashion.

Calculating the Backlog

At face value, calculating the backlog appears to be a relatively simple process. The reasonable expectancy (R/E) per unit multiplied by the number of units in the backlog will give the hours in the backlog. This figure, compared to the person and/or machine hours available to produce it, will demonstrate whether or not the department is in a healthy position. But this is too simple. Additional information is needed.

The percentage of performance of the unit against the standard is required to properly evaluate the backlog. Here's how it works:

> Step 1.   There are 1,000 tons of work in the backlog. The R/E is 0.4 hours per ton. This means that there is a standard measure of 400 backlog hours.
>
> Step 2.   The departmental performance is running at 85% on a historical basis. Therefore, the 400 backlog hours must be divided by 85% to determine the actual labor hours required. Thus, 400 divided by 85% equals 470.5 hours. This is true value of the backlog.
>
> Step 3.   There are eight people in the department available 37.5 hours each, for a total of 300 hours. By dividing the 470.5 by 300, we find that the department has an actual backlog of 1.57 weeks of work.

The same format could be used to show individual departments with the total representing a larger entity. This format allows for the pyramiding of the reports.

The economic staffing level (ESL) is shown in number of people and regular hours. This figure is the budgeted figure for the department. If the budget has been based on a variable volume, that is, hours per ton, the figure may well be valuable. If the budget has been developed on an average basis and is not readily subject to change, then this will be a fixed figure. In the example shown earlier, the figure of 14 people at 37.5 hours per week is a fixed staffing figure.

The actual hours worked are shown in regular and overtime categories to alert management to any serious or continuing overtime situations. In this case, a three-day absence caused 22.5 lost hours. Because 7.5 hours of overtime were used, the total actual hours of 510 resulted in a net loss from the staffing level of 15 hours. This would not be considered serious, since it is a loss of less than 3 percent compared to a plus or minus 5 percent goal.

The hours on schedule represent the actual hours spent on scheduled (measured) work. *The scheduled hours produced are the result of the volume produced times the R/E. Percentage performance is determined by dividing the scheduled hours produced by the actual hours on schedule. The nonscheduled hours is the difference between the actual hours on schedule and the total hours worked and is shown in hours and as a percentage.*

In the example used, the goal for performance is 90 percent so the department is below par. The goal for nonscheduled hours is 5 percent, so we have a double-below-par situation.

The backlog is shown in tons and hours. In the total column or in any area where the backlog is made up of a variety of different units, the unit column is not used. The 3,500 units represent 1,400 hours of work at an R/E of 0.4 hours per unit.

The required hours needed to complete 1,400 hours of work, based on a *performance factor* of 83.8 percent is 1,671 hours. Since one given week's performance may not be indicative of the general performance of the department, it is recommended that a five-week rolling average be used for this calculation.

Another factor has been introduced here—the percentage of nonscheduled hours. Again, a five-week rolling average is recommended, although in the example, the current figure is used. To calculate the hours required, an additional 9 percent is added, which makes the hours required 1,821.

10

INVENTORY CONTROLS

PROPER INVENTORY INVESTMENT

Five Variables

There are five variables to be considered when trying to simulate or calculate the proper inventory level:

1. Ability to forecast customer needs, as represented by the forecast error;
2. Desire to give prompt delivery service, as represented by the planned in-stock service level;
3. Accuracy of inventory perpetual records, compared to actual balance on hand, as represented by percent of parts that deviate;
4. Amount of "vertical" integration of the product line, as represented by the amount of manufactured versus purchased parts; and
5. Completeness of documents; as represented by accuracy of bills of material, route sheets, and so on.

Proper Inventory Level

The purpose of establishing an inventory investment standard is to set a level to prevent the build-up of extra inventory that, at some point, would become excessive and eventually obsolete material. There are three methods applicable for determining that proper level.

Day's Usage Method. The calculation worksheet shown on the following page should be completed by the materials manager and submitted to the vice president of manufacturing for approval. The recent historical and/or forecasted "dollar usage per day" should be obtained by taking the total inventory issues in dollars last, and dividing by the number of work days. Insert this number next to the appropriate "type inventory." By using the desired "days supply" column, an extension is made to determine the "standard in dollars." The "actual dollar inventory" should then be posted and the "deviation" from the "standard in dollars" determined.

Forecasted Sales Method. Although the second procedure is more judgmental, you can establish target levels by ascertaining the amount of inventory desired by sales to meet anticipated customer orders. To use this method, take the historical sales last year, establish months' supply targets, and calculate dollar inventory by various categories.

Calculation Method. The preceding two methods can easily be utilized. However, it often is desirable to perform a more complete target determination. This procedure is described below.

At any given point, for the items in stock, some will be at maximum amount (for example, the reorder quantity of 6,000 items, plus safety stock of 600 for a total of 6,600), some at the reorder point (1,800), some at the safety stock level (600) and, of course, all sorts of other levels. The average quantity on hand for an item can be determined by dividing the reorder quantity by two and adding to it the safety stock quantity. If we reordered 6,000 sheets of paper, the average quantity on hand would be 3,600 (6,000 divided by 2 plus 600 safety stock). If we determine the average quantity on hand plus the safety stock quantity and multiply this amount times the unit cost for each item on hand, we then can determine the dollar inventory target standard for all items kept in the stockroom, merely by adding each item's average quantity on hand. This determination can be done by the various inventory groups—raw material, product line, storage location, and so forth.

Most organizations have to maintain additional inventories for the special needs of their customers. This material can be for sales promotions, unusual emergency requirements, prebuilding for seasonal goods, hedges for possible strikes, reserves for special customers, and so forth. Even the most perfect inventory control systems end up with surplus (slow-moving items), as well as obsolete material due to changing customer needs, or even design engineering needs.

One of these groups is the "desired" inventory, two more are "permissible," and the last two are "not desired." Group 2 is under the control of manufacturing or operations, while Group 3 is the responsibility of the sales or special users department. Thus, with permission from management, special inventories can be maintained over and above the normal inventory item balances in Group 1. (Refer to Exhibits 10.1 through 10.4.)

Five Inventory Groups for Determining Proper Investment Targets

Group 1: Normal, Planned Inventory (Desired). To calculate the inventory for this group, you obtain the reorder quantity and safety stock for each of the departments allowed to maintain inventory. Each reorder quantity is divided by two to get the average on-hand amount.

The planned safety stock is added to this amount to get a unit total, which is multiplied by the unit cost to obtain the dollar value. Then, all dollar values are added by department to get departmental and grand totals for Group 1.

Group 2: Manufacturing Preference Items (Permissible). Some departments in the company are permitted by management to maintain certain items where no

EXHIBIT 10.1 Calculation Worksheet

	Dollar Usage Per Day	×	Days Supply	=	Standard in Dollars	Actual Dollar Inventory	Standard to Actual Deviation	
Type Inventory							Less	More
Raw materials								
Local suppliers	$ 1,760		30		$ 52,800	$ 41,673	$ 11,127	
Distant vendors	4,150		70		290,500	402,693		$ 112,103
Purchase components	2,180		60		130,800	196,532		65,732
Work-in-Process—Parts	1,870		30		56,100	187,961		131,861
Manufactured components	4,700		45		211,500	399,711		188,211
Work-in-Process—Assembly	9,600		60		576,000	781,003		205,003
Finished assemblies	16,100		30		483,000	716,943		233,943
Replacement parts	4,360		90		392,400	181,296	211,104	
Totals	$44,720		49		$2,193,100	$2,907,812	$222,231	$ 936,943
						Net		$ 714,712
						Absolute		$1,159,174

stock-out can be permitted. The projected dollar value of these items should be obtained and listed by each storing department.

Group 3: Sales Department Preferences (Permissible). In any organization, some departments require what we call "preference" items. The actual dollar value of these permitted items upon sales and management approval, such as special finished goods for a favorite customer, should be listed on the worksheet.

Group 4: Surplus Inventory (Not Desired). There is no perfect inventory system; in any organization, surplus or excess material will develop through the normal chain of events. Surplus inventory is defined as good, usable inventory for which you have too much on hand. The maximum amount of inventory on hand for any item should be the reorder quantity plus the safety stock. Thus, surplus inventory is that amount on hand that exceeds the reorder quantity plus safety stock dollar value—so list the actual dollar value by department and total of all surplus material.

Group 5: Obsolete Inventory (Not Desired). This last group includes items no longer required, due to changes in supplies used and/or equipment required. In this group—also by department—you should list the actual (book or original) value of all obsolete material by department and in total.

In summary, the inventory standard target is the total of groups 1, 2, and 3. Groups 4 and 5, by being identified, can eventually be disposed of through exchanges, substitution, scrapping, and so forth. The total actual inventory of $3,107,019 (at FIFO) represents a turnover of 2.2 times, since the annual inventory usage was $6,979,316 worth of material. However, if the investment was decreased to the target of $2,168,470, turnover increases to a more respectable 3.2 times.

Work-in-Process Inventory Target

This calculation (which is necessary for most companies) can be made by determining two statistics: (1) the value of the average daily usage (called day's supply), and (2) the average manufacturing actual cycle time in days. The work-in-process target is then calculated.

Work-in-Process Material Target Calculation

1. Divide annual value of raw material and purchased component issues by the number of work days in a year to get "average daily usage" of these materials. For example:

$$\frac{\$6,978,733}{240} = \$29,078$$

2. Determine the average production "cycle time" (sometimes called the "manufacturing lead time"). We'll use nine days in this example.

EXHIBIT 10.2   The Five Inventory Groups

| **PLANNED** |

Desired

Group 1   • Normal inventory items

| **EXCEPTION** |

Permissible

Group 2   • Manufacturing preference: Long runs, vendor rework, emergency items, new products strike hedge

Group 3   • Sales preference: Stocking plans, favored company, promotion, credit holds

Not Desired

Group 4   • Surplus: Excess of current needs
Group 5   • Obsolete and phased out material

---

3. Multiply the average daily usage times the average cycle time to obtain the work-in-process inventory target:

$$\$29,078 \times 9 = \$261,702$$

How to Calculate Excess and Obsolete Inventory

The question often raised is how to establish the "classical" procedure to calculate obsolete inventory. You should not have the finance department responsible for the determination of the proper obsolete inventory reserve, for the following three reasons:

1. It removes the responsibility for obsolete inventory from operations, where it belongs.

2. It lessens the responsibility of marketing to provide a forecast or historical customer demand for each item expected to be ordered in the future.

3. It eliminates the independent check-and-balance review, which is a prime duty of the finance department.

The following details the proper method to select the items and make the obsolescence calculation. Since any obsolete calculation is very sensitive to (and dependent upon) a correct forecast, this procedure begins in marketing. Projections for future customer demands (orders) come from a combination of:

• A forecast for assembly products;
• Historical activity for spares; and
• The existing open customer orders.

EXHIBIT 10.3 Inventory Target Worksheet

| | Normal Planned (Desired) Group 1 | | Exception Inventories | | | | |
| | | (Permissible) | | | (Not Desired) | | |
Type Inventory	Average	Mfg. Preference 2	Customer Preference 3	Total Target	Surplus 4	Obsolete 5	Grand Total
Raw material							
Purchase components							
Work-in-process							
Finished goods							
Total							
Calculation	a +	b +	c =	d +	e +	f =	g

EXHIBIT 10.4 Inventory Targets

| | Normal Planned (Desired) Group 1 | | Exception Inventories | | | | |
| | | (Permissible) | | | (Not Desired) | | |
Type Inventory	Average	Mfg. Preference 2	Customer Preference 3	Total Target	Surplus 4	Obsolete 5	Grand Total
Raw Material	$ 481,616	$ 41,600	$ 0	$ 523,216	$221,064	$ 47,683	$ 791,963
Purchase components	775,503	61,100	0	836,630	214,336	47,145	1,098,111
Work-in-process	462,037	0	0	462,037	110,325	19,642	592,004
Finished goods	126,087	50,000	170,500	346,587	78,611	199,742	624,940
Total	$1,845,270	$152,700	$170,500	$2,168,470	$624,336	$314,212	$3,107,018
Calculation	a +	b +	c =	d +	e +	f =	g

This information is given to manufacturing, which makes a gross requirement master schedule for the life of the inventory specified by finance. Manufacturing compares the schedule needs versus the inventory on hand, and makes a "Tentative Obsolete List." Since the obsolete item determination is dependent upon the forecast, a double-check should now be performed to ascertain if any item/product was inadvertently missed. The finalized, recommended list should then be given to finance.

REDUCING INVENTORY TO THE CALCULATED LEVEL

The raw material, work-in-process, and finished-goods inventories in most companies are excessive, usually at least 20 percent too high. The challenge is to reduce carefully the inventory investment with the following steps.

Create an Inventory-Reduction Team

The initial set-up is to establish the inventory-reduction team that will review all areas and activities affecting the factory and warehouse inventory levels. The team is not assigned any operating responsibility for the inventory-control function, but is to serve as a strong assistance to the production and inventory-control departments. The team objectives are to:

- Review and analyze specific inventory-management problems.
- Suggest immediate and obvious steps to balance and reduce inventories.
- Assist in formulation of inventory-management programs.
- Develop necessary procedures to implement recommended changes.
- Provide systems and procedures needed to carry out inventory policies as established by the inventory policy committee.
- Recommend changes for improvements to the inventory policy committee.
- Provide for accomplishment of corporate inventory objectives, while improving the level of service to customers.

Although the ideal time to reduce inventory is during good economic conditions (it is much easier to use up the excess and write-off the obsolete inventory), most companies undertake inventory-reduction programs during a poor business climate. The efforts should be on both a broadly gauged (macro) basis and a specific item (micro) approach. Timing is short, intermediate, and longer range. Usually a substantial decrease can be achieved after three months of work, followed by a relatively slow period—in terms of reduction—for the next three months (the first plateau). Good reductions are then achieved during the seventh to twelfth month (a second plateau), and then steady but smaller decreases until the optimum level is reached at about eighteen months after starting.

Short-Range Reductions

An example of the initial efforts that gain short-range reductions can be classified into three groups. The first are tasks that give tangible results, such as:

- Review order before final release;
- Reschedule orders-in-process;
- Cancel or reschedule slow-moving products;
- Cancel or reschedule open purchase orders; and
- Fill branch requisitions from plant inventory.

The second group includes work that cannot be readily measured. These include:

- Hold up purchased materials for delivery;
- Review steel and shop order coverage;
- Return rejected material rapidly;
- Audit inventory analyst's decision; and
- Return supply inventory from field warehouse to central warehouse.

In the third group, on-the-job training of employees should be increased, policies reviewed and emphasized, and supervision efforts magnified.

Intermediate-Range Reductions

Intermediate-range results can be achieved by using these 39 reduction techniques:

1. Buy at a smaller economic order quantity or at the EOQ—if you weren't before.
2. Reduce the protective, safety stock level.
3. Reschedule shop or purchase orders to later deliveries.
4. Telegram vendor to stop delivery for "X" days.
5. Substitute one type of raw material on hand for another.
6. Clean up the shop, scrapping or reworking old material.
7. Reject all overshipments on purchased items.
8. Police the over-issues of material.
9. Buy more items on a short-range basis.
10. Reduce ordering costs.
11. Review high order points and high order quantities.
12. Use old stock first.
13. Use just-in-time (JIT) quick delivery flow principle, telling suppliers the day and time to deliver.

14. Deliver by truck or air freight, not by railroad car.

15. Review all A items daily, B items weekly, and C items monthly for excess coverage.

16. Review weekly all purchase orders valued above $300.

17. Cancel all unneeded shop and purchase orders.

18. Modify excess or obsolete parts into another part number.

19. Arbitrarily reduce lot sizes and requisitions by "X" percent.

20. Maintain list of items in all warehouses and move goods from one warehouse to supply another.

21. Accelerate the scrap-processing program.

22. Speed up the receiving inspection process.

23. Rework rejected material rapidly.

24. Send to customers a list of certain items you wish to sell at special prices in a "preinventory clearance" sale.

25. Obtain material from vendors on a delayed-invoice-payment basis.

26. Use the run-out ratio to prioritize various items in process.

27. Use the critical ratio to provide last-minute priority for production sequence.

28. Break critical machine capacity bottlenecks.

29. Review the posting accuracy on ledger cards.

30. Cancel excess "float" on orders.

31. Use line balancing, milestones, or Gantt charts for control of in-process items.

32. Study purchasing statistics for poor vendor deliveries or quality.

33. Speed up sales order entry and engineering document processing time control.

34. Cease supplying old service parts; send customer blueprints instead so they can produce the parts themselves.

35. Set up more blanket orders.

36. Conduct group brainstorming meetings for idea selection.

37. Decrease time span between filling of order and replacement of stock sold.

38. Utilize where-used lists.

39. Control the inventory investment carefully on single-customer-use items.

Exhibits 10.5 through 10.17 illustrate various ways to analyze your inventory carrying costs. Pick the analysis method that's right for you. After you've had a chance to evaluate the results review pages 147–159 and choose strategies that will reduce inventory for your operations. Keep in mind that the balance between inventory turns and holding the correct amount of inventory should be considered and performed accordingly.

EXHIBIT 10.5 Results of Three Inventory-Reduction Programs

Program	Inventory Type	Duration of Program—Months	Value of Inventory ($000)		Reduction		Turnover	
			Start	Finish	Dollars	Percent	From	To
1.	Raw material	12	$ 4,358	$ 3,050	$1,308	30.0	2.4	3.4
2.	Raw material WIP & FG	9	2,500	2,005	495	19.8	2.8	3.5
3.a	Raw material	24	2,022	1,518	504	24.9		
b	Work-in-process	24	3,200	2,210	990	30.9		
c	Finished goods for prod assembly	24	2,884	2,285	599	20.8	2.4	3.0
d	Finished goods for service	24	2,561	1,669	892	34.8		
e	Branch plant RM & WIP	24	6,931	5,942	989	14.3		
Subtotal			$17,598	$13,624	$3,974			
Grand Total			$24,456	$18,679	$5,777	23.6	2.5	3.3

EXHIBIT 10.6   Calculation of Cost Factor for Carrying Inventory in Your Company—A Worksheet

Warehouse Space $ _____
   The annual expense of warehouse space in your company. If all
   your space is owned, then it's the cost you'd expect to pay to
   lease equivalent space in your locale.

Taxes $ _____
   Actual taxes paid in the last fiscal year on your inventory. Taxes
   on buildings should be part of the warehouse space cost figure.

Insurance $ _____
   Insurance premiums paid in the last fiscal year on the inventory.
   Again, insurance for buildings is part of the warehouse space cost
   calculation.

Obsolescence/Shrinkage $ _____
   How much inventory value was written-off at the end of last year,
   either because your physical inventory count came out short, or
   because certain material was determined to be nonsalable?

Material Handling $ _____
   The total annual expense in labor and material handling
   equipment (lift trucks, etc.) needed to receive and put away all
   incoming merchandise, or to move it around during the year.
   Customer order-filling expense is not included.

Cost of Money $ _____
   Your current interest rate for borrowing money (whether you
   actually borrowed or not) applied to the average value of the
   inventory throughout the year.

   Total Costs $ _____

$$\frac{\text{Total costs}}{\text{Average inventory value}} \quad \frac{\$ _____}{\$} = _____ \%$$

Note: The answer represents your *cost* for carrying $1 of inventory for a year. Acceptable range of answers: 25% to 35%.

EXHIBIT 10.7   Cost of Carrying Inventory—An Illustration

Warehouse space	$130,200
($10,850 per month × 12)	
Taxes	65,000
Insurance	40,000
Obsolescence/shrinkage	60,000
Material handling	64,800
Cost of money	240,000
(12% × $2,000,000 Inventory)	
Total Annual Costs	$600,000

$$\frac{\text{Total costs}}{\text{Average inventory value}} \quad \frac{\$600,000}{\$2,000,000} = 30\%$$

Note: This company spends .30¢ for every $1.00 of inventory carried for a year. Since, on the average, they have $2,000,000 in inventory throughout the year, the costs listed amount to $600,000. The 30% *rate* is used in other calculations in order to keep the total costs as low as is practical, consistent with the Costs of Ordering and with the service objectives. Rather than making this calculation, you may elect to use 20% plus prime rate.

EXHIBIT 10.8   Computing Your Company's Inventory Turn Rate—A Worksheet

Single Location:
1. Cost of goods sold (from stock only) this month $ _____
2. Cost of goods sold—Annualized (No. 1 × 12) = $ _____
3. Current inventory in dollars $ _____

Calculation:

$$\frac{\text{Annualized cost of goods sold from stock}}{\text{Current inventory in dollars}} = \text{_____}$$

Central Warehouse That Supplies Other Branches:
1. Cost of goods sold (from stock only) this month $ _____
2. Cost of goods sold—Annualized (No. 1 × 12) = $ _____
3. Transfers-out to other branches this month $ _____
4. Transfers-out—Annualized (No. 3 × 12) = $ _____
5. Current inventory in dollars $ _____

Calculation:

$$\frac{\substack{\text{Annualized cost of goods sold} \\ \text{from stock and annualized transfers-out}}}{\text{Current inventory in dollars}} = \text{_____}$$

Note: The answer represents how many times per year your inventory investment is "turned" or utilized through sales or, for a warehouse, supplying needs of other branches. It's a measurement of inventory use. Acceptable answers depend on the gross margin distributors develop. At 30% gross margin, 5 to 6 turns per year is considered good. At 20% margin, the turn would have to be 6 to 8 for good performance.

**EXHIBIT 10.9   Turnover's Impact on Net Profit and Extra Sales
Needed to Offset Poor Inventory Control**

Here's an average performance for a distributor:

$2,000,000 in cost of goods sold from stock for a year.

$1,000,000 invested in inventory.

The turnover rate is 2.0 ($2,000,000 ÷ $1,000,000 = 2.0)

Let's see what happens to profit if cost of goods sold stays the same, but inventory control performance improves the turn rate:

$$\frac{\$2,000,000 \text{ CGS}}{\$666,666 \text{ INV}} = 3.0 \text{ turns}$$

Inventory savings = $ 333,333

At 30% carrying cost per year, that would save:

$100,000 in *Net profit*

$$\frac{\$2,000,000 \text{ CGS}}{\$500,000 \text{ INV}} = 4.0 \text{ turns}$$

Inventory savings = $ 500,000

At 30% carrying cost per year, that would save:

$150,000 in *Net profit*

$$\frac{\$2,000,000 \text{ CGS}}{\$400,000 \text{ INV}} = 5.0 \text{ turns}$$

Inventory savings = $ 600,000

At 30% carrying cost per year, that would save:

$180,000 in *Net profit*

How many additional sales dollars would have to be generated to produce $180,000 Net profit?

- If it were Gross profit, then a 30% margin would bring $180,000 from $600,000 additional sales, but,
- To get $180,000 *Net profit*, the additional sales needed would likely be nearly $2,000,000!

EXHIBIT 10.10   Service Level Measurement—An Illustration

Week: <u>11-6-87</u>

Sales orders received	<u>160</u>	
Number of line items		<u>482</u>
Transfer requests	<u>72</u>	
Number of line items		<u>216</u>
(1) Total number of line items		<u>698</u>
(2) Number of lines filled complete		<u>446</u>

Calculation:

$$\frac{\text{Lines filled complete (2)}}{\text{Total No. of line items (1)}} \quad \frac{446}{698} = \frac{64\%}{\text{Service level}}$$

Note: This company is filling 64% of the "demand" against their *stock items*—represented in sales orders from customers and transfer needs to other branches . . . the very purpose for which the inventory was established.

Admittedly, this measurement is quite harsh. It gives no credit for a line filled partially, as, for example, filling 82 out of an order for a 100 quantity.

It is, however, a defendable measurement. No one could argue that the figures are "padded." And who's to say what negative impact a partial shipment has on a customer? Find out where you are under this measurement and then watch it improve as new controls are put in place.

EXHIBIT 10.11   Calculation of Usage Rate

Current Year

Regular item:

Mar.	Apr.	May	June	July	Aug.	Sept.	Usage Rate = 23
29	17	37	15	20	20	↑	

You're Here
Now

Last Year's Equivalent Months

Seasonal item:

Sept.	Oct.	Nov.	Dec.	Jan.	Feb.	Mar.	Usage Rate = 102
↑	67	84	119	137	127	77	

You're
Here
Now

Add to this base rate, the growth or decline percent of this line, product group, or business in general—last year to this year.

Usage Rate is expressed in number of units sold/transferred (moved) per month. This rate is then used in both the order point and order quantity calculations for proper control of the stock item.

Usage Histories That Need to Be Qualified: Some Examples

Potential Problems

Mar.	Apr.	May	June	July	Aug.	
12	14	10	6	18	118	Nonrecurring sale in August for 100 pieces

Usage rate: 30/month   Revised rate: 13/month

Mar.	Apr.	May	June	July	Aug.	
7	13	10	0	0	0	Out of stock since May

Usage rate: 5/month   Revised rate: 10/month

Mar.	Apr.	May	June	July	Aug.	
50	0	0	50	0	0	One dominant customer!

Usage rate: 17/month   Revised rate: Not figured (Ordering controls set to fit customer's buying pattern)

Mar.	Apr.	May	June	July	Aug.	
0	0	0	0	1	0	Low usage item! Sell very low number per year.

Usage rate: .17/month   Revised rate: Not figured (Order point set at zero;) (Order quantity set at one.)

EXHIBIT 10.12   Basic Order-Timing Control: The Order Point

Basic Formula:

$$(\text{Usage rate} \times \text{Avg. Lead Time}) + \text{Safety allowance (50\%)}$$
$$\text{Example: } 100 \times 1 + 50 = 150$$

Complicated Formula

$$\begin{aligned} &\text{Usage rate} \times \text{Average lead time} \\ &+ \left(\text{Usage Rate} \times \text{Lead Time} \times .7 \times \frac{\text{Maximum lead time} - \text{Average Lead Time}}{\text{Average lead time}} \right) \end{aligned}$$

- - - - - - - - - - - - Delivery Delay % - - - - - - - -

- - Safety Allowance - -

Example: $100 \times 1 + \left(100 \times 1 \times .7 \times \dfrac{1\frac{1}{2} \text{ Months} - 1 \text{ Month})}{1 \text{ Month}} \right)$

$100 \times 1 + (100 \times 1 \times .7 \times .5)$ Maximum lead time is the
$100 + (100 \times .7 \times .5)$ worst delivery experienced
$100 + (70 \times .5)$ on this item during the
$100 + 35$ last year.
$135 = \text{Order Point}$

What the Order Point Does

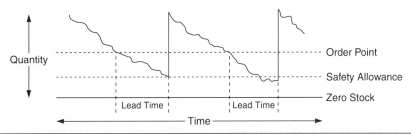

EXHIBIT 10.13   A Higher Order-Timing Control: The Line Point

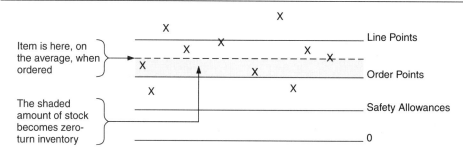

Line Point Formula

Line Point = Order Point + (Usage Rate × Review Cycle)

$$\text{Review Cycle} = \frac{\text{Total Annual Purchases (\$)}}{\text{Buying Target (\$)}}$$

Review cycles for seasonal product lines vary when you are *in* or *out of* the purchasing season. As you enter the season, the review cycle shortens and all item line points change. As you leave the purchasing season, the review cycle lengthens and line points change once again.

Definition of a seasonal product line: 80% of the annual sales occur in six consecutive months.

EXHIBIT 10.14   Cost of a Replenishment Cycle ("R" Cost)

One-Half the

Total annual expense of setting-up and maintaining records
of stock on hand. This includes the cost of all personnel,
office space, telephones, supplies, computer time if you're
automated, etc. $ _____

The portion of the Purchasing Department's annual expense
expended on purchase orders for stock merchandise. Again,
this includes the personnel costs, office space, long-distance
calls, computer time, etc. $ _____

Annual expense of expediting stock merchandise $ _____

That portion of the Accounts Payable Department's annual
expenses devoted to processing, clearing questions on,
paying, and writing/calling vendors about invoices for stock
merchandise. This should be about 50% of the total cost of
the department (people, office space, supplies, telephones,
computer time, etc.) $ _____

The *fixed* portion of the Receiving Department's annual
costs devoted to filing, posting to, making receiving copies
of purchase orders for stock merchandise. Receiving must
perform some steps to every P.O., regardless of size, number
of dollars involved. $ _____

                                    Total costs in these categories $ _____

1. Number of purchase orders issued for stock merchandise
   in a full year   _____

2. Average number of line items on a purchase order for
   stock items   _____

   Total lines ordered in a year (No. 1 × No. 2)   _____

   Calculation: $\dfrac{\text{Total Ordering Costs}}{\text{Total Lines Ordered}}$: $ _____ = $ _____

Your answer represents the number of dollars you will spend   "R" COST
in your company each time you go through the ordering cycle
on one stock item.

**EXHIBIT 10.15   Internal Cost and Turnover Control
Economic Order Quantity (EOQ)**

Formula: $$EOQ = \sqrt{\frac{24 \times \text{Cost to replenish (R)} \times \text{Monthly usage rate}}{\text{Cost of carrying inventory (K)} \times \text{Unit cost}}}$$

Examples:

High Cost & Usage Item		Low Cost & Usage Item	
Usage rate	100	Usage rate	10
Unit cost	$10	Unit cost	.15¢
Carrying cost	35%	Carrying cost	35%
Cost to order	$ 5	Cost to order	$ 5

$$\sqrt{\frac{24 \times \$5 \times 100}{.35 \times \$10}} \quad = EOQ = \quad \sqrt{\frac{24 \times \$5 \times 10}{.35 \times .15¢}}$$

$$\sqrt{\frac{12000}{3.5}} \quad = EOQ = \quad \sqrt{\frac{1200}{.0525}}$$

$$\sqrt{3428.57} \quad = EOQ = \quad \sqrt{22857.14}$$

$$59 \quad = EOQ = \quad 151$$

Little over 2 weeks' supply   15 Months' supply

What the EOQ Does

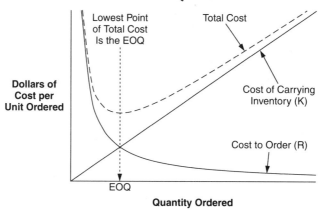

EXHIBIT 10.16   Buying in Accord with Inventory Class

Classification Steps

1. For all stock items, or a 10% random sampling, multiply the annual usage in units by unit cost to determine the annual dollar amount moving through the inventory for each item.

100 Units sold in a year × 4.20 Cost = $420

2. Sequence all items according to the dollar-movement answers. The best items with most dollars moving through the inventory are at the top of the list. Zero's are all at the bottom.

3. Decide where the "Dead" item breakpoint is to be. Suggestion: Any item that sells less than $10 at cost for a whole year is considered "D" Class (Dead, Defunct, Dog, etc.)

4. Remove all D items from the classification exercise. They are now to be handled under the Disposition Program.

5. Assign each item remaining on the list (after the D's are removed from the bottom) an Inventory Class as follows:

Top	7½% of the items	Class 1
Next	7½%	Class 2
Next	10%	Class 3
Next	10%	Class 4
Next	8%	Class 5
	8%	Class 6
	8%	Class 7
	8%	Class 8
	8%	Class 9
	8%	Class 10
	8%	Class 11
Last	9%	Class 12
	100%	

The percentages are of the total number of items on the list. If, for example, you had 5,000 items remaining in the study after taking out the D's, Class 1 would have 7½% of 5,000 or 375 items. Class 2 would also have 375. Class 3 would have 500 items, etc.

6. If you have used a 10% random sampling of your stock items to work out the inventory classes, you must now determine the breakpoint for each class in terms of annual dollar-movement through the inventory.

> The breakpoint, for example, between Class 2 and 3 might turn out to be $1,827 moving through the inventory in a year.

7. When the breakpoint between each class is known, you may assign any and all other stock items to their proper class, simply by determining the annual sales X unit cost for each one.

Annual sales (250) times unit cost ($.05) = $12.50

This item will likely be Class 12 if you removed all items selling less than $10 in a year. The breakpoint between Class 11 and 12 might be much further up the list of remaining items . . . perhaps somewhere around $30 per year.

EXHIBIT 10.17 Inventory-Control Survey

Action Focus	N/A	Strong	Satisfactory	Needs Some Improvement	Weak: Needs Major Improvement	Action Plan, Responsibility
Calculate degree of investment of inventory versus earning assets						
Use proper mix of raw materials, work-in-process, finished goods						
Improve accuracy of sales forecasts for proper service levels						
Tighten controls over movement, processing, storing of parts and materials						
Set lead time for systematic replenishment						
Calculate sufficient inventory for satisfactory customer service						
Coordinate inventory control with manufacturing process						
Pinpoint cost of capital relative to excess inventories						
Improve timing of raw material deliveries to plant						
Use Economic Order Quantity (EOQ)						
Use optimum # of annual purchase orders calculation						
Employ reorder point-order up to level system						
Compute carrying costs: capital						
Compute carrying costs: inventory service (taxes, insurance)						
Compute carrying costs: storage space (warehouses, etc.)						
Compute carrying costs: inventory risk (obsolescence, damage, pilferage, etc.)						
Computer carrying costs: inventory risk (security, relocation costs)						
Integrate with order entry, sales analysis, cost accounting						

Action Item				
Improve database management: adding, deleting, changing records				
Use exception reporting back-order reports, automatic order generation				
Explore personal computer with electronic spreadsheets for "what if" simulations				
Try computer simulations of "goal-seeking" for optimum stock levels				
Employ electronic coding for identification and/or physical inventories				
Use optical scanning for inventories, distribution, document preparation				
Conduct cycle inventories rather than all at once				
Store supplies, raw materials off site (occupancy, labor costs)				
Generate automatic or on-line requests for materials replenishment				
Profitably dispose of scrap/surplus to dealers				
Contribute scrap/surplus to charitable institutions				
Contribute scrap/surplus to educational institutions				
Periodically review inventory budget versus actual				
Take action on production workers' waiting time for raw materials				
Provide special care for delicate components				
Place fast-moving parts near production area				
Use inventory locator file to easily find desired item				
Emphasize increasing rate of inventory turns				
Correlate physical inventory to accounting records				
Report slow-moving items, obsolete products, and overstock				
Clear up written instructions for inventory taking and maintenance				

INVENTORY CONTROL GUIDELINES WORKSHEET

		Yes/No	Commentary
1.	Is materials handling a specialized activity in the company or unit; that is, at least one person engaged full time in the activity?	_____	_____
2.	If yes, are direction and quality of materials handling services the responsibility of one person?	_____	_____
3.	Does production planning give warehouse personnel sufficient advance notice of items and stock activity?	_____	_____
4.	Are warehouse personnel notified in advance of planned inventory changes?	_____	_____
5.	Is there any indication that the company carries varieties of stocks that lend themselves to standardization?	_____	_____
6.	If yes, is any kind of value engineering being practiced or planned?	_____	_____
7.	Is there any evidence of an excessive accumulation of materials awaiting repair, rework, or return to vendors?	_____	_____
8.	Do inventory records appear to serve a useful purpose beyond accounting; for example, are they used for purchasing materials or for rescheduling production?	_____	_____
9.	Does someone have the obligation to keep current on new methods of materials handling?	_____	_____
10.	If yes, is that person encouraged to look in other industries for equipment that could be slightly altered to meet the company's needs?	_____	_____
11.	Do materials appear to be standing around piled up unnecessarily on the receiving platform?	_____	_____
12.	Do production workers stand around waiting for materials to arrive?	_____	_____
13.	Are materials moved more often than necessary?	_____	_____
14.	Do skilled workers handle materials; that is, is expensive labor used for unskilled—and often unnecessary—manual jobs?	_____	_____
15.	Are delicate parts frequently damaged in transit?	_____	_____
16.	Are production areas cluttered with parts and materials to be used or moved to the next operation?	_____	_____

Yes/No   Commentary

17. Are all materials unloaded mechanically or with machine assistance?   _____   _____

18. If no, do materials that are unloaded manually have to be handled in that manner?   _____   _____

19. Are prepackaged cartons for simplifying counts and materials handling being used?   _____   _____

20. Are identical items stored in one location to minimize time-consuming searches by stock handlers?   _____   _____

21. If the warehouse is on more than one floor, are fast-moving stock items concentrated on one floor near the shipping area to minimize travel, retrieval time, and elevator usage?   _____   _____

22. Are storage areas and shipping areas close together, so that the storage area can act as an effective feeder to the shipping docks without costly backhauling between storage area and resultant double-handling?   _____   _____

23. If no, can the storage and shipping areas be brought closer together?   _____   _____

24. If yes, does the change appear to be economically justified?   _____   _____

25. Are lifting areas well illuminated?   _____   _____

26. Are all bins clearly labeled to facilitate order-picking?   _____   _____

27. Are materials so placed as not to overflow from one location into adjoining aisles, which would require rehandling to free blocked items?   _____   _____

28. Is merchandise that can be stored uncartoned, rather than cartoned, so stored? (If no, materials handling and production costs may be much higher than necessary.)   _____   _____

29. Are materials available to workers without waste motion?   _____   _____

30. Are bags of incoming materials palletized to avoid handling individual bags?   _____   _____

31. Is there a central locator file?   _____   _____

32. Are large portable bins available to avoid repeated handling of small containers?   _____   _____

Yes/No   Commentary

33. Are dump trucks in lieu of standard trucks
    used in unloading bulk commodities?   _____   _____

34. Is crane capacity adequate to lift the heaviest jobs? _____   _____

35. Are all the main lifting areas covered by craneways? _____   _____

36. Can forklift trucks be used with benefit in the
    warehouse and plant?   _____   _____

37. If forklift trucks are used, are a sufficient number
    and variety on hand?   _____   _____

38. When material is received, is it properly typed
    and routed?   _____   _____

39. Is material examined for conformance to
    specifications when received?   _____   _____

40. Does storage space throughout appear adequate? _____   _____

41. If materials must be moved from one machine to
    another, are they moved mechanically? If not,
    are they best moved manually?   _____   _____

42. Is scrap disposed of mechanically?   _____   _____

43. Are aisles clear, smoothly paved, and well
    lighted so that traffic can flow smoothly?   _____   _____

44. Are storage areas well lighted?   _____   _____

45. Are storages areas marked off into sections? _____   _____

46. If yes, are sections numbered or lettered
    for identification?   _____   _____

47. If yes, are records kept of what is stored in each
    area, so that parts and products can be
    located rapidly?   _____   _____

48. Are products stored in the most easily handled
    forms and in units in which they will be shipped? _____   _____

49. Are aisles wide enough to permit free movement
    of handling equipment?   _____   _____

50. Are storage areas located as close as possible
    to the production areas they serve?   _____   _____

51. Is there an adequate supply of fire extinguishers? _____ _____

52. Is warehouse space being utilized for storing
    materials that are outside the intended scope of
    storage? For example, is scrap being stored at
    substantial costs?   _____   _____

53. Are costly, long-carried items stored far from exits? _____   _____

Yes/No   Commentary

54. Is a burglary alarm system used for protection through all doors and through all windows?

55. Is there a regular schedule for cleaning the plant?

56. Does the person approving rates have a rate and routing guide covering incoming and outgoing items?

57. If yes, is the guide kept up to date?

58. If yes, is it adequate; that is, does it cover the usual raw material purchase and shipment of finished goods?

59. Are quantities checked to the proper receiving or shipping document?

60. Are the rates checked to the guide and shipping order?

61. Are the extensions checked?

62. Are bills paid within the specified time limit?

63. Are there controls such as to prevent duplicate payment of freight bills?

64. Are controls over payment of freight charges adequate but not excessive?

65. Have arrangements been made to utilize average demurrage agreement credits?

66. What corrective action has been taken to reduce demurrage expense?

67. Examine loss and damage claims and try to ascertain if there is a pattern for such claims. Can they be eliminated?

68. Are claims settled promptly?

69. Has the company used the services of an independent freight audit agency as a supplement to or instead of its own freight department?

70. Is inventory a significant company investment?

71. Can the quality of inventory management significantly affect the firm's earnings?

72. Are all material purchases delivered to central stores as opposed to direct delivery to production units?

Yes/No   Commentary

73. If yes, are the stores' records maintained by employees functionally independent of the storekeepers?   _____   _____

74. Is one person responsible for inventory management?   _____   _____

75. Is the gross inventory turnover known?   _____   _____

76. Are the turnover rates for the various inventory classes known?   _____   _____

77. If yes, do they appear reasonable as measured against industry standards, previously levels, and so forth?   _____   _____

78. Are perpetual inventory records maintained with respect to raw materials and supplies, work-in-process, and finished stock?   _____   _____

79. Are inventory records maintained on bins or in stock areas?   _____   _____

80. Are all inventory items ordered, stored, issued, and controlled on the same basis?   _____   _____

81. Are security measures that effectively control pilferage of expensive items in force?   _____   _____

82. Are material items properly identified by part number?   _____   _____

83. Are vendors' counts double-checked by the receiving department?   _____   _____

84. Does the company have adequate storage facilities?   _____   _____

85. Does the company carry varieties of stocks that lend themselves to standardization?   _____   _____

86. Is there any evidence of an excessive accumulation of material, that is, material awaiting repair, rework, or return to vendors?   _____   _____

87. Do inventory records appear to serve a useful purpose beyond accounting; for example, are they used for purchasing materials or for scheduling production?   _____   _____

88. Are perpetual inventory records checked by physical inventories at least once each year?   _____   _____

89. Is there written approval by a responsible employee of adjustments made to perpetual records based upon physical inventories? How much was the last adjustment? What was done about it?   _____   _____

	Yes/No	Commentary

90. Does the system include provision for periodic reporting to a responsible employee of slow-moving items, obsolete items, and over stock?

91. Are the following classes of inventories under accounting control: (a) consignments out, (b) materials in hand, of suppliers, processors, and so forth, (c) merchandise shipped on memorandum, (d) consignments in?

92. Is merchandise on hand that is not the property of the company (customers' merchandise, consignments in, and so forth) physically segregated, clearly marked, and under accounting control?

93. At year-end inventories, are adequate written instructions prepared for guidance of participating employees?

94. At year-end inventories, are the following steps checked on a sample basis: Quantity determinations, summarizations, additions, and summarizations of detailed sheets?

95. Are records kept for manufactured parts in subassemblies? Do the records appear justified?

96. Has the overall inventory been reconciled? For example:

Beginning inventory (at cost)		xxx
Purchases		xxx
Total available		xxx
Less sales (at cost)	xxx	
Less scrap (at cost)	xxx	(xxx)
Ending inventory		xxx

97. Has the effect of local personal property taxes been considered in the storage of inventory?

98. Does the company know the cost of maintaining inventory records (personnel, space data processing)?

99. If inventories vary substantially over the year, is a reporting form for insurance coverage used?

Exhibit 10.18 illustrates a method to reduce your inventory monthly. The purpose of the technique is to help reduce inventory carrying costs and maintain higher inventory turnover.

EXHIBIT 10.18   Quick Calculation of Inventory Targets

Inventory Class	How Determined (Annual Part Issues)	Last Year's Issues	Turnover Desired	Inventory Target	Actual	Excess
A	$5,000 and above	$4,745,936	4X	$1,186,484	$1,398,156	$ 211,672
B	$1,200–$5,499	1,405,864	3X	468,621	776,753	308,132
C	Below $1,200	827,518	2X	413,759	932,158	518,399
	Totals	$6,979,318	3X	$2,068,864	$3,107,067	$1,038,203

Note: One of the worst mistakes an executive can do is to arbitrarily set a specific inventory turnover as a target—without first calculating the proper level, based on the company's service level objectives.

INVENTORY RECORD ACCURACY ANALYSIS WORKSHEET

One way to get an overall idea of the impact of inventory value and inaccuracy is to utilize the following bits of data collected during and at the completion of the annual physical inventory. In doing any inventory calculations, use the FIFO, not year-end LIFO, inventory value.

Data Worksheet

Data Code	Explanation	Typical Data	Your Company
	Inventory Value		
A	Inventory investment (before physical inventory)	$3,107,018	_____
B	Book to physical net adjustment (last time taken)	($ 37,284)	_____
	Record Accuracy[a]		
C	Perpetual book and actual storeroom balances quantities are *within 10 percent* of each other	67%	_____
D	Perpetual book balances exceed *actual stock by more* than 10 percent	21%	_____
E	Actual stock quantities exceed *perpetual book balance* by *more* than 10 percent	12%	_____
	Total of C, D, and E	100%	100%
	Turnover		
F	Actual overall annual inventory turnover	2.246	_____
G	Desired overall annual inventory turnover[b]	3.218	_____
	Carrying Costs		
H	Company's current bank loan interest rate	10.0%	_____
I	Material handling, storage, insurance costs, and so forth	10.7%	_____
J	Total Inventory Carrying Costs	20.7%	_____

Data Code	Explanation	Typical Data	Your Company
	Purchases		
K	Annual Purchases—Production Materials	$6,979,316	_____
L	Annual Purchases—Miscellaneous Items	$1,369,637	_____
M	Total Purchases	$8,348,953	
	Tax and Profits		
N	Present Company Federal Income Tax Rate	42%	_____
O	Company profits last year	$615,000	_____

[a] Random sample permissible to obtain percentages.
[b] Obtain from company executives.

Then use the data obtained in the first step to estimate the impact on increasing company profits through better inventory control. This is accomplished using this calculation worksheet.

How to Estimate the Impact on Profits through Improved Inventory Control

Step 1: Begin by posting the data obtained from the Data Collection Worksheet.

1. Inventory investment (before physical inventory adjustments)   ($3,107,018)
   (Data A)

2. Physical inventory adjustment (plus or minus)   ($37,284)
   (Data B)

3. Subtotal (add or subtract lines 1 and 2) $3,069,734

4. Target inventory level

$$\frac{2,246}{\text{(Data F)}} \div \frac{3.218}{\text{(Data G)}} = .6979 \times \frac{\$3,197,018}{\text{(Data A)}} = \$2,168,388$$

5. Subtotal (subtract line 4 from 3) to obtain "Excessive Inventory" $ 901,346

Step 2: Determine the cost of inaccurate inventory records and excessive inventory.

11

PRODUCTION PLANNING
AND CONTROL

Production planning and control is the very essence of an operation. The purchase and use of materials, the movement and control of parts in operations, the warehousing and shipment of products to customers—these activities constitute the basic determinants of success in manufacturing. An effective production-planning-and-control function enables an organization to meet customer delivery requirements, maintain low inventories, and minimize production costs. And the core activity of production planning and control is forecasting.

Forecasting determines how much material will be purchased, stored, and processed, how large inventories will be, how well customer delivery commitments will be met, and how many people will be employed in operations. Forecasting of orders is the first activity of the production-planning-and-control systems, and its success—or lack of it—has made or broken the careers of many managers.

The most established procedure used to forecast orders is the weekly or monthly meeting between sales and operations managers. It is usually at these meetings that forecasts are made, based on sales expectations.

The problem with this method is universal; sales managers—invariably optimistic and concerned about satisfying customer commitments for fast delivery—almost always project greater sales levels than those which actually occur. The reason is that an optimistic outlook on sales will keep the plant producing at high enough levels to satisfy an increase in customer demand.

Of course, when the anticipated increase turns into a small trickle, the person held responsible won't be the sales manager. Inevitably, the manager will be blamed for high inventories and overstaffed shifts. Regardless of fancy platitudes, issued from above, concerning the responsibility of sales for issuing realistic forecasts, it will *always* be the job of management to hold down inventory and manpower costs in relation to sales. Unfair as that might be, that's the way it really is! So it behooves every manager to learn how to forecast realistically. One such method, and one I've come to admire for its relative precision, is called *cycle forecasting*.

CYCLE FORECASTING

Cycle forecasting, a technique developed almost 25 years ago by the Institute for Trend Research, recognizes that there will almost always be peaks and troughs in business orders, and that those peaks and troughs can be roughly predicted. Regardless of product or technology, cycles occur, and they appear to occur within all economic and political institutions.

Cycle forecasting predicts when those orders will expand and when they will contract. It is based on the fact that, throughout economic history, cycles have been artificially induced by businesspeople and consumers, either through their optimism or pessimism regarding the prevailing economic climate. Cycles occur, in other words, when people defer purchases because of fear, and later make those same purchases because of their belief that business conditions are improving. Exhibit 11.1 depicts cycle forecasting calculations.

In Exhibit 11.1, the plant has been using cycle forecasting for many years, to predict inventory and manpower requirements. Start by listing actual monthly order rates in dollars for several years. The next column, "Moving Annual Total," shows the current twelve-month total. As these numbers are accumulated, the total for current month is added and the total for the same month during last year is dropped. The moving annual total for January, 19X0, for example, was calculated this way:

Total for 1/X9:	$18.50 Million
Plus 1/X0 orders:	1.85 Million
Subtotal:	$20.35 Million
Less 1/X9 orders:	1.13 Million
Moving annual total—1/X0:	$19.22 Million

Finally, each current moving annual total is divided by the year-ago moving annual total, to derive the next column, (Order Level), as shown here for January, 19X1:

$$\text{1/X1 Order level} = \frac{\text{1/X1 Moving annual total}}{\text{1/X0 Moving annual total}}$$

$$\text{1/X1 Order level} = \frac{\$25.46 \text{ Million}}{\$19.22 \text{ Million}} \times 100 = 132.5\%$$

The order level tends to reduce the impact of seasonal variations and other factors affecting incoming orders such as order-processing delays. The resultant order level trend clearly illustrates basic changes in the ordering cycle alone. (See Exhibit 11.2.)

Compare actual orders for 19X1 with their corresponding order levels for the same months to see the differences. April and May, for example, show actual declines in the number of orders received, while their corresponding order levels are steadily increasing, signaling an upturn in the order cycle. This trend is verified by the higher number of actual orders received from September through December.

If the company had reduced its purchasing and manpower levels, based on decreasing incoming orders experienced in April and May, the plant would have been in poor

EXHIBIT 11.1   Cycle Forecasting Calculations

		Orders*	Moving Annual Total*	Order Level (%)
1980	J	1.13		
	F	1.42		
	M	1.66		
	A	1.46		
	M	1.50		
	J	1.68		
	J	1.58		
	A	1.39		
	S	1.66		
	O	1.57		
	N	1.64		
	D	1.81	18.50	
1990	J	1.85	19.22	
	F	2.03	19.83	
	M	2.49	20.66	
	A	2.06	21.26	
	M	2.03	21.79	
	J	2.11	22.22	
	J	1.94	22.58	
	A	1.91	23.10	
	S	1.95	23.39	
	O	2.44	24.26	
	N	2.12	24.74	
	D	2.50	25.43	
1991	J	1.88	25.46	132.5%
	F	2.59	26.02	131.2
	M	3.14	26.67	129.1
	A	2.91	27.52	129.4
	M	2.87	28.36	130.2
	J	2.95	29.20	131.4
	J	2.62	29.88	132.3
	A	2.60	30.57	132.3
	S	3.45	32.07	137.1
	O	2.90	32.53	134.1
	N	3.40	33.81	136.7
	D	3.38	34.69	136.4

Note: All numbers marked * expressed as millions of dollars.

EXHIBIT 11.2   Comparison of Open Orders and Order Levels

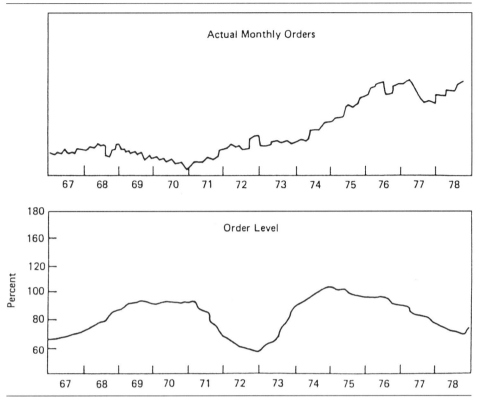

position to handle the larger influx of orders six months later. They could have failed to honor customer commitments, or they might have been forced to extend customer delivery dates while they built-up inventories and hired and trained additions to the workforce.

The Business Cycle

Cycle forecasting is predicated upon the inevitability of peaks and valleys in the business cycle. As seen in Exhibit 11.3, there are six distinct phases, each recognizable, and each possessing its own unique characteristics:

1. *Expansion.* This phase occurs during a period of optimism. It is recognizable by gains in employment, business increases, and a rapidly improving gross national product (GNP). Productivity increases and purchasing agents contract for additional orders.

2. *Maturity.* The end of the expansion period is marked by narrower gains on the chart for a period of approximately three months, and most gains thereafter are balanced by some downturns. The curve "flattens out." During this period

EXHIBIT 11.3   The Business Cycle

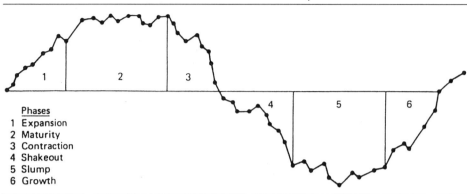

Phases
1 Expansion
2 Maturity
3 Contraction
4 Shakeout
5 Slump
6 Growth

employment and business activity remain high, demand triggers inflationary price increases, and plants are near full capacity.

3. *Contraction.* Three consecutive months of decline on the chart mark the start of a period of business contraction. Purchasing levels drop-off slightly, inventories increase, plants stop hiring people, overtime is drastically reduced, and businesses curtail capital improvement plans. Business, though, continues to be good, but not at the level of the preceding period.

4. *Shakeout.* When the order level drops below 100, and subsequent points on the chart continue to fall, the business cycle has reached its shakeout period. This phase is recognizable by plant layoffs, sales declines, inventory reductions, decreases in the prime rate, and a general sense of pessimism. Business plans are generally curtailed and unemployment levels begin climbing.

5. *Slump.* This is the roughest period of all; if business conditions are severe enough a depression ensues. Plant layoffs continue, employment rates begin to alarm the politicians, capital improvement plans are virtually nonexistent, and inventories continue to climb to discouraging levels.

6. *Growth.* Usually three successive points of growth on the chart signal the faint beginnings of a period of economic growth and recovery. Plant layoffs stop and some companies begin to slowly rehire skilled employees. Purchasing agents see the first glimmer of hope through small increases in buying levels. Inventories begin to decline and business makes new capital improvement plans. The GNP begins to rise.

A normal business cycle lasts about four years, with two-and-one-half years below 100. Obviously, the duration of a business cycle is influenced by a great many variables, such as whether the country is at war or peace, the strength of the dollar both home and abroad, the type of product being manufactured, and literally dozens of other factors. *The business cycle curve, therefore, must be individually interpreted by each company using its own product demand and in the context of its own situation.*

Use of the Business Cycle

The manager can use the business cycle curve to plan ahead. Listed below are typical actions that can be taken by the manager during each of the six phases of the business cycle:

1. *Expansion*

   Build or expand manufacturing facilities

   Install new machine tools

   Expand the labor force

   Build inventory

   Sub-contract work

   Write-off obsolete inventory losses

   Develop new vendors

   Start training programs

2. *Maturity*

   Sell surplus machinery

   Maintain—but not increase—inventories

   Freeze all expansion plans

   Freeze salaried hiring

   Develop plans for business downturn

   Plan to reduce subcontract work

   Get machinery in top condition

   Work overtime

3. *Contraction*

   Begin layoffs

   Start reducing inventories

   Stop training programs

   Reduce purchasing levels

   Establish tight budgets

   Avoid long-term purchasing contracts

   Reduce fixed costs wherever possible

   Begin cost-reduction program

   Stop all overtime

4. *Shakeout*

   Continue layoffs

   Continue reducing inventories

   Reduce purchasing levels further

Freeze capital improvement programs

Get tougher on customer returns

Reduce indirect labor activities

Reduce management deadwood

Combine functions

5. *Slump*

Stop layoffs. Hold onto skilled people

Consider eliminating a shift

Set tighter budgets

Make new expansion plans

Begin purchasing capital equipment

Keep cost reduction programs moving

Locate better vendors

6. *Growth*

Begin rehiring skilled employees

Build inventories

Move ahead with expansion plans

Place added purchasing orders

Prepare training programs

Hire new salaried employees

Introduce new products.

CONTROLLING OUTPUT THROUGH WORK MEASUREMENT

One of the most important decisions a manager will ever make concerns the selection of the work measurement system he will adopt to control output. Common to all is the proper use of a work measurement system to control and improve manufacturing output. Without such a system, output, at best, would be sporadic and, generally, inconsistent. A work measurement system, tailored to the individual organization, is what puts it all together.

Types of Work Measurement Systems

The predicament of the manager is this: Which work measurement system should be selected? The options are these:

1. No work measurement system;

2. Measured daywork;

3. Short-interval scheduling;

4. Incentive systems; and

5. Profit-sharing plans.

1. *No Work Measurement System.* The first option, "No work measurement system," isn't as ridiculous as it may appear to be at first sight. Many businesses have operated successfully without application of any work measurement at all, and some will continue to do so in the future.

In a business owned by the workers themselves (there are quite a few of these companies operating successfully), work measurement is generally not required, because all employees are motivated to produce high quantities of output. Obviously, their success is geared to high-production quantities and low costs, provided that sales demand remains high.

Companies that have low labor content in their products normally have production machinery available that set the work pace. Automated equipment, for example, where labor is used to load hoppers only, establishes how high production will be. The influence of operators on output for such machinery is minimal. Under this circumstance, work measurement will not pay for itself. Only 10 to 20 percent of manufacturing companies can sustain relatively high output without the use of some form of work measurement.

2. *Measured Daywork.* Under measured daywork, work standards are established for production operations, but no financial inducements are offered to operators to meet or exceed those standards. The attainment of work standards is left to the varying abilities—and interests—of individual foremen. With measured daywork, skillful supervisors can convince operators to meet established standards; other foremen either cannot or will not. If a foreman knows how to use the standards to increase the work measurement system, then chances are measured daywork will control and improve production output. That is not usually the case.

Measured daywork, however, is normally preferable to no work measurement system at all. It has demonstrated its ability, over the years, to increase output in the range of 20 to 60 percent; but it should be pointed out that many of its successes were attributable, in part, to methods improvements, which accompanied the installation of the measured daywork system.

3. *Short-Interval Scheduling.* Short-Interval Scheduling (SIS) is just as it sounds, scheduling short intervals (i.e., a day or less). SIS combines the best features of a measured daywork system with a proven control technique that sharpens the ability of foremen and managers to increase output. SIS is measured daywork at its best. It is highly recommended that any major application of measured daywork be implemented through the framework of SIS to achieve maximum savings.

4. *Incentive Systems.* For most production operations, incentive systems appear to offer the best chance for increasing labor performance, when compared with other work-measurement programs. The chief advantage of the incentive system is that it offers financial rewards for operators who achieve output above established work standards.

5. *Profit-Sharing Plans.* These plans enable all hourly people in manufacturing, both direct labor and indirect labor alike, to share the rewards of increased productivity. They are based on plant-wide productivity improvements. If a plant, for example,

had labor content equal to 30 percent of its cost of sales, and known productivity improvements resulted in a reduction of that labor content to 25 percent of its cost of sales, then both management and labor would participate in the profit gain.

The prime advantage of profit-sharing plans is that it includes all hourly employees in the plant, while management does not have to spend money needed to support an incentive system or measure daywork plan.

The basic detraction from this type of plan is that it does not usually produce output improvements anywhere in the range of incentive systems and, in fact, may not even have the savings potential of an effective measured daywork system.

In summary, listed below are the conditions favoring each type of work measurement system:

No Work Measurement System

1. Worker-owned business;

2. Mostly automated machinery;

3. Low labor content;

4. Strong desire for labor peace (assuming company is profitable); and

5. Management convinced (often wrongly) that administrative costs of work measurement exceed benefits.

Short-Interval Scheduling

1. High labor content;

2. Company losing money;

3. Large indirect labor force; and

4. Measured daywork system in place ineffective (or none being used).

Measured Daywork

1. High labor content;

2. Mostly machine-produced product;

3. Strong, well-trained foremen;

4. Strong interest of upper management;

5. Large indirect labor force; and

6. No work measurement system in place currently.

Incentive Systems

1. High labor content;

2. Well-trained industrial engineers;

3. Many manual operations;

4. Strong desire of management for extra production; and

5. Expressed desire of union and employees for incentive earnings.

Profit-Sharing Plans

1. Large indirect labor force;

2. Company unwilling to commit resources to support other work measurement systems, but needs to increase output; and

3. Management–employee–union spirit of cooperation very high.

CONTROL OF QUALITY

Quality today is the last frontier for profit improvement and cost reduction, and nowhere is this more so than in manufacturing. Improvements in manufacturing have focused on manpower reductions, tooling and methods improvements, incentive systems, materials requirement planning (MRP) programs, and a host of other approaches and programs designed to reduce costs and improve manufacturing profitability. But relatively little has been accomplished in the area of quality to achieve the same goals. While some progress has been made, the full potential of quality as a contributing factor to manufacturing success has not been realized. Effective quality techniques and controls can contribute both to improved profitability and repeat sales (through enhanced customer satisfaction).

To be successful, the quality program needs to encompass the following elements:

- A cost-of-quality reporting system that indicates the success (or failure) of the quality program.
- A thorough and ongoing and detailed evaluation of the quality system.
- A quality plan, which lists all improvements needed to upgrade quality, including objectives, responsible parties, and timetables.
- A company (or divisional) quality board to establish quality policy, and which concerns itself with major quality problems and opportunities.
- A successful vendor quality program.
- An effective production quality program.
- A responsive quality audit of outgoing products to customer (responsive in the sense that it is timely and evokes immediate corrective action of problems found).

Let's examine each of the above elements in some detail:

Cost of Quality

Cost of quality means exactly what it says—a detailing of all quality costs. (See Exhibit 11.4.) Unfortunately, in many organizations, many of the elements of the true cost picture are omitted. Some companies claim only scrap and rework costs, while others include cost of inspectors, and so on. To be properly inclusive, an effective cost-of-quality report should include the following elements:

1. *Warranty costs* are those costs that reflect failure of the product to perform its intended function (or those which displease the customer aesthetically). Included are those costs attributable to customer complaint investigations and of returned goods inspection, sorting, and testing.

2. *Scrap costs* are incurred when parts and materials are deemed to become totally worthless (disregarding scrap value) because of quality problems. Scrap costs should always include materials, labor, and overhead apportioned to the product.

3. *Rework costs* also include material, labor, and overhead that results when defective product is sorted, inspected, tested, and reworked to recover the parts or materials for usable inventory. This does *not* include costs billable to vendors for their quality errors.

4. *Appraisal costs* are those associated with inspecting the product to assume compliance with company specifications for purchased parts and materials, and finished product. Also included are costs to inspect the process and costs to determine vendor quality capability. Since both of these latter costs directly influence the quality of products, they are considered part of appraisal costs.

EXHIBIT 11.4   Cost of Quality—Division Level Performance

A. COQ Summary

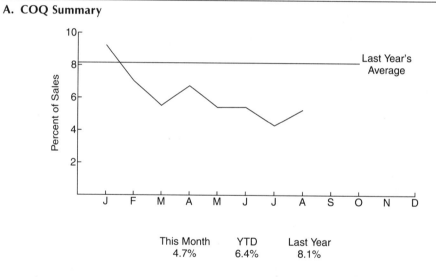

This Month	YTD	Last Year
4.7%	6.4%	8.1%

B. Major COQ Categories

COQ Category	Dollars		Percent	
	This Month	**YTD**	**This Month**	**YTD**
Warranty	$ 3,200	$ 45,600	.4	.4
Scrap	8,800	88,500	1.1	1.8
Rework	7,200	57,300	.9	1.3
Appraisal (Inspection)	14,400	160,950	1.8	2.1
Administration	3,120	26,910	.4	.6
Engineering support	805	14,025	.1	.2
Total COQ	$37,525	$393,285	4.7	6.4

5. *Administration costs* are essentially quality control budgetary costs less inspection labor. Typical administrative costs are salaries for quality control managers, foremen, technicians, and engineers, and support costs such as testing costs, gauging costs, calibration costs, and other miscellaneous costs reflected in the quality control budget.

6. *Engineering costs* are those costs incurred in both marketing and engineering to improve product quality. Typical engineering costs are:

Design reviews: These are costs incurred in the review of new products or major design changes of existing products to improve quality and eliminate quality problems prior to the release of product drawings.

Product qualification: This refers to costs incurred in the testing, pilot plant, and qualification of new products or for major changes in existing product lines.

Design changes: These costs occur when design changes are necessary to correct original design inadequacies.

Section "A", "COQ Summary" of Exhibit 11.4 shows COQ as a percent of sales. Since COQ numbers, by themselves, are absolute numbers, they are meaningless until related to some base figure such as sales. This is because a company with $100,000 quality costs and a sales base of $1 million has a COQ of 10 percent, while another company with $50,000 quality costs and a sales base of $250,000 has a 20 percent COQ.

The divisional COQ summary publishes statistics for the current month, YTD, and last year's average. The chart also illustrates monthly COQ readings and the COQ trend.

The next section, "COQ Categories," lists costs for all COQ categories and indicates what their percent of sales are for the current month and YTD. This refinement of COQ dollars shows where the "COQ dollars are." It helps managers to focus on meaningful categories for quality cost reduction.

The last section of the report "Highlights" indicates the major actions, improvements, and problems of the month. It is a good tool for quality control people to get their message across and get management's attention.

Quality is much more than designing, manufacturing, and servicing a product that meets company specifications. Ask any manufacturing manager. Quality, today, is the final frontier of reducing costs in manufacturing. Every other aspect of cost reduction has been approached: design, production, purchasing, inventory, manufacturing engineering, and production planning and control. What's left is quality. Quality has the potential to strip millions of dollars of costs given the right perspective, a good and effective operating plan, and aggressive execution. Although it is hard accurately to assess cost of quality for most companies that do not have an effective quality program, it is *not* unusual to see figures at 10 percent of the sales range. If a company sells $20 million, for instance, quality costs in an uncontrolled situation could *easily* be as high as $2 million. Quality costs, for many different reasons, remain undiscovered and unchallenged in the overwhelming number of manufacturing companies operating today.

Effective quality practices, then, have the potential of slashing manufacturing cost significantly. To be considered in this category, the manufacturing quality program must contain the following four elements:

1. A painstakingly thorough analysis of the capability (see Exhibit 11.5) of the manufacturing quality program, and a candid assessment of its effectiveness.

2. A quality plan that describes all of the fundamental techniques which must be adopted to improve the effectiveness of manufacturing quality.

3. Reporting systems capable of characterizing, on a timely basis, all of the strengths and weaknesses of the quality effort.

4. A responsive and timely quality audit of product being delivered from manufacturing into customer's hands—a tool that manufacturing management can use to launch a well-targeted quality-improvement program.

Analyzing the Quality System

The first step to be undertaken is an assessment of the capability of the quality function in manufacturing. This involves the answers to many detailed questions, along with evaluation of the effectiveness of the function. The evaluation takes the form of a rating technique, which allows manufacturing management to assess strengths and spot weaknesses. The rating technique is shown below:

Effectiveness Quartile	Points	Rating Explanation
85–100%	10	Highly effective
50–84%	6	Acceptable results
25–49%	3	Marginal results
Under 25%	0	Poor results

Notice that the ratings are based on *results;* this tends to rate the activity realistically rather than upon any apparent degree of sophistication.

The final results of the quality capability study shown in Exhibit 11.5 culminate in a numerical rating, which assesses the strength of the quality system. A review of the system's maximum points is given below (of course, the minimum point would be zero):

Function Evaluated	No. of Questions × 10 =	Maximum Points
Organization and Administration	4	40
Receiving Inspection	7	70
Operator Workmanship	8	80
Manufacturing Quality	15	150
Packing and Shipping	6	60
Gauge Control and Calibration	9	90
Warehousing and Delivery	8	80
Quality Reporting	8	80
Purchasing	6	60
Quality Planning	8	80
New Product Quality	5	50
Process Audit	6	60
Product Audit	10	100
Total	100	1,000

EXHIBIT 11.5   Quality Capability Survey

Organization and Administration
1. Is the quality organization organized properly to accomplish its objectives?
2. Is there a quality plan, and is it working?
3. Is there a quality manual that explains all techniques, practices, and procedures used by QC?
4. Are QC employees trained well, and do they know their jobs?

Receiving Inspection
5. Are product drawings used up-to-date?
6. Are all tests performed written in a procedures manual?
7. Are records maintained by vendor showing quality history for each?
8. Is there rapid feedback of rejected material to vendors via the purchasing department?
9. Is there evidence of vendors correcting quality problems?
10. Is rejected material segregated from accepted stock, and is it locked-up?
11. Are sample plans meaningful and easy-to-use by inspectors?

Operator Workmanship
12. Are production operators well trained in product quality techniques?
13. Do they sample-inspect their own production?
14. Do they have adequate gauges for measuring their own work?
15. Are there written inspection procedures and quality standards for operator use?
16. Are inspection results told to operators?
17. Is their performance adequately adjusted to improve quality at individual work stations?
18. Are operators who produce faulty work given additional guidance and counseling to improve their performances?
19. Does each operation have adequate process instructions and product drawings?

Manufacturing Quality
20. Are tests and inspections in the form of written instructions to inspectors?
21. Is first piece inspection practiced on operations where the setup of the machine determines the quality of the parts, such as metal stampings?
22. Is roving inspection used to gather quality data (as it should be) instead of control of operations?
23. Do all production batches funnel through a finished-batch-inspection station (tollgate)?
24. Are the inspections made sensitive and timely enough to detect shifts in the production process?
25. Is corrective action of substandard operations timely and effective?
26. Is defective material subjected to material board review prior to disposition?
27. Are production operators made aware of defective parts they have produced?
28. Are routine investigations made of recurrent defective parts and operations by QC?
29. Is defective material reworked by the same operator who produced the defective material?
30. Are inspection buy-off stamps used for accepted product?
31. Does the combination of operator and inspection sampling provide needed quality protection?
32. In assembly operations, is analysis made of defective parts, to determine which department (and operation) is the cause?
33. Are quality standards the same between fabrication, machining, and assembly operations?
34. Do inspections and tests simulate end-use of the assembled, finished product?

Packing and Shipping
35. Are written packing and shipping specifications available and used?
36. Are packing and shipping containers and methods adequate to prevent corrosion and damage?

(continued)

EXHIBIT 11.5   *(Continued)*

37. Are picked parts checked against master parts shipping list to assure correct parts and quantity shipment?
38. Are shipping cartons well identified to prevent mix-ups in deliveries?
39. Are all appropriate documents included with the shipment?
40. Is release to ship authorized by QC?

Gauge Control and Calibration
41. Are gauge masters traceable to the National Bureau of Standards?
42. Is there a written system for gauge control and calibration?
43. Are production gauges, as well as QC gauges, calibrated?
44. Are the frequencies of calibration adequate?
45. Are gauge calibration records maintained?
46. Are all gauges marked with the last date of calibration?
47. Are all new gauges calibrated before their use in production?
48. Are calibration tests conducted under the proper environment of temperature and humidity?
49. Are employee-owned and subcontractor gauges calibrated?

Warehousing and Delivery
50. Are handling methods for stock in place so that damages are minimized?
51. Are all parts bins and storage locations adequately marked to identify stored parts?
52. Are handling, storage, picking, and delivery operations specified in writing?
53. Are export packaging requirements identified?
54. Are receiving and shipping operations adequately separated to prevent mixes?
55. Is defective stock quarantined?
56. Is accepted stock under lock to prevent contamination, pilferage, and loss of control?
57. Is release to stock authorized by QC?

Quality Reporting
58. Is cost-of-quality information published on a timely basis, and does it identify all major costs?
59. Are performance reports (batch acceptance and sample percent defective) reported at all key operations?
60. Are quality records retained for sufficient lengths of time to satisfy all regulatory and company requirements?
61. Are quality reports used effectively for quality improvement?
62. Are records maintained in a protected area?
63. Are the results of inspections and tests recorded in a manner suitable for defect analysis?
64. Are scrap and rework data summarized and then used to reduce defect levels?
65. Are suitable summary reports prepared for top management, so they can monitor and control quality improvement?

Purchasing
66. Does purchasing have the latest drawing revisions to give to vendors?
67. Are vendors aware of the company's quality standards for purchased parts and materials?
68. Are quality standards included in purchasing contracts?
69. Do vendors submit their test results with shipments?
70. Are vendors promptly made aware of rejections?
71. Do vendors move quickly to correct their mistakes?

Quality Planning
72. Are written tests and inspection methods prepared for all new products and processes?

EXHIBIT 11.5 *(Continued)*

73. Does quality engineering plan the inspection stations in the manufacturing process, including location, sample technique and sizes, gauging, methodology, and reporting practices?
74. Does quality engineering review all new tooling in the plant to assure its ability to consistently produce acceptable products?
75. Is quality taken into account in work standards so operators can (a) sample their own output, and (b) recognize that incentive payments will not be made for defective product?
76. Does the paperwork process allow for traceability of defective work to individual operators and work stations?
77. Does quality engineering train inspectors, operators, and foremen in effective work habits aimed at producing a top-quality product?
78. Has quality engineering determined the best testing equipment and gauging to be used in product inspection?
79. Has quality engineering assured the availability of test and product specifications, visual standards, models, and samples?

New Product Quality
80. Are critical quality characteristics specified on engineering drawings?
81. Have quality standards and inspection requirements been planned for the new product, along with tooling and gauging?
82. Have potential quality problem areas been identified and corrected?
83. Are design reviews made sufficiently ahead of production to allow QC to adequately prepare for manufacturing quality requirements?
84. Are prototypes run in production so manufacturing and quality capability can be improved?

Process Audit
85. Are process audits made that evaluate the capability of the manufacturing process to provide a consistently high-quality product that meets company expectations?
86. Is this process audit conducted by people outside of the manufacturing organization to assure its impartiality?
87. Are the audits made at random so no preparation can be made by production people?
88. Are reports made to the functions that are in the best position to correct problems?
89. Is the corrective action timely and effective?
90. Are steady improvements being made?

Product Audit
91. Are audits made of completed and approved products ready for shipment?
92. Are the auditors apart from the regular QC organization to assure their impartiality?
93. Do field service and marketing people participate in the audit so the "view" is tilted toward customer acceptance?
94. Are prepared checklists made which list those quality characteristics wanted on machines by customers?
95. Are those characteristics weighted to show the differences among critical, major, and minor defects?
96. Is a final numerical rating achieved so that comparisons among audits and trends can be observed?
97. Do manufacturing people from diverse functions participate in the audit so they can learn the importance of quality?
98. When defects are discovered, are they quickly corrected in the manufacturing process?
99. Are these product audits summarized for management review?
100. Do all QC people rotate turns in conducting product audits so they can keep in touch with customer expectations?

Finally, total points are correlated to the following ratings:

Rating	Points
Highly effective	840–1,000
Acceptable	491–839
Marginal	251–490
Poor	0–250

The Quality Plan. To be really successful, a company just completing its quality system evaluation must identify its weaknesses and establish a plan to overcome them. Problems are identified, actions are specified, persons responsible for the actions are identified, and dates for completion of the actions are indicated. (See Exhibit 11.6.)

The quality plan should *always* have the blessing and support of top management if anything is to get done. This point is particularly relevant when it is recognized that manufacturing people alone cannot make all the needed improvements; engineering and marketing people are also involved.

The Quality Board. Any ongoing quality program needs direction. It is simply not enough to turn full responsibility for quality improvement over to the quality control manager; too many other people are involved. The quality control manager cannot design, manufacture, or sell and service the product. These jobs rightfully belong to engineering, manufacturing, and marketing. These are the people who have the primary influence upon quality and, consequently, they affect quality results the most. They must become involved.

EXHIBIT 11.6   Quality Plan

Problem	Action to Be Taken	Persons Responsible	Date for Completion
No identification of quality costs	Develop a COQ report	QC Manager	3/81
Inspectors are confused about relative seriousness of quality characteristics	Identify critical quality characteristics on engineering drawings	QC Supervisor and Engineering Manager	1/82
Excessive defective parts are escaping the machine shop	Improve sampling plans used by inspectors	Quality Engineer	6/81
There is no early warning of quality problems found by customers	Start a finished goods audit	QC Auditor	2/81

Each company or division of a company needs a quality board to direct the quality efforts of its people. The quality board should become involved with quality in the following areas:

Quality policy;

Quality improvement; and

Major quality problems.

The quality board, then, assumes the mantle of responsibility for the quality success of the company. Their job is to monitor major actions and results to assure the right things are done by the right people at the right time. It assures direct involvement in quality of every operating and support arm of the company.

The quality is very important to the manufacturing manager. There is a tendency in any manufacturing company to lay the total blame for poor quality on the doorstep of manufacturing. In almost every case that is not true. Sloppy design practices, misunderstandings between marketing people and customers regarding product needs, poor service—these and a host of other factors are directly attributable to engineering and marketing. The quality board provides an opportunity to objectively analyze quality problems and assign responsibility for corrective action to the right parties.

The quality board should generally have this composition:

General manager—Chairman

Quality control manager—Secretary

Operations manager

Engineering manager

Marketing manager

It is essential that the general manager assume responsibility for quality results by chairing the quality board. His leadership will also preclude the dominance of vested interests above actions best for the company.

Vendor Quality.   Experience shows this measurement is the simplest and best to use for evaluation of vendor quality. Other complex ratings have been developed by quality practitioners but tend to become so hard to understand that they lose their meaning. The use of acceptance rates, shown below, tells it all about vendor performance.

$$\text{Percent lot acceptance} = \frac{\text{No. of lots accepted}}{\text{No. of lots inspected}} \times 100$$

The control of vendor quality also demands some other activities:

1. Use of vendor history files to list lot acceptance rates by part numbers on dates received, rejections made, visits to and by vendors and listing of problems

discussed, actions taken by vendors to correct quality problems, and a summary of their effectiveness.

2. Insistence by *purchasing* people that vendors correct quality problems, that timetables be established for corrective action, and that vendors will be eliminated as a source of supply if quality doesn't improve.

3. Evaluation of new suppliers' quality capability and their full understanding of the company's quality requirements.

4. Fast correction of rejected quality parts by vendors, through rework of shipment of replacement parts.

Production Quality Program.   There are just a few basic ways that parts and materials can be inspected in processing. These are discussed below.

First-Piece Inspection. When the quality of the production run is dependent on the machine set-up, a first-piece inspection needs to be made. Almost any operation utilizing tools, dies, jigs, and fixtures needs a first-piece inspection. This type of inspection is usually best performed by a combination of set-up people *and* machine operators, the operators rechecking and verifying the adequacy of the set-up made by set-up people. Inspectors (quality control people) are best left out of this sequence, unless the first-piece inspection demands specialized testing equipment. Once production people come to depend upon inspectors to check set-ups, they will not pay as close attention to the job. If they are held responsible for set-ups, they will do a better job and higher quality will result.

Roving Inspections. Here, inspectors move from machine to machine during the production run, checking. When production is generating either very-high-quality or very-low-quality parts, this type of inspection is very effective. If quality is high there is no sense in using other more costly methods of inspection. Roving inspection is generally the least expensive method of inspection; a few inspectors can cover a lot of territory. If quality levels are very poor, roving inspection will quickly detect failures, and inspectors will then be able to quarantine defective lots. The high rejection rate assures that defects will be found.

Tollgate Inspection. For most operations, quality is neither very high nor very low; it falls somewhere in the middle. In this case inspectors, using the roving inspection method, are less likely to detect poor-quality parts. When this is the case, tollgate inspection is called for.

In tollgate inspection, all completed lots of parts are funnelled through a stationary inspection point at the end of each department. The product flow shown below illustrates tollgate inspection:

Grinding department	$\rightarrow$	Grind pins
		Tollgate
Milling department	$\rightarrow$	Mill slots in pins
		Tollgate
Polishing department	$\rightarrow$	Polish pins
		Tollgate
		Deliver to assembly dept.

Tollgate inspection is obviously most applicable to operations grouped together. For example, if all grinding machines are in one department, a tollgate inspection can follow grinding. If many different types of operations are combined in one production department, tollgate inspection will probably be placed after key operations. To have it follow, each and every operation would be too costly. For example:

Small parts department   →   Automatic chucker—Thread fitting
                               Chamfer machine—Chamfer fitting
                               Tapping machine—Tap
                               Tollgate
                               Deliver to assembly department

Automatic Inspection—In this type of inspection, equipment inspects parts. This method of inspection is the fastest and most reliable, but also the costliest. It is generally applied to high cost, tight-tolerance parts, where assembly operations are highly dependent on good parts.

Operator Inspection—It is *always* best to have operators check their own parts, whenever possible, using an established sampling plan. This is probably one of the best inspection methods. It assures the interest of operators in quality, and reduces the number of inspectors needed in operations. Operator inspection is generally used in partnership with either roving or tollgate inspection.

Finished Goods Audit. The finished goods audit is a final inspection of the product the way the customer sees it when he gets to use it. It's always conducted on product ready for shipment, and it is a reflection of (1) the quality level of products reaching customers, (2) the effectiveness of operations in building a high-quality product, and (3) the effectiveness of the quality organization in releasing only high-quality products for customers. The finished goods audit is composed of quality characteristics important to customers and, hopefully, those same quality characteristics which are inspected in processing. The finished good audit allows operations management the opportunity to preview quality problems customers will find, and gives operating personnel the opportunity to correct those problems before the finished goods warehouse is flooded with defective products.

Developing a Quality Plan. Once the capability of the quality system has been evaluated, the weaknesses of the function must be addressed to improve quality results. The plan prioritizes needed action, establishes key events, sets timetables, and shows specific individuals responsible for corrective action. (See Exhibit 11.7.) A quality plan can be made for almost any period of time, but, in the opinion of a great many users it should cover a period of two to three years, normally an optimum period. Anything shorter will probably not be inclusive enough to cover the many key events that need to happen. Anything longer is speculative. Too many things can change in four or five years; the planning of events that far down the road is vague, at best.

The Best Early-Warning System. Early-warning systems are designed to do just that—provide an indication of your product's outgoing quality level, as well as

EXHIBIT 11.7   Machining Subcontractor Quality Plan

Problem	Key Event	Date Completion	Responsibility
High in-plant failures of vendor material	Establish effective receiving inspection system	3/91	J. Barnes, Quality Engineer
High rejection rates in coils and bars	Implement a statistical Bar X & R program	5/91	M. Jones, Quality Engineer
Many false readings of inspection gauges resulting in rejection of acceptable coils	Train inspectors to read and handle testing gauges	6/91	P. Shore, Assistant Quality Manager
Management complaining about poor quality reports	Start improved quality reporting system	7/91	S. Pauley, Quality Control Manager

highlight current quality problems. In most cases it is months, and sometimes even years, before products reach customers' hands. If companies rely mostly on warranties and complaints to assess customer satisfaction, the pipeline between the plant and the customer might be clogged with products that have a multitude of defects, undiscovered by the factory, and inordinately costly in terms of repair costs and irritated customers.

Many firms conduct product audits to assess product quality levels, but few conduct them properly. They are seeking the best early-warning system to suit their particular needs but, for one reason or another, they fail to do the right things.

A well-designed product audit is the best method yet devised to provide early warning of outgoing quality levels and problems. To be successful, however, it should contain the following five elements:

1. Products must be selected randomly after they have been accepted by the line quality assurance organization and are ready for shipment to distributors or customers. The product audit is, after all, an indication of the effectiveness of the quality assurance organization as well as the operating effort.

2. The product auditor must be independent of the line quality assurance organization that accepts the product. Ideally, the product auditor should work directly for the general manager, but, in practice, that arrangement would be too cumbersome. Not enough direction would be provided by the general manager. He is too busy. There is nothing wrong with having the product auditor report directly to the top quality person in the organization. It is important, however, for him to be independent of the line quality assurance organization responsible for product buy-off and free from any pressure from it or from operating people.

3. The quality characteristics being rated during the product audit must be the same characteristics that are important to the customer. *This is an extremely critical point that is most often missed by the majority of early-warning systems.*

Most quality systems are geared to product specifications; acceptance is based on whether or not the product meets specifications. But the customer is totally indifferent to his supplier's internal specifications. What he wants is a product that functions properly, is aesthetically pleasing, and is safe to use. While product specifications are generally defined in terms of customer needs, that is not always the case. As products mature, they become subject to all sorts of compromises and modifications. Engineering changes, for example, are made to reduce costs. These changes may substitute materials that may not be acceptable to some customers; or part functions may be modified to accommodate manufacturing operations, and those changes might affect product function in customers' hands. All kinds of changes occur. Eventually, some product specifications become monsters on their own. They become self-perpetuating, with no consideration of their intended purpose—that is, to consistently produce customer satisfaction.

Quality characteristics for product audits, therefore, should be established *jointly* by quality assurance *and* marketing. Salesmen and servicemen, in particular, will be most sensitive to customer wishes and customer needs. Many times the listing of quality characteristics important to customers will come as a surprise to quality assurance people, simply because they have been trained to think in terms of specifications and, as we have come to see, specifications drift over a period of time. The exercise of establishing meaningful quality characteristics will generate positive changes in product specifications.

4. The quality characteristics should be rated as to their importance. There are four classifications of defects ranging from "very serious" to "incidental." Each class is assigned a weight in points, with the most points assigned to the most serious classification of defects. During the product audit each characteristic is evaluated and actual points are assigned. Should the product auditor decide to assign partial points to a 50-point characteristic, he can do so, provided that, in his judgment, some, but not all, of the quality characteristics have been attained. At the conclusion of the audit, standard points and actual points are totaled and divided to establish the rating.

5. Defects found during the product audit must be aggressively traced and eliminated. This is the most important segment of the audit. While it is relatively easy to reinspect the finished product for defects found in the audit, it is much more difficult—but more necessary and more rewarding—to eliminate the cause of defects. The constant recurrence of the same defects signals higher rework or scrap costs, more defective products finding its way to customers, and, most importantly, a discouraged and dispirited management team that becomes increasingly frustrated watching the same defects recur.

A product audit constructed with the elements just described will be a powerful tool for management to use to upgrade quality levels and assess the effectiveness or the organization. A smart management team will take full advantage of this early-warning system.

Points

100 Class A—Very Serious

1. Will surely cause an operating failure of the unit in service that cannot readily be corrected in the field.
2. Will surely cause intermittent operating trouble, difficult to locate in the field.
3. Will render unit totally unfit for service.
4. Is liable to cause personal injury or property damage under normal conditions of use.

50 Class B—Serious

1. Will probably cause an operating failure of the unit in service that cannot readily be corrected in the field.
2. Will surely cause an operating failure of the unit in service that can readily be corrected in the field.
3. Will surely cause trouble of a nature less serious than an operating failure, such as substandard performance.
4. Will surely involve increased maintenance or decreased life.
5. Will cause a major increase in installation effort by the customer or serviceman.
6. Has defects of appearance or finish that are extreme.

10 Class C—Minor

1. May cause an operating failure of the unit in service.
2. Is likely to cause trouble of a nature less serious than an operating failure, such as major degrees of substandard performance.
3. Is likely to involve increased maintenance or decreased life.
4. Will cause a minor increase in installation effort by the customer or serviceman.
5. Has major defects of appearance, finish, or workmanship.

1 Class D—Incidental

1. Will not affect operation, maintenance, or life of the unit in service (including minor deviations from engineering requirements).
2. Has minor defects of appearance, finish, or workmanship.

A quality control analysis is shown in Exhibit 11.8. If the analysis indicates several weaknesses, management should develop action plans based on priorities.

EXHIBIT 11.8   Quality Control

Action Focus	N/A	Strong	Satisfactory	Needs Some Improvement	Weak: Needs Major Improvement	Action Plan, Responsibility
Call customers to find out how your products are working						
Designate a quality control manager and hold accountable						
Measure cost of quality by component						
Emphasize prevention rather than appraisal						
Calculate rework expenses over time to determine trend						
Employ Quality Circles productively						
Try a "bragging session" to highlight success stories						
Reward superior suppliers of quality materials						
Train resources in quality improvement						
Use statistical sampling for inspection						
Establish upper control limits and exception reports for rejects						

EXHIBIT 11.9 Maintenance Labor Report—Week Ending 3/24

Craft	Number of Men	Total Hours Worked	Planned Hours Routine	PM	Unscheduled Hours	Earned Hours	Percent Labor Performance	Percent of Time on Standards
Machinists	10	430	205	40	185	220	89.8	60.0
General maintenance	6	210	180		30	190	105.6	85.7
Electricians	6	240	100	40	100	130	92.9	58.3
Pipefitters	4	130	60		70	50	83.3	46.2
Truck mechanics	2	80			80			
Total Department	28	1,090	545	80	465	580	92.8	57.3

CONTROL OF MAINTENANCE

The control of maintenance operations is essential to good plant performance. Reports designed to disclose all important aspects of maintenance are needed by operations managers, in order to stay on top of maintenance costs and performance. These reports are:

- Labor performance (see Exhibit 11.9);
- Schedules missed (see Exhibit 11.10);
- Craftsman performance (see Exhibit 11.11); and
- Machine maintenance costs (see Exhibits 11.12 and 11.13).

Labor Performance

Labor performance in maintenance operations is one of the most difficult of all operating jobs to achieve. The work is highly nonrepetitive, there is a good deal of judgment involved for most maintenance tasks, there is still a good deal of art involved in the application of crafts rather than science alone, and—last but not least—most maintenance workers consider themselves a cut above most plant workers and resent the intrusion of management-control systems in their work, similar to control systems the ordinary plant operator is exposed to.

EXHIBIT 11.10   Schedules Missed Report for Maintenance Work Orders—Week Ending 3/24

Work Order Number	Work Description	Planned Hours	Earned Hours	Percent Labor Performance
80-12	Repair 6″ drill press	50	40	80.0
80-28	Install monorail system	121	86	71.1
80-34	Rebush boring mill	168	122	72.6

EXHIBIT 11.11   Craftsman Performance Report—Week Ending 3/24

Craftsman Name	Current Week Performance				YTD Performance	
	Planned Hours	Earned Hours	Percent Labor Performance	Percent of Time Standards	Percent Labor Performance	Percent of Time Standards
Jones	32	30	93.8	80.0	91.7	51.5
Rawlins	18	16	88.9	45.0	90.5	46.7
Fanton	22	17	77.3	55.0	86.9	48.3

EXHIBIT 11.12   Maintenance Work Classification

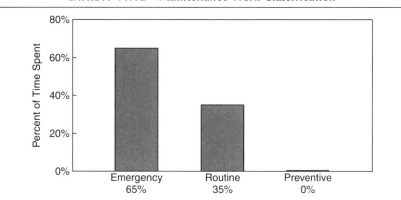

EXHIBIT 11.13   YTD Machine Maintenance Costs—Week Ending 3/24

Machine	Maintenance Labor Costs	Material Costs	Total Costs	Replacement Costs
Grinder #2R	$280.50	$ 6.75	$ 287.25	$12,500.00
Miller #3F	660.35	225.30	885.65	16,750.00
Tapper #4G	106.50	85.90	192.40	17,200.00
Reamer #7T	675.90	910.32	1,586.22	10,900.00

For all of these reasons alone, control is important. In fact, a maintenance organization exposed to the discipline of effective control techniques costs significantly less to operate when compared with an uncontrolled department. That is a matter of record.

The first two columns of the weekly report shown in Exhibit 11.9 indicate the type of craft and the number of people in each craft, while the third column lists the hours each craft and the entire department worked during the week.

The next two columns show just how many of these hours worked were spent on planned activities for both routine and preventive maintenance (PM). Planned activities, in hours, are those activities planned ahead of time by maintenance supervisors, to which work standards have been applied.

The next column, Unscheduled, reflects those hours spent on emergency and unplanned maintenance work. Adding this column to the two previous columns under "Planned Hours" results in the hours listed in the "Total Hours Worked" column.

Earned Hours, the next column, shows hours earned on work standards. The next column, Percent Labor Performance, is derived by dividing earned hours by planned hours, as follows:

$$\text{Percent labor performance} = \frac{\text{Earned hours}}{\text{Routine + PM hours}} \times 100$$

The final column shows how much time was actually spent on hours being measured by work standards. Since hours on work standards is equivalent to planned hours, time on standards is derived like this:

$$\text{Percent of time on standards} = \frac{\text{Routine} + \text{PM hours}}{\text{Total hours worked}} \times 100$$

Notice that only 57.3 percent of all maintenance time was spent on planned work with work standards. This is not unusual. The object, of course, is to approach 100 percent, but it will never quite be reached, because the nature of maintenance work is that emergencies will always occur, and that emergency work is unplanned and essentially hard to measure for work standards.

Returning to labor performance, it can be stated that 92.8 percent for the entire department is a respectable performance, and that an examination of labor performance for individual crafts does not reveal any exceptionally poor performances, although the 83.3 percent performance of the pipefitters, and 89.8 percent performance for machinists can certainly be improved.

Schedules Missed

Analysis of the maintenance labor report is likely to indicate areas of performance, which management will want to examine closely.

This report automatically prints out those work orders whose earned labor performance falls below a stated percentage. Management selected 90 percent as the lowest percentage it considers acceptable performance. Any work order performance level slipping below that point is programmed to be displayed automatically on a computer report.

The schedules missed report describes work order performance as contrasted with the maintenance labor report, which describes labor performance by craft. Between the two, maintenance management is given sufficient information to detect weak spots, make corrections, and control overall performance. Both reports, then, attack collective labor performance from different angles.

The schedules missed report starts with a listing of the delinquent work order numbers and a description of the tasks contained in the work orders. It then goes on to list planned hours, earned hours, and percent labor performance, as shown in the maintenance labor report.

Craftsman Performance

While the maintenance labor performance report and the schedules missed report focus on overall work order and departmental labor performance, the craftsman performance report details individual craftsman performance.

The left-hand column lists each craftsman's name, and the following columns calculate his labor performance and percent of time on standards for both the current week and year-to-date (YTD). This report shows maintenance supervisors which craftsmen need additional training and direction. The YTD columns allow supervisors to track individual performance over the course of the year. Craftsman Ferguson, for example, had a labor performance of 77.3 percent for the current week and is only at 86.9 percent for the current year—a poor performance.

Machine Maintenance Costs

Machine maintenance costs report is seen in Exhibit 11.13. This report shows how much it costs to maintain individual pieces of production (or support) machinery. The columns of the report show, from left to right, machine, labor costs, materials costs, total costs, and replacement costs. By comparing total costs with replacement costs, manufacturing and maintenance managers can determine when the purchase of new machinery is more economical than repairing existing machinery.

This report also helps managers spot developing problems in machinery. It helps managers recognize the principle that, when maintenance costs increase, so does machine downtime, and that maintenance costs can be reduced significantly when machinery failures are minimized. Smart maintenance managers recognize that a thorough preventive-maintenance operation on production machinery, coupled with the replacement of parts that exhibit high failure rates, are the prime ingredients in the reduction of machinery maintenance costs.

How One Company Saved 30 Percent by Installing a Maintenance Work Classification System

A service center in New England classifies all maintenance work in one of the following categories:

- *Emergency.* Work needed to immediately restore production such as machine breakdown, loss of air supply, or electrical failure. This category of maintenance receives preference over the other described below.

- *Routine.* Work needed to improve the functional characteristics of a working piece of equipment. A slitter, for example, currently producing at 60 percent efficiency can be scheduled for upgrading to increase its efficiency rating to 80 percent. This type of maintenance work can be scheduled to repair at the convenience of both production and maintenance people.

- *Preventive.* Service of machines and equipment before they need repairs. Preventive maintenance aims to increase equipment uptime through scheduled, periodic servicing including adjustments, lubrications and overhauling.

The company at one time had an uncontrolled maintenance function. Early analysis of the amount of time spent on each of the three categories of maintenance revealed, graphically, what is shown in Exhibit 11.12.

The company soon installed a maintenance work order system coupled with effective time estimating of work to be done by craft, Gantt chart scheduling of longer-term maintenance work, and training for crafts members in these techniques. The results,

EXHIBIT 11.14   Maintenance Results—Two Years Later

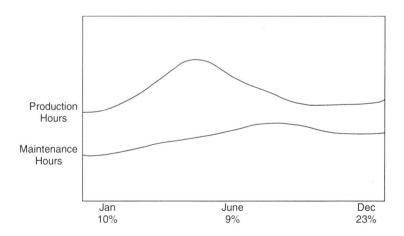

within a period of two years, are displayed in Exhibit 11.14. Their estimated savings in dollars by craft exceeded 30 percent for total maintenance dollars. Dollars expended were reduced by $275,000 per year.

Measuring Maintenance Effectiveness with
Three Control Charts

It is not enough simply to install effective disciplines within the maintenance activity. Controls must be established to monitor progress. A company in the Midwest uses the following controls to maintain the large savings in labor it achieved.

1. *Maintenance hours as a percent of production hours.*

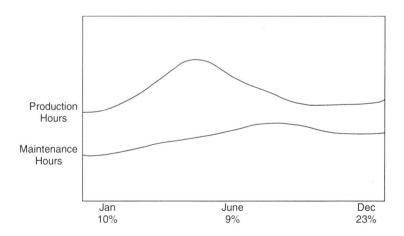

In this case, maintenance hours showed an unfavorable trend. Not enough dollars were shaved from the maintenance budget to keep in pace with the downturn in production hours beginning mid-year.

2. *Total maintenance dollars as a percent of cost-of-sales.*

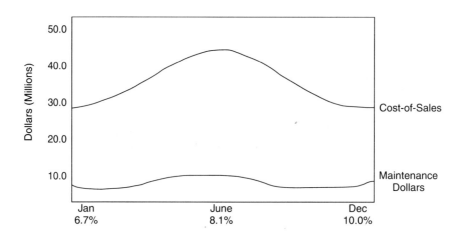

Here, too, the trend is up, although the total percentage average (about 8 percent) is considerably below the prior year's performance of 12 percent. Again, industry or regional averages are not really significant. What counts is *improvement*. So long as a company's maintenance department's control indicators are constantly improving, criticisms cannot be leveled.

3. *Maintenance supply costs as a percent of total maintenance dollars.*

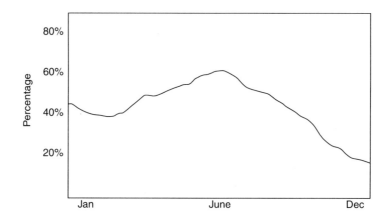

Here, a steady and noticeable trend is evident. Maintenance management exercised good control over the expenditure of maintenance supply costs.

Exhibit 11.15 on pages 222–223 is a maintenance checklist.

COST-SAVING MEASURES FOR CONSERVING ENERGY

This section presents some important fundamentals, pointing out places to look for conservation opportunities, showing how to set up an energy-conservation program, and examining alternate sources of energy, all the while keeping an eye on the bottom line. While delving into the particulars of these topics, you are advised to keep some basic truths in mind.

- *Conservation* is the most powerful tool. Almost every manufacturing plant abounds with opportunities to reduce energy consumption without switching fuels, and without making major changes in equipment or process.
- Oil and gas are fuels of *convenience,* and when the price of the convenience exceeds its value there should be no hesitation to replace them.
- Energy problems have not changed the *rules* of economics, only the numbers. Equipment additions that will cut the use of energy must still be economically justified and proposed operating changes must be shown to enhance, not reduce profitability.

Plant buildings may house offices, laboratories, warehouses, and production operations. Heating will usually be required in the winter months and, for some of the building space, air conditioning in the summer. Look for energy-conservation opportunities in the following key areas.

How to Stop Unwanted Air Movement

Reduce the infiltration of outside air (or flows between parts of a building) by following the four steps:

1. Applying caulking and weatherstripping to holes in the building walls and to poorly sealed windows and doors. Look for holes around window and door frames, and where pipes and conduit pass through walls.
2. Installing strip curtains in doorways and wall openings, such as those for a conveyor, which must be left open for traffic but, at the same time, allow unwanted air currents to move. The strip curtains will part to allow personnel and objects to pass, but close up again as soon as they are through.
3. Sealing off doorways in plant areas that must handle frequent traffic by installing impact doors consisting of two flexible sections, each covering half of the opening. The sections part when contacted by a moving object, such as a lift truck, automatically resealing after it passes.
4. Installing dock seals and shelters at the warehouse loading docks. They consist of blocks of flexible foam insulation covered with a resistant fabric, and placed on the outside wall of the dock in an inverted U at the dock opening. The truck

EXHIBIT 11.15 Maintenance Checklist

Action Focus	N/A	Strong	Satisfactory	Needs Some Improvement	Weak: Needs Major Improvement	Action Plan, Responsibility
Categorize productive versus nonproductive hours						
Check maintenance assignments and degree of supervision						
Improve workload identification, measurement, management						
Use planning, scheduling, and control techniques (e.g., PERT/CPM)						
Increase accuracy/timeliness of maintenance information						
Increase Engineering's role in plant planning, installation						
Investigate pros and cons of contract maintenance						
Perform major maintenance at regular intervals						
Teach production workers simple preventive maintenance						
Establish standard times and costs for routine repairs						
Take appropriate action on major cost variances						
Emphasize preventive maintenance philosophy at all levels						
List machines that shut down key parts of production						
Use colored tags to mark equipment needing repair or service						
Recharge batteries on vehicles such as materials handlers, etc.						
Combine and/or consolidate vehicle delivery routes						
Place computer equipment away from open windows (sunlight, dirt, temperature, humidity changes)						
Keep computers away from electrical machinery to prevent interference						
Cover printers, consoles, floppy disks, personal computers, etc.						
Enforce no smoking rules in computer centers						

222

						Install anti-static mats; spray carpeting
						Periodically clean read/write heads with special diskettes
						Put printing elements (including daisy wheels) into cases
						Clean print wheels, chains, and platens periodically
						Use nonabrasive solutions and lint-free cloths on terminal screens and keyboards
						Maintain floppy disks in envelopes and avoid writing on them
						Keep staples, paper clips off disks to keep from demagnetizing
						Identify equipment with high price tags
						Report on machine conditions at shift end
						Condense maintenance list and post at selected machines
						Ensure that vehicles are serviced at or better than prescribed intervals
						Use mobile repair kits (bicycles, etc.)
						Employ activity analysis and auditing
						Standardize and document maintenance instructions
						Provide pocket pagers or walkie-talkie devices to summon personnel quickly
						Fit machinery with attachments to record running time cumulatively
						Have operators record problems on special forms at the machinery
						Consider reconditioning used equipment
						Sell obsolete machines to scrap dealers
						Remind operators of machine cost, use a sign showing replacement value
						Have Engineering approve or originate design specs for buildings and equipment
						Request a formal work order to improve planning and chargebacks
						Examine "backlog report" for critical items to be expedited
						Perform periodic safety checks

is backed up to the dock so that the edges of its sidewalls and roof contact the blocks, sealing off air flow from the outside while the truck is being unloaded.

Techniques for Blocking Solar Radiation

When buildings must be kept as cool as possible by natural means, or when they require expensive energy for air conditioning, use these five techniques to reduce the heat load imposed by incident sunlight:

1. Change the color of exterior surfaces exposed to sunlight. Light colors reflect more of the sun's radiation, with aluminum and white-colored surfaces reflecting most of all. One building owner in the Southwest found that the use of white roof gravel would reduce absorbed heat from sunlight by 42 percent.

2. Be sure that windows are provided with shades or blinds, that their reflecting surfaces are kept clean, and that they are used.

3. Provide exterior shading of walls and windows with awnings, canopies, overhangs, and plantings.

4. Install reflective or tinted glass in windows, to reflect incident sunlight or to block those wavelengths that produce the greatest heating effect.

5. For larger buildings, adjust the responses of heating and cooling systems to the variation in loads in different parts of the building. As the sun moves through the sky in a normal workday, various parts of the building receive different amounts of solar heat. People working in the north end of the building may complain, winter and summer, that they are "always cold"; those on the south side may have just the opposite complaint. Concentrations of people and the activities they perform may vary in different parts of the building at different times of the day. The solutions can be as simple as putting separate zone controls in those parts of the heating and cooling systems, serving various parts of the building and as sophisticated as installing entirely new control systems operated by computers, which constantly monitor changing conditions and direct the most economical response to them.

Tips for Using Solar Radiation

In those areas, and at those times of the year when heating loads are the most important energy consumers, the sun's energy can be used in these ways to help carry the loads:

1. Reverse as many as practicable of the techniques mentioned above to block solar radiation—use darker exterior colors, remove exterior and interior shading of windows and doorways.

2. Install skylights, so that sunlight can help with the lighting load. A refinement is to add light-sensitive dimmer switches to the artificial lighting controls, so that

they contribute more light when the sunlight is weak and less when it is strong, maintaining a constant level of light in the illuminated areas.

3. More elaborate passive-solar-heating systems can be installed. Their fundamental components are (a) an unoccupied area of the building, (b) a large roof or wall section fitted with glass or other transparent material through which the sun's rays can pass to heat the air in the unoccupied section creating a "greenhouse effect," and (c) a means of circulating the air thus warmed to the occupied sections of the building. Control systems can be as simple or as complex as desired.

How to Reduce Conduction/Convection Losses

The object here is to cut down the losses or gains of heat through walls, roofs, and floors—the "building envelope"—primarily through the use of insulation.

1. *Roofs.* The upsurge in fuel costs which occurred in the early 1970s have caused building designers to take a more careful look at the amount of roof insulation provided. One owner of an industrial building complex built on the U.S. Gulf Coast found that, by increasing the standard one inch of roof insulation to three inches, he could cut heat gain or loss by 20 percent, and thus achieve the best balance between additional construction cost and fuel savings.

2. *Walls and floors.* Uninsulated concrete floors laid on ground can be expected to have a heat loss of about 2 BTU per hour per square foot, assuming room temperature at 70°F and the ground at a constant 50°F. Uninsulated brick and concrete walls exposed to outside temperatures down to 0°F can be expected to lose 15 BTU per hour per square foot; insulation thicknesses of $1\frac{1}{2}$ inches, once considered adequate for industrial buildings, have been increased in some cases to two or three times that amount, depending upon the cost of fuel, and the severity of the climate.

3. *Windows.* Ordinary window glass comes in thicknesses of $\frac{1}{16}$ or $\frac{1}{8}$ inch. Even if the thermal conductivities of glass and building brick are roughly the same, a $\frac{1}{8}$-inch thickness of glass will conduct 96 times as much heat as the same area of a 12-inch brick wall. That is why many newer industrial buildings (especially if they are conditioned) are designed without any windows at all. "Double glazed" or *thermal pane* windows, which consist of two (sometimes three) sheets of glass separated by dead air space, can be used (when the building must have windows) to reduce heat loss or gain, but their high cost has tended to limit industrial applications.

4. *Ceiling height.* In buildings (particularly older ones) with high ceilings, a great deal of energy can be wasted in heating successive layers of warm air, which rise to the ceiling, until they fill the air space down to the level at which personnel are comfortable. One way to avoid this loss is to install a false ceiling at normal room height, cutting off the space above from the flow of air. If this cannot be done for some reason, another solution is to install fans in the upper air space to direct the warm air back to the lower levels.

Lighting Conservation Measures

Look for energy savings in these areas:

1. *Reduced illumination.* Do you really need all that light? One company found that it could reduce the "normal" standard of illumination of 100 foot candles to 70, without interfering with worker effectiveness; it also provided three levels of lighting in office and general work areas, and added "task lighting" at specific work stations. The drop from 100 to 70 foot candles resulted in a reduction of 30 percent in energy consumption.

2. *Fluorescent lighting.* Fluorescent lamps will provide the same illumination as incandescent types, for about one-third of the energy consumption.

3. *Windows.* Ordinary window glass comes in thicknesses of $\frac{1}{16}$ or $\frac{1}{8}$ inch. Even if the thermal conductivities of glass and building brick are roughly the same, a $\frac{1}{8}$ inch thickness of glass will conduct 96 times as much heat as the same area of a 12 inch brick wall.

4. *Heat from lights.* In buildings that have extensive lighting systems, advantage can be taken of the heat given off by the lamps. Blowers are set up to move air across the banks of lights, and the air thus warmed is distributed for space heating. Economies are realized, not only in the reduction of heat that must be supplied from other sources, but also in the prolonged life of the lamps, which results from their operation at lower temperatures. In the cooling season, this warm air is diverted to the exterior of the building, reducing the load on the air conditioning system.

Three Ways to Save Energy with Heating and Cooling Systems

Here are three ways you can work with the system you have to save energy:

1. Adjust temperature settings in unoccupied spaces. There will be a number of areas of the plant not occupied at all during some parts of a 24-hour day, or occupied only sparsely and intermittently. Heat control settings should be lowered and cooling control settings raised in such areas, and automatic controls are usually the cheapest method of adjustment. Of course, nothing beats shutting them down altogether—there is no greater energy saving than zero consumption—but the savings must be compared with the costs of wear and tear caused by frequent start-ups and the extra energy required to bring the space back to its normal controlled temperature.

2. Lower control settings in winter, raise them in summer. In times of energy shortages, Americans are asked to heat occupied buildings only to 68°F, and cool them to 78°F. While these temperatures may not be comfortable for everyone, you can set up a test program, to see how closely these settings can be approximated without an undue number of complaints.

3. Establish adjustment and preventive-maintenance programs. Make sure that fuel–air ratios, dampers, vanes, and valves are properly adjusted on a regular basis; that heat exchange surfaces are cleaned; and that filters and belts are replaced or adjusted.

Energy Savings in Plant Operations

Steam generation and distribution: Conservation in the steam system starts with the question: How much of the energy paid for in the purchased fuel is lost? Look for ways to recover it in the answers to the following questions.

- How much energy is going up the stack?
- How much energy is lost in steam leaks and malfunctioning steam traps?
- How completely used is the steam you generate?
- How much energy is lost through poor insulation?

Electrical system: Most plant managers are not building new plants and must address the problem of conserving electrical energy in an existing installation. The first and probably most remunerative action to take is to look at is the plant *power factor,* which is the ratio of the electric power company.

Plant processes: No matter what industry your plant is a part of, it probably has its own literature—books, trade magazines, and technical journals. Your technical staff should review the literature for energy-conservation ideas specific to your industry. At the same time, here are some general lines of attack that can be pursued in most plants.

1. *Don't throw away energy you have already paid for.* Too often a hot process stream at the end of the production process is cooled with water or air, and its heat rejected to the atmosphere. With heat-exchange equipment, this energy can be recovered and used profitably, e.g., to preheat cold feed streams or provide hot water for various purposes. And, don't forget that heat can be reclaimed from hot solid products, as well as from fluids—usually by air (or other gas) streams which, when warmed, can be fed to furnaces and burners, cutting their energy consumption, or for space heating. The same idea applies to energy in the form of pressure; one plant, which operates a large air compressor for process use, achieved flow control by blowing off some of the compressed air to the atmosphere. As part of an energy-conservation program, it connected the compressor vent to the plant's utility air system, allowing it to shut down completely that system's smaller compressor, and found a process use for the remaining vented air. In the first year alone, cost savings were four times the capital costs incurred in making the necessary changes.

2. *Keep heat-transfer surfaces clean.* Process streams can deposit undissolved solids on heat-exchanger surfaces by a silting process, or dissolved materials can precipitate on them, along with decomposition products. More efficient use of these heat-transfer surfaces may be achieved by more thorough cleaning of the stream before it starts through the process, or, if the product can tolerate it, addition of antifouling chemicals to resist deposition on heat-transfer surfaces. If neither of these works, periodic shutdowns to permit physical scraping and brushing may be necessary. If one of the heat-transfer surfaces consists of fins exposed to the air, they should be periodically washed or blown to remove dust and grease accumulations.

3. *Consider energy consumption when purchasing new process equipment.* Makers of industrial equipment have been giving more attention to the energy efficiency of their products since the high-priced energy era began. Request energy-consumption information from the manufacturer whose equipment you are considering, and include energy usage per unit of output in the purchasing decision.

4. *Look for energy-saving opportunities in the way process and utility flow streams are controlled.* Prior to the arrival of expensive energy, industrial practice was to pump liquids and gases at higher pressure than needed, and insert a throttling valve in the line to reduce flows to desired levels. Although not as obvious to the naked eye as a stream leak blowing to the atmosphere, throttling valves waste energy by converting it to heat, which is dissipated in the flow stream or lost to the atmosphere. One way to reduce these losses is to install variable-speed motors on the pumps and blowers in the system, whose output can then be adjusted to changing flow demands, reducing the need for throttling. For an elaboration on this and other ideas for saving process system energy, see F. G. Shinskey, *Control Systems That Save Energy,* in Elias P. Gyftopoulos and Karen C. Cohen, eds., *Industrial Energy Conservation Manuals: No. 2,* (Cambridge, MA: MIT Press, 1982).

Heat pumps: Under favorable conditions, the heat pump can deliver four times as much energy as it absorbs in running the compressor, which makes it an attractive energy-conservation device. In the winter mode, however, when it absorbs heat from the outside air, its efficiency drops off rapidly if the outside temperature falls below freezing. An ideal situation for the heat pump exists when a large supply of noncorrosive underground water is available (which will have a steady temperature close to 50°F) for the external heat exchanger. Then the working fluids can reject heat to the water (summer) or absorb heat from it (winter) at good efficiencies.

Although heat pump systems have been designed and built since the 1930s, they did not come into widespread use until the era of high energy prices, and their application has been mostly for residential and commercial space heating and cooling. Some industrial applications have been reported in low-level heating processes, and in distillation and evaporation.

Switching fuels: A recent U.S. Department of Energy survey found that 70 percent of large industrial boilers in the United States were capable of burning more than one fuel, and the most popular combination was the ability to burn natural gas or fuel oil.

Natural gas is the most widely used industrial boiler fuel, because it is clean-burning, requires the least operator attention, and the least capital investment in burning equipment. However, industrial users may find that for economic reasons or through a requirement of the gas supplier, they must contract for gas on an "interruptible" basis. This means that, during periods of peak demand, the gas company may require industrial users to stop using it, forcing plants either to shut down or switch to an alternative fuel.

For boilers capable of using only natural gas, the addition of an alternative fuel is easiest when the new fuel is oil. Although gas-only and oil-only boilers are built somewhat differently, the design parameters are usually within 20 percent, and only minor modifications to the internal structure of the boiler are needed as the alternative burning equipment is added. But the process is not entirely without complications: Fuel oil tanks will need to be installed; soot blowers may need to be installed to remove ash deposits from the boiler tubes; and the smokestack may need to be lengthened to reduce the air pollution effects at ground level.

Converting a gas boiler to use coal as an alternate fuel is a much more difficult problem. Here the design parameters vary by 50 percent, and extensive changes to the furnace and the boiler tubes will be required. Installation of a soot blower will be mandatory. Before proceeding very far with such a project, a thorough study should be undertaken by a competent engineering group; they may ultimately recommend installing a second coal-fired boiler alongside the gas boiler, rather than trying to modify it. Another possibility would be to consider a coal-water slurry as the fuel, rather than dry coal; conversion to this fuel might involve much less modification of the original boiler.

How to Set Up a Successful Energy-Conservation Program

By looking back through this chapter, you can see that energy conservation is (1) an *engineering* problem that involves replacing and redesigning equipment; (2) a *maintenance* problem, in keeping insulation, steam systems and other possible energy-loss sources in good repair; (3) an *operating* problem, requiring energy-conservation discipline among the people who throw the switches and open the valves that control energy flow; (4) a *cost* problem, because so much capital and operating expense is involved; and (5) a *management* problem, because all these elements must be combined into a coordinated effort to achieve visible results.

Five Steps to Take in Beginning Your Program. These are the five basic steps to take in setting up an energy-conservation program.

Step 1: Make an energy survey of the plant. (See Exhibit 11.16.) This step readily breaks down in two phases. Phase One will consist of a physical inspection of the plant and an examination of its records to answer the following kinds of questions:

- How much energy is being used?
- What kinds of energy are consumed?
- Where in the plant is it being consumed?
- Are there leaks, sloppy operating practices, or other energy-losing situations readily observable?

Phase Two consists of examining the information obtained in Phase One to answer these questions:

- Which units are operating at the lowest levels of efficiency and, therefore, offer the greatest opportunities for energy conservation?

EXHIBIT 11.16   Energy-Saving Survey

Department _____   Surveyed by _____   Date of Survey _____

Fuel Gas or Oil Leaks	Steam Leaks	Compressed Air Leaks	Condensate Leaks	Water Leaks	Damaged or Lacking Insulation	Excess Lighting	Excess Utility Usage	Equipment Running and Not Needed	Burners Out of Adjustment	Leaks of or Excess of HVAC	Location	Date Corrected

- Are there cost saving or security of supply benefits to be obtained by changing or adding to the types of energy purchased by the plant?
- What additional electric meters, steam flow meters, and other types of instrumentation must the plant install to be able to measure the effects of energy-conservation measures?

Step 2: Identify capital projects that will improve the plant's energy position. Typical projects would include (1) modification of existing equipment, such as adapting boilers to use alternate fuel; (b) replacement, such as retiring production equipment that may be still operable, but is obsolete in terms of energy consumption; and (c) installing new equipment, such as heat exchangers and electric capacitors, to make more efficient use of energy. (See Exhibit 11.17.)

Step 3: Identify operating changes. These are the measures that can be taken without changes to plant equipment, and might include shutting down certain energy-consuming units for part of the day, operating equipment at lower temperatures and pressures, and modifying operating procedures and rules, so that a higher degree of energy conservation discipline is actually obtained. (See Exhibit 11.18 on pages 234–239.)

Step 4: Establish goals for energy improvement. Steps 1 through 3 provide the tools for making things happen to improve the plant's energy situation. Now it is up to management to establish the goals which the program is expected to accomplish. They must be expressed in clear, measurable terms (preferably units of energy consumption), have a stated time period for accomplishment, and be realistic—too difficult, and a sense of frustration will set in; too easy, and no one will be motivated to work very hard.

Step 5: Train and motivate plant personnel at all levels. Everyone in the plant must understand what it is you are trying to accomplish, why you are conducting the program, and what it means to them to contribute all they can, if the program is to be successful.

How to Organize Your Plant's Energy Program. This job cannot be accomplished by appointing a "plant energy committee," having it meet once a month, and hoping that something comes of it all. The job of upgrading the plant to optimum efficiency with respect to energy consumption is clearly one for the line organization, and only that group can be expected to accomplish the program's goals.

In a small plant, the plant manager himself may head up the energy-conservation group. In larger plants, an assistant plant manager or operations manager may be available to take charge; if so, that manager must carry the full delegated authority of the plant manager to implement the program. Each production, utility, and staff department head is automatically a member of the conservation group, and is responsible for carrying the program in his department.

None of this is to say there should not be staff assistance. A Plant Energy Coordinator can be appointed, whose job is to assist the line organization by keeping records of progress, disseminating information and new ideas on conservation techniques, reminding line managers of upcoming deadlines, preparing reports of the program's progress, and participating in the training effort. In the larger plants, this may constitute a full-time

EXHIBIT 11.17   Energy-Conservation Capital Projects

Department _____   Form Completed by _____   Date _____

Project Number	Project Description	Energy Savings BTU/Year	Capital Cost $	Ratio BTU/Year Savings $ Capital	Percent ROI	Priority	Status

job. Some plants have found it useful to have each department head appoint a subordinate to handle the working details of the conservation effort, and to have these people form a liaison group, which meets regularly to exchange ideas, identify problems, and report progress. The important point is to not allow the Coordinator or the liaison committee to become bogged down in trying to carry out conservation projects themselves.

Keeping Track of Progress.   The program will require its own special record-keeping system in order to provide a coherent picture of past performance and provide a justification for future activity. Follow these steps in setting up the system:

Step 1: Adopt a standard energy use statistic for all departments of the plant. The unit that probably has the widest applicability is BTU per unit of production (pounds, tons, or item count). Users of various forms of energy such as steam, electricity, and natural gas, would convert all their consumption rates to BTU and divide the number of BTU by the production units. A cautionary note is in order here, however, which is best illustrated by an analogy from ordinary life. If an automobile is driven over a 50-mile course at 65 miles per hour, it will consume considerably more gasoline per mile than if it were driven over the same course at 40 mph. Production equipment may react in much the same way—consuming more energy per unit produced if it is driven over the same course at 40 mph. Production equipment may react in much the same way—consuming more energy per unit produced if it is driven harder to meet special time or quality requirements. Provisions must be made for these variations in the record-keeping systems, if valid performance comparisons are to be made.

Step 2: Establish uniform recording methods for all departments. Not only should they report for the same time periods and in the same units, but they should use the same energy-conversion factors and the same formulas for calculating such measures as boiler and process equipment efficiency. The record-keeping system may also have to conform to rules issued by corporate headquarters, if the company owns more than one plant. (See Exhibits 11.19 on page 240 and 11.20 on page 241.)

Step 3: Establish a baseline for energy consumption before undertaking energy improvement projects. The energy survey mentioned above should provide sufficient data to establish the preprogram energy consumption levels of the various plant units.

Step 4: Computerize. The number of items to be kept track of, the calculations and data manipulation required, and the frequency of reporting all make the energy reporting system a natural application for the computer, especially for the mini-computer. An undue amount of energy reporting in industry is still being done manually—in small manufacturing units, because no computer is available, and in large operations, because access to the mainframe is not readily available and sufficiently informal. The declining costs and rapidly expanding power of mini-computers make them a tool for energy-management programs that should not be overlooked.

Inform the Players.   General support for the program will lag, if only a few insiders know what is going on. Management will demand matter-of-fact reports, which report the energy usage and dollar-value achievements of conservation measures employed by the program, as well as any progress made toward security of operation—the ability to keep the plant running if one of its sources of energy is suddenly cut off or curtailed.

EXHIBIT 11.18 Energy-Saving Plans of Action

Action Focus	N/A	Strong	Satisfactory	Needs Some Improvement	Weak: Needs Major Improvement	Action Plan, Responsibility
Energy						
Stop leaks of heat and air conditioning						
Reduce temperature on thermostats during certain periods						
Insulate walls, floors, pipes, etc.						
Use solar heating where applicable						
Print employee reminders to put lights off						
Use automatic light dimmers and/or shutoff switches						
Employ timers to shut off equipment after prescribed time						
Appoint departmental "energy-watchers" to coordinate program						
Use alternate fuels including production by-products (waste)						
Audit energy bills and meters						
Examine equipment power requirements						
Upgrade wiring						
Use heat exchangers, etc.						
Track energy bills for unusual increases in costs						
Use different temperature standards for winter versus summer						
Keep doors and windows closed						
Encourage employees to wear suitable clothing						
Install air seals at loading dock entrances						
Check energy efficiency ratings of electrical equipment						
Convert lighting fixtures to more efficient types (mercury, sodium)						
Remind employees to shut off vehicle engines when not in use						

Obtain heating and air conditioning from a single unit			
Recognize outstanding employees with appropriate awards			
Upgrade furnaces for greater fuel efficiency			
Seal up cracks around windows and doors, change to double insulated			
Plug up leaks in steam lines			
Clean and service boilers, fans and blowers			
Use window coverings and insulating film to reduce energy consumption			
Try spring loaded faucets to shut off water automatically			
Reduce hot water temperature; avoid mixing with cold water			
Consider premium awards for energy suggestions			
Reduce exterior lighting to minimum safe levels			
Use variable speed motors where applicable			
Clean or replace air filters			
Convert from ambient to task lighting			
Turn off vending machine lights			
Employ a variable air volume system			
Use infra-red scanning to locate sources of heat loss			
Take advantage of off-peak utility discounts; shift work accordingly			
Machines and Equipment			
Pinpoint pros and cons of equipment purchase vs. rental vs. leasing			
Train machine operators thoroughly; maintain progress reports			
Evaluate availability and reliability of vendor service			
Keep detailed records on dependability of spare parts			
Provide backup priority list for critical equipment			
Replace inefficient machines with newer ones			

(continued)

235

EXHIBIT 11.18   (Continued)

Action Focus	N/A	Strong	Satisfactory	Needs Some Improvement	Weak: Needs Major Improvement	Action Plan, Responsibility
Conduct safety training on hazardous equipment to reduce accidents						
Question equipment features for cost effectiveness						
Use posters and other media to dramatize need for equipment care						
Chart workflows to isolate wasted steps						
Chart workflows to see if straight line method is used						
Project cash flow through relationship to Purchasing subsystem						
Provide for Just-In-Time applications to reduce inventories						
Allow random stores feature to handle multiple locations						
Automatically select vendors to keep acceptable mix of resources						
Maximize cash discounts and vendor credits						
Enter input on-line to reduce data entry costs						
Post financial information directly to journals, ledgers						
Prepare balance sheets, P&L, budgets as by-products of system						
Generate all mandated and optional payroll forms, reports						
Provide proper audit trails for internal and legal purposes						
Allow downloading to personal computer for electronic spreadsheets, etc.						
Produce depreciation schedules for fixed assets (land, building, equipment)						
Integrate with comprehensive order-entry system						
Evaluate sales performance by person, geographic area, customer, product						
Age accounts receivables, print reports on inactive or delinquent customers						

Integrated Manufacturing Information Systems				
Meet raw material requirements of production process				
Prevent excess inventory accumulations				
Provide current, accurate stock status				
Highlight significant variances between book and physical inventories				
Indicate fast and slow sellers				
Produce preprinted count tags				
Allow flexibility in count cycles (annual, monthly, cyclical, etc.)				
Generate timely, accurate master production schedules				
Permit modeling ("what if") to simulate effects of changes				
Calculate bills of material value				
Compare planned versus actual labor hours in detail				
Schedule parts shipments on a planned rather than crisis basis				
Avoid extra shifts and overtime by adjusting capacity				
Check off receipts to appropriate purchase order				
Packaging/Materials Handling				
Improve product protection: more durable packaging				
Improve product protection: more weather resistant packaging				
Study distribution center layouts and space requirements				
Study distribution center systems for materials handling				
Make packaging more attractive at same or lower cost				
Enhance identification of cartons' contents to save time in picking stock				
Material Handling/Warehouses				
Adjustable shelves to allow for different package sizes				
Adjustable shelves for volume peaks and valleys				

(continued)

237

EXHIBIT 11.18 (Continued)

Action Focus	N/A	Strong	Satisfactory	Needs Some Improvement	Weak: Needs Major Improvement	Action Plan, Responsibility
Adaptable loading dock ramps for different heights of vehicles						
Gravity feed instead of manual movement of inventory						
Ball-bearing conveyors						
Kit of commonly used items (tape machines, cutters, package markers)						
Clear assignments for production employees' simple equipment maintenance						
Solicit suggestions from employees						
Receiving/Shipping						
Emphasis on quality control to reduce damaged shipments						
Suppliers show weight on cartons to speed stocking						
Legibility of shipping addresses to reduce handling time						
Standards for receiving and storage time of inventory						
Manufacturing Resource Planning						
Measure current system effect on expense reduction						
Check present system effect on cash flow improvement						
Evaluate MRP Re: productivity						
Feasibility of MRP for better systems and data processing						
Practical use of simulation ("what if")						
Reduce excess paperwork						
Tighten controls on inordinate overtime						
Decrease routine Purchasing expenses						
Interact with Product Engineering on better bills of material						
Coordinate production plan (units) with business plan ($)						
Measure goals, actuals, variances of production						

Take action on significant variances			
Order materials on planned (not crisis) basis			
Track number of inventory turns versus comparable periods			
Compare inventory mix to customer demand			
Check if customer delivery dates are met			
Make provision for standard versus actual costs			
Assign accountability for production plan			
Prepare production timetables for 12–24 months			
Review frequency of production plan relative to sales forecast			
Check practicality of inventory lead times, safety stock			
Evaluate master schedule for proper units by product			
Verify performance of facilities planning			
Employ dispatch list for production work centers			
Set production priorities wherever appropriate			
Integrate MRP with accounts payable to properly reimburse vendors			
Provide for reports of stock status and back-orders			
Interact with payroll system to pay employees accurately			
Set up easily understood parts numbering system			
Examine input/output costs this year versus last year			
Consider pilot versus parallel system for conversion			
Brief supervisors/managers on benefits, operation of MRP			
Identify and rectify production bottlenecks			
Transportation/Construction			
Reduce freight rates through conversion to full carloads			
Traffic department scheduling to lower distribution costs			
Audit of freight bills to uncover overcharges			
Preventive maintenance of company vehicles			
Standards for construction of distribution facilities			
Standards for creation of parking lots, building security			

Form Completed by ————————————————— ———— Date ————

EXHIBIT 11.19   Monthly Plant Energy Consumption Log

| Year | Electric Power | | Natural Gas | | | Fuel Oil | | | Coal | | | Total BTU | Number of Units Produced | BTU per Unit of Production |
	kWh	BTU/kWh	BTU	k cu ft	BTU/k cu ft	BTU	gal	BTU/gal	BTU	Tons	BTU/lb	BTU			
Jan.															
Feb.															
Mar.															
Apr.															
May															
June															
July															
Aug.															
Sep.															
Oct.															
Nov.															
Dec.															
Year															
Jan.															
Feb.															
Mar.															
Apr.															
May															
June															
July															
Aug.															
Sep.															
Oct.															
Nov.															
Dec.															

EXHIBIT 11.20   Energy-Conservation Project Evaluation Summary

Capital _____ or Expense _____

Department _____

Date _____

Project No. _____ Person Responsible _____

Project Title _____

Description of Project _____

_____

_____

_____

_____

_____

_____

_____

_____

Location _____

_____

_____

Financial Evaluation

Estimated

Energy saving (electric power kWh/yr, steam lb/yr, etc.)

Utility or Raw Material	Saving	
_____	_____	/yr
_____	_____	/yr
_____	_____	/yr
Total energy saving	_____ MBTU/yr	
Total energy cost saving	_____ $/yr	
Other cost saving due to:		
_____	_____ $/yr	
Additional cost due to:		
_____	_____ $/yr	
Net cost saving	_____ $/yr	
Cost of project	_____ $	

The general plant population will want something more informal and easier to understand. Some useful ways of communicating, to keep interest alive, are monthly newsletters, plant billboards, signs in each department showing past usage and future goals, foremen's meetings, and department or plantwide general meetings.

Newer Developments in Energy Supply

Solar Energy.   Some very broad definitions of solar energy have appeared, including not only the direct energy received from sunlight but extended also to include indirect effects, such as wind, ocean waves, and biomass conversions. This section will deal only with the direct use of sunlight.

The main limitations on the application of solar energy to industrial uses have not been technological factors, but cost. Although a number of pilot units have been constructed that demonstrate the technical feasibility of generating hot water and steam, industrial development has awaited very large reductions in the capital cost of the required equipment. The following are main types of solar devices, which may find ultimate industrial/commercial use.

Flat-plate-solar collector: This, which resembles a large window frame lying on its side, usually mounted on a roof or similar structure, so that it faces the sun. At the top of the frame are one or two sheets of glass or plastic, through which the sun's rays pass. Below that is a flat metal plate painted black. If water is the working fluid to be used, the metal plate is attached to pipes or tubing containing water. Below them is a thickness of insulation supported by a base plate. The radiant energy is received by the blackened plate and converted into heat, which is transmitted to the water; the transparent plates prevent the loss of this heat back to the atmosphere by convection and, to some extent, by radiation. Flat-plate collectors have been commercially applied to residential hot water heating, and could be applied for the same purpose in industrial situations, where they are cost effective. They are, however, generally limited to producing fluid temperatures below 200°F.

Thermal power central receiver system: This system consists of a steam boiler mounted on an outdoor tower. It is surrounded by a field of mirrors, shaped to focus the sun's rays on the boiler, and equipped with mechanisms that allow them to follow the sun as it moves through the sky. Steam is generated in the boiler and can be used for process purposes or to drive an electric power generator. Much higher temperatures—up to 2000°F—can be generated. These systems require a great deal of land space, and will probably find their greatest use in the Southeast.

There is an obvious gap between the need of a manufacturing plant for a steady supply of energy and the fluctuation of energy available from sunlight, caused by changes in the length of day and variable cloud cover. Solar power systems, therefore, usually require a conventional backup system (electric power from a utility or fossil-fuel-burning equipment), or a means of strong surplus solar energy for later use (electric batteries, or, in a hydroelectric system, a pumped storage facility).

Fuel Cells.   Basic courses in chemistry often include a demonstration in which an electric current is passed through water, decomposing the water into its constituent elements, hydrogen and oxygen. The fuel cell works in just the opposite way—hydrogen is passed over one electrode of a cell, oxygen over the other, and electricity is produced. Thus, the fuel cell is a means of converting chemical energy into electrical energy, and, in practical applications, it produces heat as well. The oxygen can be supplied pure or contained in an air stream. The hydrogen is obtained from natural gas, oil refinery products (naphtha), or coal; since this brings us right back to the use of fossil fuels, the question may well be asked, "Why bother with the fuel cell—why not just burn the fuel directly?"

The answer lies in efficiency of the process. The efficiency of fuel utilization in a fuel cell will run from 10 to 40 percent higher than in a conventional system. The higher number applies when both the electricity and heat generated in the cell are used. The electricity is generated as direct current (usually at less than 500 volts), and, for plants using that kind of power, there is an additional saving over the efficiency loss suffered when alternating current purchased from a utility is converted to direct current. These devices are expensive, and widespread application will await steep declines in the capital cost of the cells.

Economics: The Bottom Line Still Counts

Throughout this chapter we have dealt with the two basic goals of the energy-conservation program, the first goal being to find ways of reducing the suddenly very high costs of supplying fuel to the plant. This is a cost-reduction effort, and its projects are expected to generate a return on capital investment at least competitive with, if not superior to, other possible cost-reduction opportunities requiring capital. Although the search for new energy-conservation methods is challenging and often fascinating, money is the yardstick that tells us when we have gone far enough.

The second goal is to protect the company against going out of business altogether, if the primary form of energy used by the plant is threatened with interruption or curtailment for any length of time. When survival is the issue the rules can be bent rather sharply, but, even in this situation, there are economic limits. If, for instance, the annualized cost of installing a backup fuel system is greater than the company's expected earning for the next eight years, then the risk of being shut down for a period may have to be borne. In a less extreme situation, if the cost of the backup system is not actually prohibitive, but would preclude a very attractive investment in production equipment that would increase the company's market penetration, then a more careful study of the risks must be made. It would involve making estimates such as the probability of an energy supply failure occurring and its length, and its severity expressed in dollars—loss of sales, diminished competitive position.

Operating Example: Determining the Cost Effectiveness of an Energy-Conservation Proposal.   Following the plant energy survey, a plant manager was presented with the following proposal from his powerhouse superintendent: An economizer can be installed on the main boiler to heat the incoming feedwater and thus recapture some of the heat now going to the atmosphere in stack gases. The installed cost of the equipment is estimated at $302,000. The area engineer estimates that approximately

18,000 barrels of fuel oil will be saved per year, yielding annual cost savings of $223,560. For investment analysis purposes, the plant manager assumes that the economizer will have a useful life of 210 years, with no salvage value and, using the economic justification method, makes the following evaluation:

Return on Investment

Total pretax profit over life of project (10 × $223,560)	$2,234,600
Less depreciation	302,000
Taxable profit	$1,933,600
Income tax at 34%	657,424
After-tax profit	$1,276,176
Average annual after-tax profit (Divide by 10 years)	137,618
Return on investment (127,618 divided by 302,000)	42.2%

Payback Period

After-tax profit	$1,276,176
Plus depreciation	302,000
Cash Flow	$1,578,176
Average annual cash flow (Divide by 10 years)	157,818
Payback period (302,000 divided by 157,818)	
(Investment divided by Annual cash flow)	1.91 yr

With a 42 percent return and a payback period of two years, this might be an attractive investment to management. But there could be other economic considerations that would create serious second thoughts about proceeding with it. For instance, if capital funds are very hard to obtain for some reason and only enough money is available for this project or for the installation of new production machines needed to keep the company competitive in its business, then the company may have to forego the energy savings as a matter of survival.

Monitor Fuel-Saving Ideas

- By developing more efficient processes for its use, which takes time and money;
- By rationing or reducing demand for it through pricing, so that only a few can afford to buy it; and
- By operating existing processes more efficiently, which requires the dedicated enthusiasm of all.

Lighting.   Lighting usually represents a small faction of the total energy requirement of a factory, but economies are easy for all to see and can give impetus for conservation of less tangible items. Good lighting design improves productivity, but glare can lead to accidents.

- Make the best use of daylight by keeping windows and roof lights clean, also by suitable arrangement of working places near windows.
- Keep lamps and fittings clean.
- Replace lamps when their efficiency drops through aging.
- Use suitable reflectors and diffusers, which transmit light in the desired direction.
- Avoid dark background colors, which absorb light.
- Have separate switches to control lights near windows.
- Make sure that light is adequate, but that it is switched off when not required. (Frequent switching reduces the life of lamps.)
- Consider automatic switching of lighting.
- Use fluorescent or discharge lamps, rather than filament lamps.

Space-Heating.   Excessive temperature variation with hot and cold spots needs to be controlled by strategically placed thermostats.

- Block off unoccupied working areas and do not heat them.
- Limit maximum temperature to the legal limit of 19°C. Check the accuracy of temperature control. Minimize variation in temperature.
- Use warm air curtains in conjunction with automatic door closing, where possible, to improve comfort without draught or excessive loss of hot air. Dispatch bays are often the cause of excessive heat loss.

Ventilation.   A ventilation system, which includes heating, humidification, and filtration is expensive to install, but a good system will improve the working environment, as well as productivity.

- Avoid drafts by a properly sealed system, sealing doors, windows, etc.
- Doors and windows should normally be closed in cold weather.
- Excessive ventilation, caused by leaving windows open, involves excessive space-heating. Consequently, the number of changes per hour in a room should be restricted.
- In air-conditioned buildings, ensure that the controls for moisture content, temperature, and direction of air flow are effective.
- Avoid air leaks in ducts by sealing them.
- On nonworking days do not switch on air heating and ventilation too soon, but maintain a level just sufficient to give frost protection.
- Switch off the air conditioning system up to one hour before the building is due to be vacated for a long period.

Electrical Equipment.   Electricity costs are based on the rate as well as the amount of consumption. This requires a company to balance the costs of the maximum demand and the load factor. Maintaining a high power factor is important in reducing costs, by increasing efficiency of usage.

- Switch off equipment which is not required for any prolonged period.
- Lower the maximum demand by regulating the intermittent use of equipment.
- Match electric motors to their required duties.
- Use higher voltage, where possible, to reduce transmission losses.
- Match the size of transformers to their load requirements.
- Make the best use possible of the three-phase system for power distribution.
- Obtain advice on power factor control and most advantageous tariff.

Thermal Insulation.   The material chosen has to be of low thermal conductivity and suitable for the temperature of operation, so that it does not shrink, melt, or otherwise deteriorate.

- Except for heat-transfer units such as space-heaters and refrigerators, heated and cooled pipes should be lagged.
- Any exposed surface not at room temperature should be thermally insulated. Included should be valves, flues, and chimneys.
- Protect thermal insulation from damp, inclement weather, and mechanical damage.
- Use cavity insulation in buildings.
- Apply thermal insulation to lofts or roofs (100 mm recommended).
- Double-glazing provides thermal saving, also reduces drafts and noise levels.
- Make exterior doors self-closing.
- Consider the use of double doors or revolving doors in the entrances to buildings.
- Consider the replacement or enhancement of thermal insulation for low, medium, and high temperature, using material of low thermal conductivity.
- Cover the surface of a hot liquid with a lid or a floating insulator to reduce the heat loss.
- Apply cold-face insulation to the exteriors of furnaces and ovens.
- Use where possible hot-face insulation inside ovens and furnaces, which are intermittently heated, so as to reduce the heat storage loss.
- Prevent radiation escape by closing apertures such as inspection holes and doors.
- Use polished metal exterior surfaces to minimize radiation loss.

Steam, Compressed Air, and Other Services.   Oversized steam and other heated pipes, even if lagged, may have a low delivery temperature because of heat losses. Undersized pipes also have losses, but, in this case, are due to friction, which has to be overcome by a higher-than-normal pumping pressure, or by a low delivery pressure, which may fluctuate excessively with flow changes. All common services should be regularly inspected for leaks, since they are often not attended for long periods, due to poor accessibility.

- Take particular care to avoid leaks. Check thoroughly for leaks and repair, where necessary.
- Inspect and maintain stream traps.
- Seal off redundant pipework and ducts.
- Ensure that steam mains are properly sized.
- Recover steam condensate and return it to the boiler, if not contaminated.
- Avoid the use of steam-reducing valves for low-pressure steam. Back-pressure engines or calorifiers should be considered.
- Switch off compressed air services when they are not required to run continuously.
- Clean air filters and renew packing to reduce pressure losses.
- Mechanical efficiency falls with use, hence renew valves, springs, rings, glands, etc.
- Avoid overheating air in a compressor, by returning it through a by-pass to the inlet.
- Multiple-stage compressors are more efficient with intercooling between stages; regularly clean the heat exchangers to ensure minimum pumping cost.
- Ensure that fan rotating parts are in balance.
- Fan impellers often become dirty and corroded. Surface cleaning and polishing will improve efficiency.

Boilers for Steam and Hot Water. Where more than one boiler is in use, it may be possible to shut one down for part of the time. Hot water storage of a boiler will vary with the load on it and is greatly affected by the efficiency of combustion and by the transfer of heat from the waste gases to the water or steam, hence the need for regular cleaning and setting of controls.

- Stagger the demands for steam as much as possible, to give a more even loading on the boilers.
- Avoid boiler safety valves blowing unnecessarily, by proper control of firing.
- Controls should be serviced and adjusted to maintain optimum efficiency, temperature, pressure, etc.
- Is the treatment of feedwater appropriate?
- Do not have excessive blowdown.
- Can the temperature of hot water be reduced with an improvement of efficiency?
- Where superheated steam is appropriate, this should be provided at a high steady temperature.

Combustion.   The efficient combustion of a fuel demands that the combustion apparatus be suitable for the fuel concerned. Solid fuel has to be of the correct size and hardness, and have suitable moisture, ash, volatile matter, and sulfur contents. The ash fusion temperature of coal may be critical, leading to loss of unburned fuel, and problems with fly-ash, grit, and permeability of the fuel bed. Variable quality of fuel poses additional problems. High volatility in fuel can lead to incomplete combustion of waste gases, unless the supply of combustion air is suitably distributed.

- Switch off unwanted burners.
- Excess air in fuel-fired equipment is probably the chief cause of energy waste in industry. Therefore, the control of air–fuel ratio should provide only sufficient of each for complete combustion consistent with proper mixing.
- The percentage carbon dioxide, etc., in waste gases should be monitored regularly to check that combustion is efficient.
- Air leaks in brickwork and flues and around dampers should be stopped.
- Furnace drafting should be balanced; fit flue dampers to isolate boilers not on line to prevent a natural draft pulling in cold air.
- Fuel supplied for combustion should be in the proper condition to achieve optimum heat release.

  Coal—uniform mix of suitable size range, volatile matter, ash and moisture content, hardness, and reactivity;

  Oil—constant temperature to control viscosity, constant pressure; and

  Gas—constant pressure.
- A combination of different fuels calls for mixing control.
- Burners should not overheat. Their efficiency is maintained by adjustment, cleaning, and replacement of worn parts.
- Adequate mixing of fuel and air at the burner is necessary for proper direction of the flame and completion of heat release from the fuel within the combustion chamber.
- Multiple burners and multiple-zone heating need balancing to produce even heating.

Furnaces and Ovens.   For heat-transfer efficiency the hearth area of a furnace needs to be completely covered with the charge, but overloading is undesirable, as it slows the rate of heating. Control of temperature to give uniform heating aids productivity and minimizes rejects. Machinery associated with heating process is itself subject to overheating, and this is often overlooked.

- Hearth coverage is increased by proper loading.
- Doors should be left open for as short a time possible, for loading, and unloading, and should be well maintained so as to minimize radiant heat loss and air in-leakage.

- The mass of carriers, trays, etc., can often be reduced without loss of control.
- Steady operation by planning throughput is desirable.
- Heating cycles, particularly in batch furnaces, should be short but consistent with the maintenance of product quality.
- Consider the possibility of changing to a more efficient form of heating by changing the burners, or fuel, or by using an electrical method.

Reduction of Waste. Hot water wasted means energy wasted. Is the water temperature higher than necessary? Besides placing notices to discourage waste on washroom doors, the fitting of spring-loaded taps and of low-throughput showers, together with a high standard of insulation and maintenance, can be of assistance.

- Closer specification in the use of all materials saves in many ways. Energy is directly saved with those involving a high consumption of energy in their production, such as metals, rubber, plastics, paper, glass, cement, and refractories.
- Sort waste materials at source ready for recycling.
- Incinerate refuse and recover its heat, e.g., for space-heating.
- Fermentation of organic waste could provide methane gas as a fuel to drive stationary engines for power.

Waste Heat Recovery. When energy is rejected in the form of pressure, temperature of waste gases and other products, or unburned fuel from one process, it may be possible to harness it to reduce the energy needs of the same or some other process. An investigation is necessary to establish the facts before recovery of energy in the form of preheat of charge, combustion air, fuel, hot water, steam, or unburned fuel is attempted. Waste heat recovery involves capital investment. Criteria on which this investment could be justified are as follows.

- The source must provide sufficient energy at a high enough temperature or pressure, or, in the case of unburned fuel, at a high-enough calorific value.
- The quantity of energy saved must be worth more than the equivalent cost of fuel, which would otherwise be burned directly.
- The energy in the form recovered must be needed for some processes, or adaptable for that need.
- The pattern of energy demand for the waste heat recovery must comply with the pattern of availability (storage of energy in a tank or accumulator, standby plant, or auxiliary fuel firing may be possible).
- There must be space available for the recovery equipment.
- The return on capital must be acceptable.
- A loan for the capital has to be available. Government grants and short-term loans are available for approved energy-saving projects.

General Comments.   An Energy Management Department is usually to be found in a large company; its role will be to promote efficiency in the use of heat and power. A small firm requiring external advice may obtain it from appropriate government departments, advisory councils, energy and fuel suppliers, insulation manufacturers, polytechnics and universities, or research organizations and trade organizations.

- Investigate the various tariffs available for the supply of fuels, to ensure that they are those that best meet the needs of the process.

- Keep a regular record of stocks, purchases, and consumption of energy.

- Provide instrumentation to measure and control the consumption of energy. Regularly maintain and check the calibration of the instruments.

- Examine the records to pinpoint any change in the energy consumption, making use, where appropriate, of computer database packages, to relate energy consumption to production.

- Carry out efficiency tests on machines and other plant equipment to verify that they are not deteriorating.

- Institute or revise planned engineering maintenance, to reduce energy waste, improve safety, and to enhance general working conditions.

- Ensure that energy conservation has due consideration in production planning.

- Encourage all personnel to save energy, by investigating any suggestion that might reduce energy consumption in the long term.

- Be prepared to argue a case for the installation of capital equipment, which can reduce energy consumption; investigate what grants are available from regional and government sources.

- Use persuasion and incentives to achieve desired results and, above all, maintain the pressure for fuel economy.

INDEX